High-Level Language Computer Architecture

CONTRIBUTORS

Howard M. Bloom
Carl R. Carlson
Yaohan Chu
Robert W. Doran
Theodore A. Laliotis
Bernard J. Robinet

High-Level Language Computer Architecture

Edited by

Yaohan Chu

*Department of Computer Science
and
Department of Electrical Engineering
University of Maryland
College Park, Maryland*

ACADEMIC PRESS   New York   San Francisco   London   1975

A Subsidiary of Harcourt Brace Jovanovich, Publishers

Figure 1, p. 32, adapted by permission from Lonergan and King, *Datamation* 7, 28–32, Copyright 1961 Association for Computing Machinery, Inc.

Figures 6 and 7, pp. 42, 43, adapted by permission from Sugimoto, *Proc. ACM*, 519–538, Copyright 1969 Association for Computing Machinery, Inc.

Figure 9, p. 51, adapted by permission from Nissen and Wallach, *Proc. Symp. High-Level Language Computer Architecture*, 43–51, Copyright 1973 Association for Computing Machinery, Inc.

ACADEMIC PRESS, INC.
111 Fifth Avenue, New York, New York 10003

United Kingdom Edition published by
ACADEMIC PRESS, INC. (LONDON) LTD.
24/28 Oval Road, London NW1

Library of Congress Cataloging in Publication Data
Main entry under title:

High-level language computer architecture.

    Includes bibliographical references and index.
    1.   Electronic digital computers—Programming.
2.   Programming languages (Electronic computers)
3.   Electronic digital computers—Design and construction.   I.   Chu, Yaohan,   (date)
QA76.6.H53   001.6'42   75-3580
ISBN 0–12–174150–8

PRINTED IN THE UNITED STATES OF AMERICA

To REX RICE and WILLIAM R. SMITH,
whose team at Fairchild designed and constructed
the revolutionary SYMBOL computer system.

Contents

Concepts of High-Level Language Computer Architecture

Yaohan Chu

Design Concepts of Japanese-Language Data Processing Systems

Yaohan Chu

A Survey of High-Level Language Computer Architecture

Carl R. Carlson

List of Contributors

Numbers in parentheses indicate the pages on which the author's contributions begin.

HOWARD M. BLOOM (187), Management Information Systems Group, Harry Diamond Laboratories, Adelphi, Maryland

CARL R. CARLSON (31), Computer Sciences Department, Northwestern University, Evanston, Illinois

YAOHAN CHU (1, 15), Department of Computer Science and Department of Electrical Engineering, University of Maryland, College Park, Maryland

ROBERT W. DORAN (63), Department of Computer Science, Massey University, Palmerston North, New Zealand

THEODORE A. LALIOTIS (109), Systems Technology Division, Fairchild Camera and Instrument Corporation, Palo Alto, California

BERNARD J. ROBINET (243), Institut de Programmation, Université Pierre et Marie Curie, Paris, France

Preface

As W. M. McKeeman pointed out, it was an accident that the digital computer was organized like a desk calculator. As a result, the digital computer of today requires a multitude of software. As software gets less reliable and consumes more memory, it needs more time to debug, takes more system programmers, and spends more overhead computer time. The progress of computer utilization and applications is now greatly limited to the development of software. Yet, the progress of software development is handicapped by the desk-calculator-like organization. The computer community, as also pointed out by McKeeman, could be worse off if the digital computer were organized like a Turing machine. In this case, a lot more programmers would have been needed. A great deal more effort would have been spent in improving arithmetic routines, in discovering ways of tape memory addressing and allocation, in creating more levels of programming languages, and in facing an unmanageable maze of software. Obviously, the airplane today would not fly at sonic speeds or supersonic speeds if we were continuously improving piston engines. Likewise, the problem of air pollution by tens of millions of today's automobiles could not be resolved if we continue to build the conventional internal combustion engines. Thus, could we expect carefully engineered, very fast, automatic desk calculators to be very good for implementing compilers or operating systems?

A modern digital computer consists of a data structure, a control structure, and a processing structure for executing algorithms. If the computer is going to execute programs written in a high-level programming language such as FORTRAN or ALGOL, there is no need to have the structures for executing programs written in an assembly-type language (i.e., a conventional machine language) or to compile the high-level language program into an assembly-type language before execution. The structures of the computer might as well have been conceived and designed for directly accepting and executing programs written in the high-level language. Such a computer architecture is called a *high-level language computer architecture.* A high-level language architecture mirrors closely the data, control, and processing structures of the high-level programming language or languages, and the high-level programming language is indeed the machine language.

This volume aims to fill a current need of tutorial material on high-level language computer architecture. The first chapter presents a classification of high-level language computer architecture according to the proximity of the machine language and the programming language. This classification gives four types: von Neumann architecture, syntax-oriented architecture, indirect execution architecture, and direct execution architecture. In order to illustrate the possible evolution of computer architecture, design concepts of Japanese-language data processing systems are chosen as an example and presented in the next chapter.

The chapter by Carlson surveys the high-level language computer architecture. That by Doran describes the syntax-oriented architecture. The chapter by Laliotis is a tutorial on the historical SYMBOL computer system that was developed by Fairchild Corporation and is now being evaluated by the Iowa State University. The SYMBOL system makes use of an indirect execution architecture. The chapter by Bloom presents design concepts of direct-execution architecture for the ALGOL 60 language. Lastly, the chapter by Robinet describes the architecture for the processor for an APL subset.

The editor would like to acknowledge the help of Ms. Joanie Fort in the preparation of the manuscript.

Concepts of High-Level Language Computer Architecture

Yaohan Chu

Department of Computer Science
and
Department of Electrical Engineering
University of Maryland
College Park, Maryland

1. INTRODUCTION

In this volume, the term "high-level language" (HLL) refers to those computer programming languages that not only allow the use of symbolic operators to signify operations and of symbolic names to represent data and data structures, but also are structured with syntax and semantics to describe the computing algorithm. Examples of such programming languages are FORTRAN, ALGOL, and COBOL.

1

1.1 What Is a HLL Computer System?

A high-level language computer system is one that can accept and execute a high-level language program. There are many high-level language computer systems today, such as those IBM, CDC, and UNIVAC computer systems that are provided with compilers for these and other high-level programming languages. There are others, such as the Burroughs B5700/6700, that are claimed to be more efficient in handling some high-level programming languages. Finally, there are research computer systems such as the SYMBOL computer system developed by Fairchild and now being evaluated at Iowa State University and those now being studied at the University of Maryland.

1.2 Is the HLL Computer a General-Purpose Computer?

The general-purpose digital computer of today is a stored-program computer that has an instruction set (commonly called the machine language) and a hierarchy of storages for storing the program and the data. The instruction set is capable of describing algorithms for solving a problem in a large class of application areas. It is limited by the capacity of the storage and by the program that can be written with the instruction set. Therefore, if storage capacity is adequate, the question to ask of general-purpose computers is how universal is the instruction set.

High-level programming languages can be as general purpose as the conventional general-purpose computer instruction set. For example, FORTRAN has been commonly used for solving scientific problems, while COBOL has been widely used for solving data processing problems. Another high-level programming language, SNOBOL, has been developed for describing symbol string manipulations, while ESPOL (a dialect of ALGOL) was developed and used to describe the operating system of the Burroughs B5500 computer system. High-level programming language PL/1, which incorporates language features of FORTRAN, ALGOL, and COBOL, has been developed for both scientific computing and data processing and has also been used to describe an operating system. High-level language CDL (Chu [1965, 1972]) has been used to describe the processor, control, and storage structures of a computer. Therefore, the implementation of a high-level language as the machine language instead of a conventional machine language could make the HLL computer system general purpose. In other words, it is the machine language(s) that determine whether the computer system is general purpose or not.

1.3 Classification

The high-level language that is used by the programmer is referred to as the *virtual language,* while the language that is physically implemented in hardware is called the *machine language.*

There is a great difference in the architecture of the various high-level language computer systems, whether they are commercially available or under research and development. These computer systems may be classified by their architecture into the following four types:

Type 1: von Neumann
Type 2: Syntax-oriented
Type 3: Indirect execution
Type 4: Direct execution

The above four types are classified by the *proximity of lexicality, syntax, and semantics* between the virtual language and the machine language. This proximity is chosen as the criterion because it can greatly influence the complexity of the translator (or compiler) that translates a HLL into an object code or machine language. It is so chosen because it can considerably affect the ease of using the computer system. The meaning of proximity of lexicality, syntax, and semantics is now briefly discussed.

1.4 Language Proximity

The lexicality of a computer language here refers to the arrangement by which the terminal alphabet, such as letters and digits, is permitted to form the lexical units, such as numbers, names, op-codes, and delimiters. It also refers to the rules by which the terminal alphabet and lexical units are permitted to form other lexical units, such as multiple-character operators, base addresses, identifiers, and reserved words. Proximity of lexicality between two computer languages refers to the similarity of the terminal alphabet and the lexical units of these two languages.

The syntax of a computer language is the set of rules by which the lexical units are permitted to form syntactical units (nonterminal alphabet) such as terms, factors, and expressions. It also refers to the rules by which the lexical units and syntactical units are permitted to form other syntactical units such as instructions, syllables, statements, and blocks. Proximity of syntax between two computer languages refers to the similarity of the syntactical units and the syntactical rules of these two languages.

The semantics of a computer language refer to the operations that the semantic units, such as op-codes, operators, and operands, call for. For example, the meaning of operator + in the arithmetic expression $(A + B)$ is the addition of two numerical operands. The meaning of operator = in the Boolean expression $(A + B) = 4$ is an equality test of two arithmetic expressions. Proximity of semantics between two computer languages refers to the similarity of the semantic operations of these two languages.

2. VON NEUMANN ARCHITECTURE (TYPE 1)

Von Neumann architecture refers to the architecture of those commercially available computer systems manufactured by IBM, CDC, UNIVAC, and others. These computer systems are characterized by a set of instructions that make up the machine language and compilers that enable the systems to accept programs in high-level languages. As described below, they employ layers of software for language translations before results can be obtained.

2.1 Compilation and Execution Process

The compilation and execution of a computer system in von Neumann architecture is shown in Fig. 1. The high-level language (HLL) code is converted into a hardware internal code, which is then translated into a relocatable code by a compiler. The relocatable code is now linked with the required relocatable subroutines from the library and translated into an absolute code by the linkage editor. The absolute code is finally loaded into the core by the loader. The in-core code is executed and the result is finally produced.

It is obvious now that the layers of language translators partly account for the software complexity in today's computer systems. Although it is

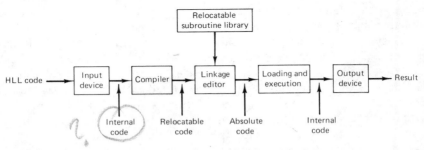

Fig. 1.   Block diagram showing translation and execution of a HLL code in a von Neumann architecture.

claimed that the user needs to know only the high-level language, the user really has to know these intermediate languages to varying degrees in order to be competent in debugging his program. For example, there is the need to read the core dump in debugging; thus, one needs to know the instructions in internal (e.g., octal) code.

2.2   An Example

As an illustration, the ALGOL program in Fig. 2 is chosen as the source code. This program computes factorial N where N is a given constant. It contains a block statement, a declaration statement, four assignment statements (one with a label), an "if" statement, an input statement, and an output statement.

```
        begin integer NUM, I, TEMP, NFACT;
                read(NUM);
                TEMP := 1;
                I := 1;
CONTINUE:   I := I + 1;
                TEMP := TEMP * I;
                if I = NUM then NFACT := TEMP else goto CONTINUE;
                write(NFACT)
        end
```

Fig. 2.   An ALGOL program for calculating factorial N.

The source code was compiled, link-edited, and executed on the UNIVAC 1108 computer system with an ALGOL compiler. The source code and the linked relocatable code are shown in Fig. 3. Notice the free format of the ALGOL program and the fixed format of the relocatable code. It is found that the original source code needs a storage of only 40 memory words. The linked relocatable code requires 69 words in addition to over 12,000 memory words for storing system routines. The need for so many words for system routines is due to the great disparity between the high-level language and the von Neumann architecture.

2.3   Language Proximity

Let us now examine the proximity in lexicality, syntax, and semantics between the ALGOL program and the relocatable code. The ALGOL program is a string of such lexical units as delimiters, operators, identifiers, and numbers in a free format; the relocatable code is a sequence of machine instructions with attached relocation information in a fixed format. Thus, the lexicality of these two codes is completely different. The ALGOL program has a precedence grammar as its syntax; the sequence of instructions of the

```
QALG, IS TEST, TEST
CYCLE  000  COMPILED BY 1204  0008  ON 11/01/72 AT 14:12:33
      B1     S1       L1
      1          BEGIN INTEGER NUM, I, TEMP, NFACT;
      2                  READ (NUM) ;
      3                  TEMP: = 1 ;
      4                  I: = 1 ;
      5      CONTINUE :  I: = I + 1 ;
      6                  TEMP: = TEMP*I ;
      7                  IF I EQL NUM THEN NFACT: = TEMP ELSE GOTO CONTINUE ,
      8                  WRITE (NFACT)
      E1
      9      END
      F1
COMPILATION COMPLETE
```

Algol Program

MAIN SEGMENT

LOAD GROUP BEGINS AT 1

Linked relocatable code

LOAD 001000 TO 003713   (NUMBER OF WORDS: 02714)

001000	270200000013	270751000001	240751000000	311051000001
	00 10 00 0	01 16 11 0	01 16 11 0	02 02 11 0
001010	271331000000	270335000000	060334000001	270360000012
	02 15 11 0	00 15 15 0	00 15 14 0	00 17 00 0
001020	061317000004	270240000014	277120040000	270140040001
	02 14 17 0	00 12 00 0	16 05 00 0	00 06 00 0
001030	060772000003	730060000022	100511000001	311111000001
	01 17 12 0	00 03 00 0	01 04 11 0	02 04 11 0
001040	270310000000	520411000000	745660006377	060300000101
	00 14 10 0	01 00 11 0	13 13 00 0	00 14 00 0
001050	050000000026	742000001055	770006040002	060660061007
	00 00 00 0	04 00 00 0	00 00 06 0	01 13 00 0

Fig. 3. Relocatable codes from the UNIVAC 1108 computer system for the ALGOL program in Fig. 2.

relocatable code has no syntax except the sequential relation of the instructions. Thus, the syntax of these two codes is also quite different. The ALGOL program uses such semantic units as operators +, :=, "begin," "if," "else," and "goto"; the relocatable code has no corresponding semantic units except the add and the store op-codes which are similar to operators + and :=, respectively. Furthermore, the ALGOL program has operands such as "NUM" and "TEMP"; the relocatable codes use no symbolic names. Indeed, they use numerical addresses where these operands are stored. Thus, the semantics is also different. In short, great disparity exists between the virtual language and the machine language.

3. SYNTAX-ORIENTED ARCHITECTURE (TYPE 2)

A great forward stride in computer architecture was made when Burroughs introduced the B5500 computer system over a decade ago. This system was specifically designed for the high-level language called Extended ALGOL, a dialect of ALGOL 60. The system has instructions in the format of 12-bit "syllables"; a string of syllables represents the Polish-string form of the source code. It uses a hardware stack to hold the intermediate results of expression evaluation and to store control words for handling interrupts and procedures. It employs a *program reference table* (PTR) to store operands and descriptors; the latter point to and describe data and code segments. It has a dynamic storage allocation for segments with nonfixed sizes. The operating system is called the *master control program* or MCP.

3.1 Compilation and Execution Process

The compilation and execution of an ALGOL program on the Burroughs B5500 is shown in Fig. 4. The compiler translates the input ALGOL program into segments of machine language code and segments of data (the main segment of which is the PTR), which form a code file. Each code segment is a series of syllables; all addressing within each segment is relative. There-fore, when a segment is brought into core by the MCP for execution, no change of addresses within that segment is required. This code is often referred to as the *Polish string*. Since this Polish-string language has been used as an intermediate language in some compilers, its use directly as the machine language eliminates one layer of software. Such an architecture is called *syntax-oriented architecture* because the machine language is or-iented toward the syntax of a high-level language. The procedure library is in relative code of Polish strings. Those procedures that are called are

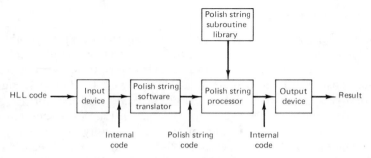

Fig. 4. Block diagram showing execution of a HLL code in a syntax-directed architecture.

linked by linking relative addresses into the Polish string during compilation and are brought into the core on demand during execution by the MCP. Significant conceptual simplicity was achieved in the Burroughs B5500 system.

3.2   An Example

As an illustration, the string of syllables from the B5500 for the ALGOL program is partially shown in Fig. 5. Notice that syllables are shown in groups with one group for each ALGOL statement.

```
I := I + 1;

opdc 22    (I)
litc 1
add
litc 22    (I)
isd

TEMP := TEMP * I;

opdc 23    (TEMP)
opdc 22    (I)
mul
litc 23    (TEMP)
isd

if I = NUM then NFACT := TEMP

opdc 22    (I)
opdc 21    (NUM)
eql
*
*
opdc 23    (TEMP)
litc 24    (NFACT)
isd

else goto CONTINUE;

litc 3
lbc
```

Fig. 5.   A string of Burroughs B5500 syllables for a part of the ALGOL program in Fig. 2.

3.3   Language Proximity

Proximity of the ALGOL program in Fig. 2 and the string of syllables in Fig. 5 is now examined. The syllable string is intermixed with lexical units of operators, literal-calls, operand-calls, and descriptor-calls. The ALGOL program consists of free-formatted statements, while the Polish string is a string of fixed-formatted syllables. Thus, proximity in lexicality is quite poor. On the other hand, the string of syllables in Fig. 5 is structured with operator precedence similar to that of ALGOL. Proximity in syntax is good.

The string of syllables has operators: "isd," "add," "mul," "eql," "lbc," and others. Except operators "add," "mul," and "eql" the other operators do not have identical semantic units in the ALGOL program. Furthermore, each constant, each variable name in an arithmetic expression, and each variable name representing an address in an assignment statement is replaced by lexical units: the literal-call syllable (of a constant), the operand-call syllable (of the contents of a PRT entry), and the descriptor-call syllable (of the address in a PRT entry), respectively. The semantics show a great disparity.

4. INDIRECT EXECUTION ARCHITECTURE (TYPE 3)

The Burroughs B5500 made a significant change in architecture. However, there still exists a large amount of software, and the problem of software complexity is only partially relieved. A new type of architecture, indirect execution architecture, was introduced by the SYMBOL computer system.

4.1 SYMBOL Computer System

During the 1971 Spring Joint Computer Conference, Rex Rice (Rice and Smith [1971]) and his group presented a series of papers that described the design and construction of the SYMBOL computer system. The SYMBOL system has a high-level ALGOL-like machine language, called SYMBOL (Chesley and Smith [1971]), which has the further capability of describing variable-length data and requires no type and size declarations (as conversion and memory allocation are handled automatically). It has no conventional set of instructions; it directly accepts programs written in the SYMBOL language. It is a functionally organized multiprocessor system (Smith *et al.* [1971]) and is designed for multiple access by terminals. In addition to an arithmetic processor, a channel controller, and a disk controller, it has a hardware translator, a hardware text editor, a hardware format processor, a hardware reference processor, a hardware system supervisor, and a hardware virtual memory. There is very little software. The SYMBOL system is now being evaluated at Iowa State University under the sponsorship of the U.S. National Science Foundation. This project has undoubtedly demonstrated the feasibility of a computer system having a high-level language as the machine language. Since there is an internal machine language, such architecture is called *indirect execution architecture*.

4.2 Translation and Execution Process

The translation and execution of a SYMBOL program on the SYMBOL computer system is shown in Fig. 6. Although the structure of the diagram is similar to that for the Burroughs B5500 in Fig. 4, there are some major

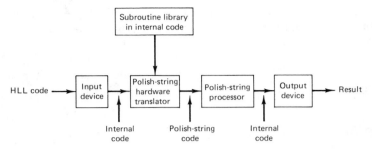

Fig. 6. Block diagram showing execution of a HLL code in an indirect execution architecture.

differences. First, the Polish-string language is different. Second, the translator in Fig. 6 is hardware implemented; the external procedures are stored in the HLL and are linked during translation. Third, the SYMBOL system is a functionally organized multiprocessor system. There are eight processors; each has a different architecture and performs a different function. For example, the translation into a Polish string is performed by a hardware translator and the execution of the Polish string is performed by the central processor. On the other hand, the Burroughs B5500 has one or two conventional central processing units that perform the processing. This makes the SYMBOL system capable of a greater throughput.

4.3 A Polish-String Language

As mentioned, the Polish-string language for the SYMBOL system is different from the Burroughs syllable string. The Polish-string language developed at the University of Maryland is used here as an example. The Polish-string language program for the ALGOL program in Fig. 2 is a string of symbol-pairs shown in Fig. 7. Each symbol-pair consists of an integer code that indicates the type of ALGOL symbol and a name or an integer that signifies the semantics; the latter is enclosed in a pair of parentheses. There is one exception when the symbol-pair is a delimiter such as { or }; in this case, there is no enclosed semantics. In Fig. 7, in each pair of lines the upper line shows the string of the original ALGOL program, while the lower line shows the string of symbol-pairs.

4.4 Language Proximity

Proximity of the ALGOL program in Fig. 2 and the string of symbol-pairs in Fig. 7 is now examined. The Polish string is intermixed with delimiters

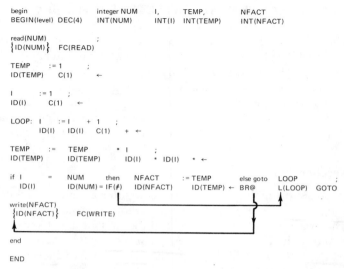

Fig. 7. Polish string from an indirect-execution computer system for the ALGOL program in Fig. 2.

such as "BEGIN" for "begin" and "INT" for "integer," and with names such as "NUM" and "TEMP," constants such as "1," and operators such as + for + and ← for :=. Some additional symbols such as "BR" are employed. Since the lexical units of these two languages are mostly identical, lexicality of these two languages is close.

The string of symbol-pairs in Fig. 7 has syntactical units similar to those in the ALGOL program. The string has expressions, statements, and blocks that are similar to those in the ALGOL program. Furthermore, the ALGOL program is structured for the most part according to operator precedence, while the string of symbol-pairs is also structured with operator precedence, except it is in a reverse Polish form. Since the rules by which the lexical units and syntactical units of these two languages are used are quite similar, the syntax of these two languages is also close.

The string of symbol-pairs has the semantic units IF, BR, INT, DEC, ←, *, +, {, and }. Some of these semantic units are ALGOL operators that perform similar actions while others are not. Thus, semantics is reasonably close.

It should be remembered that both the ALGOL language and the Polish-string language are high-level machine languages, one *external* and one *internal*. In order to understand fully the operation of an indirect execution high-level language computer system, one should know both the external and the internal high-level machine languages.

5. DIRECT EXECUTION ARCHITECTURE (TYPE 4)

Since 1967, Chu and his students at the University of Maryland have studied the architecture of the high-level language computer system (Bloom [1970], Signiski [1970], Chu [1968, 1970, 1972]). In their approach, the high-level language is taken directly as the machine language. There is no Polish-string language, no assembly language, no relocatable language, and no absolute language. *The high-level language is the machine language.* For this reason, such architecture is called *direct execution architecture.*

5.1 Execution Process

A direct execution high-level-language computer accepts a high-level language program and executes it directly without translating the input program. The execution process of a HLL program in a direct execution computer is shown in Fig. 8. The direct HLL computer scans the symbols, recognizes the syntax, and executes the operations whenever possible as specified in the program. Tables and stacks are used to store operands, operators, labels, conditionals, block structure, and loop structure in order to carry out the operations and to speed up the execution process. The procedural library is also in the high-level language; the procedure when referenced is brought into the main memory during execution.

A direct execution computer has the virtue of conceptual simplicity and avoids the need of language translations. As with the indirect execution architecture, there is no problem of software complexity because there is no conventional software.

5.2 Language Proximity

As mentioned previously, there is no intermediate language (virtual or real,

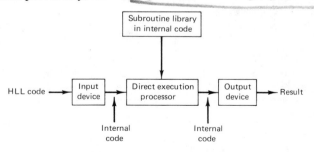

Fig. 8. Block diagram showing execution of a HLL code in a direct execution architecture.

low level or high level) in a direct execution computer. The high-level language is the machine language.

The proximity in lexicality, syntax, and semantics between the high-level language and the machine language becomes so close that they are almost identical. This gives the following advantages:

(a) It is simpler to learn to use the computer since there is only one high-level language to learn. This is true not only for the direct user and the programmer, but also true for the designers, the testers, the servicemen, the operators, the salesmen, and the instructors. This simplicity means a great reduction in cost and time to teach other computer languages that would otherwise be needed.

(b) As a result, the hardware designer and the software designer (if HLL software is needed) can talk to each other with no difficulty since the machine language and the programming language are the same. This communication between the designers may well result in fewer hardware and software errors and in less design effort and cost.

(c) It is a truly conversational system since there is no compilation of the high-level language. In fact, the debug run and the execution run are identical. The run is fast because of the hardware interpreter.

(d) It is easier to debug a program on a single HLL computer than on a conventional computer since the execution process inside the machine is simpler to understand. For example, the core dump bears a direct proximity to the input high-level language code.

REFERENCES

Anderson, J. P. [1961]. A computer for direct execution of algorithmic languages, *Proc. FJCC 1961* 184–193.

Barton, R. S. [1961]. A new approach to the functional design of a digital computer, *Proc. WJCC 1961* 393–396.

Bloom, H. M. [1970]. Design and simulation of an ALGOL computer, Tech. Rep. 70-118. Computer Sci. Center, Univ. Maryland, College Park, Maryland.

Chesley, G. D., and Smith, W. R. [1971]. The hardware-implemented high-level machine language for SYMBOL, *Proc. SJCC 1971* 563–573.

Chu, Y. [1965]. An ALGOL-like computer design language, *Commun. ACM* October, 607–615.

Chu, Y. [1968]. A higher-order language for describing microprogrammed computers, Tech. Rep. 68-78. Computer Sci. Center, Univ. Maryland, College Park, Maryland.

Chu, Y. [1970]. Microprogrammed allocating-loader, Tech. Rep. 70-135. Computer Sci. Center, Univ. Maryland, College Park, Maryland.

Chu, Y. [1972]. "Computer Organization and Microprogramming." Prentice-Hall, Englewood Cliffs, New Jersey.

McKeeman, W. M. [1967]. Language directed computer design, *Proc. FJCC 1967* 413–417.

Rice, R., and Smith, W. R. [1971]. SYMBOL—a major departure from classic software dominating von Neumann computing systems, *Proc. SJCC 1971* 575–587.

Signiski, T. F. [1970]. Design of an ALGOL machine, Tech. Rep. 70-131. Computer Sci. Center, Univ. Maryland, College Park, Maryland.

Smith, W. R., *et al.* [1971]. SYMBOL—a large experimental system exploring major hardware replacement of software, *Proc. SJCC 1971* 601–616.

Design Concepts of Japanese-Language Data Processing Systems

Yaohan Chu

Department of Computer Science
and
Department of Electrical Engineering
University of Maryland
College Park, Maryland

1. INTRODUCTION

The electronic data processing system of today involves both programs and data. The data processing systems built in the U.S.A., for example, are equipped with input/output devices that accept an American character set. Thus, the programs are in American programming languages and the data are in an American character set. When such a data processing system is used to process Japanese data, the programs can be written in an American programming language as long as the programmers know the language. However, accepting and processing the data is a serious problem when the data are in a Japanese character set. It is conceivable that data processing systems could be built for accepting programs in a Japanese programming language and processing data in a Japanese character set. When such data processing systems become available, wide use of data processing systems by Japanese people can be realized.

15

2. FIVE TYPES OF JAPANESE-LANGUAGE DATA PROCESSING SYSTEMS

The Japanese language makes use of a large set of characters. The average Japanese person has a vocabulary of at least 2000 characters. Each character consists of one to twenty or more strokes. Some of these characters are indeed difficult to write. Because of the large character set, Japanese input/ output devices are unquestionably more expensive than western input/output devices.

In this paper, Japanese-language data processing systems refer to those computer systems that can accept programs in a Japanese programming language and data in Japanese characters. Although input/output devices that accept Japanese characters are essential, there are several approaches to implementing such a system. This paper presents design concepts of five types of Japanese-language data processing systems:

Type 1. those Japanese-language data processing systems that accept assembly code in English and hand-coded Japanese data and use an expanded subroutine library.

Type 2. those Japanese-language data processing systems that accept assembly code and data, both in Japanese, by adding a preassembler and translators to the manufacturer-supplied assembler and linkage editor.

Type 3. those Japanese-language data processing systems that accept a high-level Japanese programming language and Japanese data. There are two choices: (a) those having a set of conventional instructions as the machine language (Type 3a); (b) those having a set of Japanese-language-oriented instructions as the machine language (Type 3b).

Type 4. those Japanese-language data processing systems that accept a high-level Japanese programming language and Japanese data, and have the Japanese-language-oriented postfix string as the machine language. There are two choices: (a) those using a software translator (Type 4a); (b) those using a hardware translator (Type 4b).

Type 5. those Japanese-language data processing systems that accept a high-level Japanese programming language and Japanese data, and have the high-level language itself as the machine language (i.e., one-level language).

In the above systems, Types 1 and 2 accept a low-level assembly language, while the other three systems accept high-level languages. However, Types 1 and 2 can be made to accept one or more high-level programming languages, as will be shown later.

It should be noted that these systems differ not only in the demarcation between hardware and software, but also in the proximity between the programming language that one uses and the machine language that is implemented in hardware.

3. TYPE 1: SYSTEM USING HAND-CODED JAPANESE DATA

The Type 1 Japanese-language data processing system makes use of a commercially available computer system such as those built in the U.S.A., Great Britain, and Japan. Such a computer system has a central processor that can execute a set of instructions to carry out various arithmetic, logical, and other operations. It also has a random-access memory that is a linear array of memory words for storing programs and data. It is equipped with input/output devices that accept decimal digits, the English alphabet, some special characters, and in some Japanese computer systems, some 50 Katagana characters. The program and the data, whether in English or Japanese, must therefore be represented in the set of about 60–110 characters.

Figure 1 is a block diagram showing the Type 1 data processing system. This system utilizes the manufacturer-supplied assembler, linkage editor, and loader for assembly language programming. Thus, the assembly code is in English. The input data that are in Japanese characters must be hand-coded. Furthermore, the subroutine library must be expanded to include subroutines to handle the coded data.

The Type 1 data processing system is really not a Japanese-language data processing system. The hand-coding and decoding of Japanese data are not only time consuming, but they are also sources of errors since these operations are manual. Such a system is hard to use and requires a significant amount of manual effort, but it represents the early application of western computer systems to Japanese data processing.

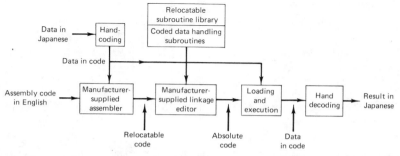

Fig. 1. Japanese-language data processing system accepting assembly code in English and hand-coded Japanese data by using an expanded subroutine library (Type 1).

4. TYPE 2: SYSTEM EQUIPPED WITH JAPANESE INPUT/OUTPUT DEVICES

The Type 2 Japanese-language data processing system is essentially a Type 1 system equipped with input/output devices that can accept Japanese characters. With the addition of these devices, the Type 2 system can now accept both Japanese assembly code and Japanese data.

Figure 2 is a block diagram showing the Type 2 data processing system. Although hand-coding of the input data and decoding of the output data are no longer required, additional software is needed. There is an input translator that converts the Japanese data from the external code of the input device into the internal code of the computer. This translator also converts the Japanese assembly code so that the manufacturer-supplied assembler, linkage editor, and loader can be used. The assembly language is now extended to include some new assembly instructions to handle Japanese data. A preassembler is provided to translate these new assembly instructions into those assembly instructions that are accepted by the manufacturer-supplied assembler. There is an output translator that converts the Japanese data from the internal code to the external code for the Japanese output device. Subroutines that handle Japanese data are still required.

The Type 2 system is rather a primitive Japanese-language data processing system. It adds three more layers of software to the multiple layers of software that already exist. As a result, it takes more computer time to execute and is thus more costly to run. Nevertheless, it is a great relief to the human coding and decoding of the Japanese characters and words. A

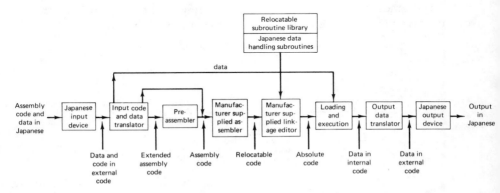

Fig. 2. Japanese-language data processing system accepting assembly code and data, both in Japanese, by adding a preassembler and translators to the manufacturer-supplied assembler and linkage editor (Type 2).

compromise solution would leave the assembly code in English but use the data in Japanese; this would allow a simpler input translator.

If the manufacturer-supplied assembler were replaced by a manufacturer-supplied compiler, both the Type 1 and Type 2 systems would accept a high-level programming language at the expense of more overhead time.

5. TYPE 3: SYSTEM THAT ACCEPTS A HIGH-LEVEL JAPANESE PROGRAMMING LANGUAGE

Both Type 1 and Type 2 systems accept low-level assembly language programs. Such programs are difficult to code and take time to debug. It has been widely recognized that high-level language programming is preferable. The Type 3 system is a data processing system that accepts a high-level Japanese programming language as well as Japanese data.

Figure 3 is a block diagram showing the Type 3 Japanese-language data processing system. This system is again equipped with Japanese input/ output devices. There are two subtypes, called Types 3a and 3b. Type 3a is similar to Type 2 except a compiler is now used to replace the preassembler and the assembler. This compiler is not the one supplied by the manufacturer. It has to be a new compiler since it is designed and implemented for a high-level Japanese programming language. The input data conversions, which are not specifically indicated in Fig. 1, are still required, but they would be carried out during compilation. Subroutines for handling Japanese data are also included as a part of the relocatable subroutine library.

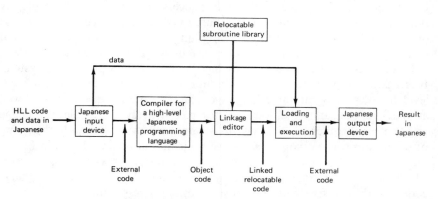

Fig. 3. Japanese-language data processing system accepting a high-level Japanese programming language and data in Japanese. There are two choices: (a) having the conventional instruction set as the machine language (Type 3a); (b) having the Japanese-language-oriented instruction set as the machine language (Type 3b).

Type 3a makes use of a commercially available computer system, but with a new compiler and an expanded subroutine library. The operations called for in the instructions of such a conventional computer system are not oriented to the operations required for the high-level programming language. If new software as well as new hardware were designed and implemented, the instruction set could be chosen to be closely oriented to the high-level Japanese programming language, and the system would produce a better throughput. The Type 3b system is such a system using new hardware and new software.

The development of high-level Japanese programming languages should be undertaken as a separate task from the design and implementation of the Japanese-language data processing system. These high-level Japanese programming languages could be simply translations of the existing high-level programming languages, such as FORTRAN, COBOL and ALGOL, with a larger character set, or they could be new ones that take advantage of the pitfalls and mistakes that have been made and since discovered.

6.   TYPE 4: SYSTEM HAVING A POSTFIX LANGUAGE AS THE MACHINE LANGUAGE

The lexicality, syntax, and semantics of the instruction set as well as the storage structure of a commercial computer system are quite different from those of a high-level programming language. This disparity is responsible for much of the software complexity of a commercial computer system. In addition, performance of the data processing system could be greatly improved if the computer architecture were specially conceived to be oriented to the high-level programming language instead of the traditional von Neumann architecture. Such a system is called the Type 4 system.

Figure 4 is a block diagram showing the Type 4 data processing system. It is again equipped with Japanese input/output devices to accept a high-level Japanese programming language program and Japanese data as well as to deliver output in Japanese. It is designed with an intermediate language to be referred to here as the "postfix string," which is essentially the string of the input program now in a reverse-Polish notation. As shown in Fig. 4, the system has a postfix-string translator and a postfix-string processor. The postfix-string translator translates the high-level Japanese language code into the postfix string. The postfix-string processor interprets the postfix string and executes the called-for operations. The result is then delivered by the Japanese output device.

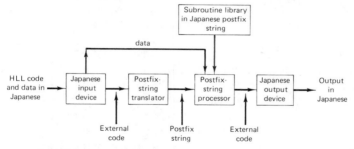

Fig. 4. Japanese-language data processing system accepting a high-level Japanese programming language and data in Japanese and having the postfix string as the machine language. There are two choices: (a) using a software translator (Type 4a); (b) using a hardware translator (Type 4b).

There are two varieties of the Type 4 system, Types 4a and 4b. Type 4a makes use of a software postfix-string translator. Thus, the machine language is the postfix-string language. Since the Burroughs B5500 (Burroughs Corp. [1968]) and B6500 computer systems also use a postfix-string language as the machine language, the Type 4a system is analogous to these Burroughs systems. Because the postfix-string language, which is the machine language, is oriented to the syntax of the high-level programming language, the Type 4a Japanese-language data processing system would be more effective and could deliver more throughput than the previous three types.

Instead of a software translator, the Type 4b data processing system uses a hardware postfix-string translator. The SYMBOL research computer system (Smith *et al.* [1971]), which makes use of such a hardware translator, is an example of this type. The Type 4b system gives some or all of the following advantages:

(a) There is no need to learn an assembly programming language since there is no assembly language. All the programs are written in a high-level programming language.

(b) Reduction in the amount of conventional software, since an assembler and a compiler are no longer needed.

(c) Elimination of overhead time for compilation and assembly of programs because neither is required.

(d) Software becomes more descriptive and thus easier to write and understand, since the software (if any) is written in the high-level language.

(e) The performance of the computer system is improved since less overhead work needs to be done by the machine.

7. TYPE 5: SYSTEM THAT DIRECTLY EXECUTES A HLJL PROGRAM

The Type 4 system translates the high-level Japanese-language (HLJL) program to an intermediate-language program such as the postfix string indicated in Fig. 4, and then executes the intermediate language program. Is the intermediate language necessary? No.

The Type 5 data processing system has no intermediate language, no assembly language, no relocatable language, and no absolute language. The high-level Japanese programming language is the machine language (Chu [1973]). A Type 5 system accepts a HLJL program and then executes it directly without translating the input program. It is equipped with the Japanese input/output devices and has a direct execution processor that scans the input program, recognizes its syntax, and then executes the operations in the program whenever the execution is possible. Figure 5 is a block diagram of the Type 5 system.

The Type 5 data processing system has the same advantages as those mentioned previously for the Type 4b data processing system. In addition:

(a)   It is a truly conversational system since there is no compilation of the high-level Japanese programming language. The debug run and the execution run are identical. The system runs fast because of complete hardware implementation in interpreting and executing the high-level Japanese-language program.

(b)   It is easier to debug a program on a Type 5 system than on a conventional computer system since the execution process that happens inside the machine is simpler to understand. For example, the core dump has a direct resemblance to the input high-level Japanese-language code.

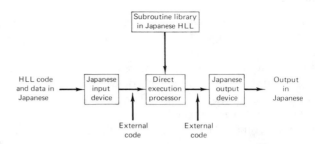

Fig. 5. Japanese-language data processing system accepting high-level Japanese programming language and data in Japanese and having the high-level language as the machine language (Type 5).

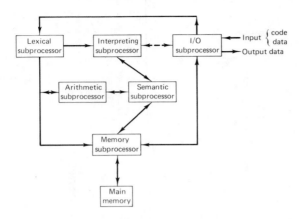

Fig. 6. Block diagram of a direct high-level language computer.

(c)   It is simple to learn to use the computer since there is only one high-level Japanese programming language.

(d)   The hardware designer and the software designer (if unconventional software is needed) communicate with less difficulty since the machine language and programming language are the same.

7.1   A Configuration

As an illustration, Fig. 6 is a block diagram of the direct execution computer of a Type 5 system with multiple subprocessors. It consists of a lexical subprocessor, an interpreting subprocessor, an arithmetic subprocessor, a semantic subprocessor, an I/O subprocessor, a memory subprocessor, and a main memory, in addition to the peripheral devices (not shown). This functionally oriented multiprocessor computer system can be visualized conceptually in the architectural diagram in Fig. 7. There are five processes: the lexical process, the arithmetic process, the interpreting process, the semantic process, and the I/O process, in addition to the input program buffer, the HLJL code area, the input data buffer, and the output data buffer. The HLJL code area stores the input HLJL program where the unnecessary blanks have been removed. The lexical process scans the HLJL code area and, when called, generates the next symbol. The interpreting process fetches the string of symbols, recognizes the syntax, and calls on the semantic process. The semantic process makes use of the block table, the operator stack, and the operand stack and performs the operations called for by the operators in the HLJL program.

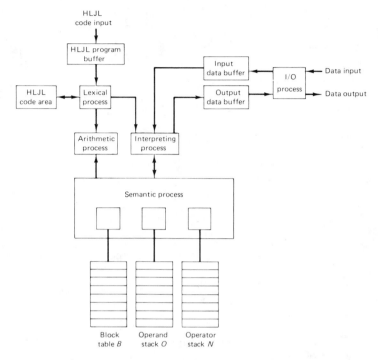

Fig. 7.   Architectural diagram of a direct high-level language computer.

7.2   A Japanese ALGOL Program

An ALGOL program is shown in Fig. 8a. It consists of one block, an integer declaration, and two assignment statements. A corresponding Japanese ALGOL program might appear as the program shown in Fig. 8b. The code of Fig. 8b, when stored in the HLJL code area of Fig. 7, might appear as shown in Fig. 9. There are nine memory words. Each word stores four characters; each character is located by the word count and character count. The lexical process scans the Japanese ALGOL program in the HLJL code area and delivers, at the requests from the interpreting process, a sequence of the symbols shown in the first column of Table I. For each request, the lexical process delivers not only the next symbol in the first column of a row, but also the word count, the character count, the hash code (if the symbol is an identifier), the type, and the value of the symbol as shown in the other five columns of the same row. The pair of numbers formed by the word count and character count is used to locate a particular

```
$ begin  integer SALARYRATE, SALARY;
         SALARYRATE := 5000;
         SALARY := SALARYRATE * 12
  end $
```
(a)

月収 := 5000;

年収 := 月収 * 12

終り $

(b)

Fig. 8. (a) An ALGOL program. (b) A Japanese ALGOL program.

character. The hash code is used to enter the identifier into the block table. If the symbol is an operator, it is indicated as type 4 and its value is its internal code. If the symbol is an identifier, it is indicated as type 3 and its value is the identifier itself.

7.3   Execution Algorithm

An algorithm for executing the HLJL code in Fig. 9 is shown in Fig. 10, where S_j denotes the symbol just fetched from the lexical processor and N_i the operator currently at the top of the operator stack. The execution begins at the "start" entry. It fetches symbol S_j from the lexical processor and determines its type.

(a)   If symbol S_j is an operator, it is saved by being pushed down to the operator stack. If the operator is "begin," the block table is set up to handle the entry of a block. The execution now returns to the start entry.

Character count

	0	1	2	3
0	$	始	め	
1	整	数		月
2	収	,	年	収
3	;	月	収	:
4	=	5	0	0
5	0	;	年	収
6	:	=	月	収
7	*	1	2	
8	終	リ	$	

Word count

Fig. 9.   The Japanese ALGOL program of Fig. 8b as stored in the HLJL code area of Fig. 7.

TABLE I

Sequence of Symbols Appearing as the Outputs of the Lexical Process

Next symbol	Word count	Character count	Identifier hash code	Symbol value	Symbol type
$	0	0		24	4(operator)
始め	0	1		23	4
整数	1	0		13	4
月収	1	3	4	月収	3(id)
,	2	1		3	4
年収	2	2	6	年収	3
;	3	0		21	4
月収	3	1	4	月収	3
:=	3	3		14	4
5000	4	1		5000	1(integer)
;	5	1		21	4
年収	5	2	6	年収	3
:=	6	0		14	4
月収	6	2	4	月収	3
*	7	0		5	4
12	7	1		12	1
終り	8	0		22	4
$	8	2		24	4

(b)   If symbol S_j is a number, the number is pushed down to the operand stack.

(c)   If symbol S_j is an identifier being declared (i.e., if operator N_i is "integer"), the variable is stored in the block table. If the next symbol is ",," the comma is ignored and the execution process returns to start; otherwise, the next symbol should be ";" and the execution process goes to entry B.

(d)   If symbol S_j is an identifier being referenced, the variable has already been stored in the block table and is now pushed down to the operand stack.

In the above, if symbol S_j is a number or a variable being referenced, the number or the variable has already been pushed down to the operand stack. Some operation is now to be performed according to the precedence relation between symbol S_j and operator N_i as described below.

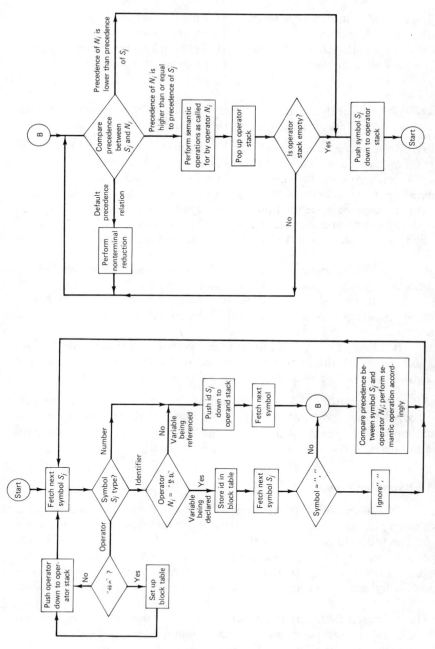

Fig. 10. Flowchart showing the algorithm used in executing the HLJL code directly by the Type 5 data processing system.

The algorithm in Fig. 10 is formulated using two properties of the operator precedence grammar: (1) no two nonterminals can exist adjacently and (2) at most one precedence relation exists between two terminals N_i and S_j that surround a nonterminal NT in the program string as shown below,

$$N_i \langle NT \rangle S_j$$

where symbol S_j at this instant is also an operator. The precedence relation between N_i and S_j determines the following action:

(a)   If the precedence of operator N_i is higher than or equal to that of symbol S_j, the operation called for by operator N_i is carried out, and as a result forms a new nonterminal. The operator in the operator stack is now popped up. If the operator stack is not empty, the execution process returns to where the precedence relation between symbol S_j and operator N_i now at the top of the operator stack is compared. If it is empty, symbol S_j is pushed down to the operator stack and the execution process returns to start.

(b)   If the precedence of operator N_i is lower than that of symbol S_j, symbol S_j is pushed down to the operator stack, because scanning of the current production must be continued to form a new nonterminal before the operation called for by operator N_i is carried out. The execution process returns to start.

(c)   If the precedence relation between symbol S_j and operator N_i does not exist (default), the current nonterminal at the top of the operand stack is reduced to another nonterminal and no other operation is required.

After the operation or operations called for by the operators are performed, the execution process returns to start. This process of fetching and handling the next symbol from the lexical process continues until the end mark of the input ALGOL string $ is reached (not shown in Fig. 10).

7.4   Execution Process

Table II is an execution table designed to show what happens during the execution process. Each succeeding entry of this table shows the next symbol from the lexical processor and the contents of the latest elements of the operator stack, the operand stack, and the block table. By referring to the algorithm shown in Fig. 10 and following the entries of the execution table sequentially, one can visualize the execution process of the ALGOL program of Fig. 8b.

The execution table has five columns. The first column shows the next symbol, and the second through fourth columns show the contents of the latest entry of the operator stack (the top element), the operand stack (the

TABLE II

The Execution Table for the Program in Fig. 8b

Next symbol S_j	Operator stack		Operand stack		Block table		Remarks
	N_i	i	O_k	k	B_r	r	
$	$ (24)	1					
始め	始め (23)	2					
整数	整数 (13)	3					
月収	整数 (13)	3			月収, 整, 64	4	Block table
					0	64	value entry
,	整数 (13)	3					Comma ignored
年収	整数 (13)	3			年収, 整, 65	6	
					0	65	Block table
;	始め (23)	2					value entry
	; (21)	3					
月収	; (21)	3	変, 64, 整	1			
:=	:= (14)	4	変, 64, 整	1			
5000	:= (14)	4	定, 5000, 整	2			
;	:= (14)	4	定, 5000, 整	1	5000	64	
	始め (23)	2		0			
	; (21)	3					
年収	; (21)	3	変, 65, 整	1			
:=	:= (14)	4	変, 65, 整	1			
月収	:= (14)	4	変, 64, 整	2			
*	* (5)	5	変, 64, 整	2			
12	* (5)	5	定, 12, 整	3			
終り	:= (14)	4	定, 60,000, 整	2			
	; (21)	3	定, 60,000, 整	1	60,000	65	
	始め (23)	2		0			
	終り (22)	3					
$	始め (23)	2					
	$ (24)	1					Stop

top element), and the block table (the latest element), respectively. The fifth column is for remarks. The formats of the first four columns are as follows:

Next symbol: This shows symbol S_j fetched from the lexical processor. The sequence of these symbols has been shown in Table I.

Operator stack: Stack N stores the operators temporarily for use in reductions. There are two subcolumns: *pointer i,* which points to the top element of the stack, and *operator* N_i, which is the operator in the top element.

Operand stack: Stack O stores operands (or nonterminals) temporarily. There are two subcolumns: *pointer k,* which points to the top element of the stack, and *operand* O_k, which is the operand in the top element. There are two types of operands in this stack: constant (3 fields: 定 , value, 整), where the second field contains the value of the constant, and variable (3 fields: 定 , hash code, 整), where the second field points to the value of the variable stored in the block table.

Block table: Block table B contains the names and values of the identifiers as they are declared or referenced. Each identifier is entered at a table location between 0 and 63; this location is determined by the hash code of the identifier's name. There are two subcolumns in this column: *pointer r,* which points to the location of the latest entry of the table, and *identifier* B_r, which has two types of entries: one containing the name of the latest entry and the other its value. The name entry contains three fields: the identifier's name, the identifier's type, and the pointer to the entry for the identifier's value, which is located beginning at location 64 of this table.

It should be cautioned that when the next symbol is fetched, changes in the entries of the execution table may occur more than once. In this case, more than one line is used or only the latest contents are shown. One can observe the occurrence of an operation by noting a change in the pointer value. If the value of the pointer to the operator stack decreases, an operation has taken place; this operation is usually preceded by some change in the operand stack or the block table. If the value of the pointer is increased, no operation occurs, but rather symbol S_j is pushed down to the operator stack N.

Acknowledgment

The author wishes to express his appreciation to Mr. Kenichi Harada of Keio University, Japan, now visiting at the University of Maryland, for his assistance in the preparation of this paper.

REFERENCES

Burroughs Corp. [1968]. "Burroughs B5500, Reference Manual."

Chu, Y. [1973]. Introducing the high-level language computer architecture, Tech. Rep. TR-227. Computer Sci. Center, Univ. Maryland, College Park, Maryland.

Smith, W. R., *et al.* [1971]. SYMBOL—A large experimental system exploring major hardware replacement of software, *Proc. SJCC 1971* 601–616.

A Survey of High-Level Language Computer Architecture

Carl R. Carlson

Computer Sciences Department
Northwestern University
Evanston, Illinois

1. INTRODUCTION

As Rosen [1968] notes, all of the features that have been designed into digital computers may be considered as reflections of software needs. However, over the past decade, there has been increased interest in using hardware and firmware to implement various computer functions that traditionally have been performed by software. The technical and economic feasibility of this approach is due to the rapid advancement of hardware technology and to recent developments in microprogramming techniques. Microprogramming, especially, has provided the computer designer with a flexible and effective tool with which to engineer a new class of computers.

Much of the research in this area has centered around the development of HLL computer architecture, i.e., computer architecture that has been

31

designed to facilitate the interpretation of one or more specific high-level programming languages. The objective of this chapter is to survey these research efforts.

2. HLL COMPUTER ARCHITECTURE

As early as 1953 (Hopper and Mauchly [1953]), researchers were investigating the influence of programming techniques on the design of computers. Since then, computers have been designed for such well-known high-level programming languages as ALGOL 60, FORTRAN, EULER, PL/1, APL, and SNOBOL.

2.1 Burroughs B5500

The first significant step in the development of HLL computer architecture occurred with the introduction of the Burroughs B5500 computer system in 1961 (Lonergan and King [1961], Barton [1961]). Many of the architectural concepts that the B5500 introduced have been further developed in the B6500/B6700 and have also been adopted in the design of various HLL computers. For example, the machine language of the B5500 consists of a Polish string of lexical units called "syllables." Each syllable has a fixed length and is of one of four types: an operator, a literal, an operand-call, or a descriptor-call. Most HLL computers have adopted some form of a Polish string as their machine language; however, they differ in their choice of lexical units.

The B5500 also introduced the idea of using a hardware stack to hold operands and intermediate results during expression evaluation and to store control words for handling interrupts and nested procedure calls. Figure 1 shows how the hardware stack is utilized in the interpretation of

Syllable executed	Contents of			
	Register A	Register B	Register S	Cell 100
L	L	Empty	100	—
M	M	L	100	—
N { Pushdown	Empty	M	101	L
N { Execute	N	M	101	L
+	Empty	M + N	101	L
× { Pushup	M + N	L	100	—
× { Execute	Empty	L × (M + N)	100	—

Fig. 1.   Execution of Polish string LMN + × (Lonergan and King [1961]).

the Polish string LMN + ×. It should be noted that only the top two elements on the stack are stored in hardware registers (registers A and B). The rest are stored in memory cells. Also, register S points to the next available memory location that the stack mechanism can use.

To solve the problem of program relocatability, the B5500 uses a *program reference table* (PRT) that is resident in memory and that holds all the actual addresses of data and program branch points. Thus, the program itself does not contain any addresses, but only references to the PRT.

It should be noted that the idea of utilizing a runtime stack was introduced at about the same time by the KDF.9 computer system (Haley [1962]) and the ADM machine (Hamblin [1960]), which was never completed as it was similar to the KDF.9 machine. Iliffe's Basic Language Machine (BLM) (Iliffe [1968, 1969]) also shared many of the design principles of the Burroughs computers but differed in several important respects. Rather than orienting the BLM hardware design towards a specific high-level language, an attempt was made to identify the types of data structures that programmers actually use and support those structures efficiently with hardware providing the necessary basic operations to generate and manipulate the structures.

2.2 ALGOL Processors

In 1961, Anderson [1961] reported on the design (at the state-transition-matrix level) of a computer that would execute ALGOL 60 programs directly. Figure 2 shows the organization of Anderson's proposed machine, which basically is an extension of the B5500 architecture.

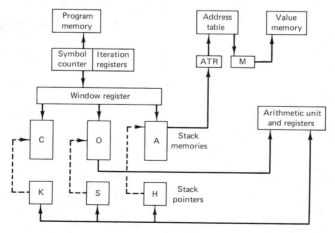

Fig. 2.   Anderson's proposed ALGOL 60 computer (from Anderson [1961]).

The *symbol counter* addresses successive symbols of the program in the *program memory* and places these symbols in the *window register*. There, the symbol type is determined and, depending upon the control state, is entered into the appropriate stack. The three stack memories (C, O, and A) and their associated stack pointers (K, S, and H) serve to record control and subcontrol states, arithmetic operators, and operands, respectively. Because of the decision to interpret ALGOL 60 directly, it was necessary to include the operator stack in order to resolve operator precedence each time an arithmetic expression was interpreted. The effort required repeatedly to resolve operator precedence, and therefore the need for an operator stack, has been eliminated in most of the other proposed HLL computers by including a language processor that converts programs into some form of Polish string prior to program interpretation.

The *address table* is used by the addressing mechanism to relate each variable to the location in the *value memory* where its value is stored. In ALGOL 60, this task has been complicated by the fact that the same identifier can be used to denote several different variables. The problem of resolving which location is being referenced with each occurrence of an identifier is a special case of the "address resolution" problem. Anderson's machine handles this problem by keeping an entry in the address table for the variable that is currently being referenced by a particular identifier and saving control-word descriptors in the value memory for each of the other variables associated with the same identifier. This means that the machine must be capable of determining which control word descriptors need to be returned to the address table when control exits from each block. Anderson omits details concerning the implementation of this mechanism. It should be noted that better software solutions to this problem have long existed and that efforts to implement these solutions in hardware have been realized (Organick [1973], McMahan and Feustal [1973], Weber [1967]).

Since 1967, Chu and others at the University of Maryland have pursued the design of an ALGOL 60 computer system (Chu [1970, 1973a], Bloom [1970], Signiski [1970], Haynes [1973]). Their approach is similar to Anderson's insofar as their proposed machine would interpret ALGOL 60 directly. However, their description is much more detailed and complete.

Figure 3 shows the block diagram of the computer system they have proposed. It consists of a *lexical processor,* an *interpreting processor,* an *I/O processor,* a *main memory processor,* and various peripheral devices. The lexical processor scans the HLL code and, when called by the interpreting processor, generates the next symbol, giving the type and value of the symbol (also the hash code if the symbol is an identifier). Under control of the interpreting processor, the semantic processor performs the

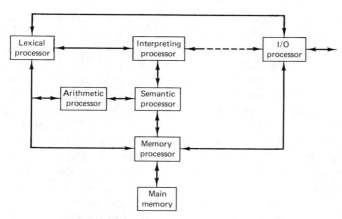

Fig. 3.   Block diagram for Chu's ALGOL computer.

operations called for by the operators in the HLL program, making use of node and block tables and operator and operand stacks.

2.3   FORTRAN Processors

In 1965, Melbourne and Pugmire [1965] reported on the design of a microprogrammed FORTRAN computer that they designed for use by inexperienced programmers who need to solve small scientific problems with a minimum of delay and cost.

The machine language that they proposed is essentially the same as FORTRAN except for the following differences:

(1) all identifiers (including array names) are replaced by storage addresses,

(2) delimiters initiating a chain of control commands are replaced by the control-unit address of that command sequence,

(3) delimiters denoting statement types are not stored,

(4) arithmetic statements are converted into reverse Polish notation.

The microprogrammed translator proposed to realize these transformations would also check statements for syntactic errors, convert lexical units such as constants, identifiers, statement numbers, etc. into standardized form, allocate space in the data storage area for all identifiers, function arguments, and arrays, and construct symbol and statement number tables.

Program execution is supervised by the *master microprogram*, which scans the instruction string looking for the next operator byte. Upon detection of an operator byte, the master microprogram puts the address of that instruction on the *instruction stack*. Control is then transferred to the appropriate microsubroutine, which interprets the instruction. When interpretation of the instruction is completed, its address is popped from the instruction stack and the master microprogram assumes control. In the case of the DO statement, this normally does not occur until all the instructions in its range have been performed the specified number of times. Occurrence of a second DO within the range of the first will increase the instruction stack. Thus, during the execution of a DO nest of depth d, the instruction stack will contain up to $d + 1$ entries. The last instruction in any DO range contains an EDR (End DO Range) flag in the operator byte. After execution of each instruction, the master microprogram tests for an EDR flag. If it is present, control transfers to the DO statement whose address is the top entry in the instruction stack; otherwise, the next instruction in sequence is executed.

As conceived of by the authors, the proposed machine would consist of a conventional register–data flow configuration together with microprograms for operation, execution, compilation, array manipulation, function execution, and stack management.

Based on some performance studies that the authors conducted with a simulator of the proposed machine, they concluded that the performance of a microprogrammed implementation of this machine would be comparable to that achievable with a software compiler on a conventional computer with similar speed.

Bashkow *et al.* [1967] also designed a FORTRAN-subset machine. However, the description of the organization of their machine, which includes the design of control circuits and the specification of registers, data representation, etc., is much more detailed than that of Melbourne and Pugmire. The Bashkow *et al.* machine is a hardware version of a one-pass-load-and-go compiler in which the machine language produced by the compiler is similar to the FORTRAN source language. Interpretation of the FORTRAN-like machine language is also performed by hardware.

Figure 4 shows the overall organization of their FORTRAN computer system. The system operates in either of two modes, LOAD or EXECUTE. The LOAD circuits control the input of FORTRAN statements, perform lexical and syntactical analysis, and construct a modified form of the FORTRAN statements in the *program area*. A scan circuit checks each successive symbol of the incoming FORTRAN statements. If the first symbol is a digit, then control is turned over to a statement number LOAD circuit, which enters the statement number together with the current value of the *program counter* into the *symbol table*. Once the statement type is determined, then control is turned over to the appropriate loading circuit.

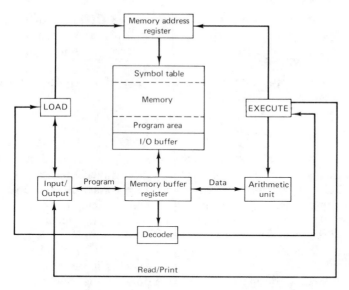

Fig. 4. FORTRAN computer system (from Bashkow *et al.* [1967]).

LOAD circuits have been designed for each of the following FORTRAN statements: DIMENSION, assignment, DO, GO TO, computed GO TO, READ, PRINT, IF, PAUSE, and CONTINUE. Noticeably absent from this list are the FORTRAN COMMON, EQUIVALENCE, and FORMAT statements, which probably can be more cost effectively implemented in software. It should be noted that Bashkow *et al.* have also avoided the problems involved in evaluating mixed-mode expressions by only allowing decimal floating-point numbers internally. All of the LOAD circuits mentioned above put the statements into the program area after replacing variable names with actual data addresses. The first occurrence of a variable name (note that subscripted variable names are found in DIMENSION statements that must precede the use of these variables in the program) causes the name to be placed in the symbol table and storage to be reserved following the name in the symbol table. Thereafter, references to these variable names are replaced by their data addresses. Because of the "one-pass" nature of the LOAD circuits, only references to statement numbers that have already been encountered in the program string are replaced by their corresponding program addresses. Thus, forward references to statement numbers are handled by indirect addressing through the statement number entry in the symbol table.

When the END statement is encountered by the scan circuit, the machine enters EXECUTE mode and begins execution of the first statement, which is always found at memory address 100. The EXECUTE mode scan circuit uses the first symbol of each statement to determine the statement type and subsequently turns control over to the appropriate statement execution circuit.

Figure 5 shows the internal representation of the following FORTRAN program segment:

$$\text{DO} \quad 5 \qquad I = 1, 150 \neq$$
$$5 \ \text{SUM} = \text{SUM} + I \neq$$

Both of these proposed FORTRAN computers make use of many techniques that have proven effective in similar software implementations. However, some techniques that were used were not the best available. For example, both machines employ a sequential search of the symbol table instead of using one of the faster techniques that software implementations usually employ. This probably means that neither of these machines could be used to interpret large FORTRAN programs efficiently. It should be noted that neither one of these proposed machines was ever implemented. However, the Bashkow *et al.* design is sufficiently complete that construction seems feasible.

2.4   EULER Processor

Another significant step in the development of HLL computer architecture occurred in 1967 with the implementation of a EULER (Wirth and Weber [1966]) processor in microcode on an IBM 360/30 (Weber [1967]). EULER, a generalization of ALGOL 60, contains additional data types (e.g., references) and data structures (e.g., a treelike data structure called a "list") and employs dynamic data-type handling. Because of the dynamic nature of EULER and the special functions that it contains that are not directly supported in 360 hardware (e.g., list processing operations), the object code produced by compilation often consumes more space and requires more execution time than object code produced for a less dynamic and flexible language (e.g., FORTRAN). In cases like this, it is generally felt that a microcoded interpreter would yield much better object-code economy and performance than that achievable through the traditional software compilation approach. In the EULER implementation, this has been shown to be true, especially in the implementation of dynamic type testing and various stack and list processing operations. The EULER system consists of three parts:

(1) a microprogrammed translator, which is a one-pass, syntax-driven compiler that translates EULER source-language programs into a string-language (reverse-Polish) representation,

Symbol table		Program area	
Address	Contents	Address	Contents
4095	Δ ⎫	0100	DO
4094	00 ⎪	0101	λ
4093	05 ⎬(a)	0102	01 ⎫
4092	01 ⎪	0103	32 ⎬(c)
4091	01 ⎭	0104	I
4090	I	0105	40
4089		0106	89
4088		0107	=
4087		0108	00
4086	00 ⎫	0109	01
4085	05 ⎪	0110	04
4084	01 ⎬(b)	0111	,
4083	16 ⎭	0112	01
4082	S	0113	50
4081	U	0114	04
4080	M	0115	≠
4079		0116	00
4078		0117	05
4077		0118	01
		0119	01
		0120	S
		0121	40
		0122	79
		0123	=
		0124	S
		0125	40 ⎫
		0126	79 ⎬(d)
		0127	+
		0128	I
		0129	40
		0130	89
		0131	≠
		0132	

Fig. 5. The internal representation for

$$\text{DO} \quad 5 \qquad I = 1,150 \neq$$
$$5 \; \text{SUM} = \text{SUM} + I \neq$$

(a) Reference to statement 5 by DO statement at program address 0101. (b) End of DO range at statement 0116. (c) Address of statement following DO range. (d) Address of SUM's data area in the symbol table. (From Bashkow *et al.* [1967]).

(2) a microprogrammed interpreter, which interprets string-language programs,

(3) a 360 machine language I/O control program, which handles all I/O requests of the translator and interpreter.

The microprogrammed compiler consists of the following four parts:

(1) *Lexical analyzer*. Symbols are read in and translated into their respective internal formats. Included in each format is a tag field that indicates the symbol type.

(2) *Syntactic analyzer*. Parsing is driven by the precedence table for the language, which is kept in memory.

(3) *Intermediate-language string generator*. When the syntactic analyzer identifies a syntactic unit to be reduced, the appropriate generation routine is called.

(4) *Error detector*. Upon the detection of a syntactic error, the compilation process terminates.

After compilation, a program consists of a reverse-Polish string of variable-length symbols. Most of the symbols that denote operators are only one byte long (e.g., +, −, begin, end, ←, go to). However, some operators require an additional two bytes to hold an absolute program address. For example, the symbol denoting the "then" operator contains the program address (PA) of the first symbol in the corresponding "else" clause.

Symbols denoting data are of yet a different length.

For example, the symbol that denotes a positive number requires three additional bytes to hold the 24-bit absolute address of the integer constant.

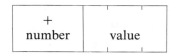

It should also be noted that symbols that denote data include a descriptor field, thus facilitating dynamic type testing and automatic conversion.

The microprogrammed EULER interpreter sequentially reads each symbol in the intermediate-language string and branches to the appropriate microsubroutine to interpret that symbol. As was the case with the previous machines, the interpreter utilizes a stack to control the processing of blocks and procedures and to store temporary values during expression evaluation.

Like ALGOL, EULER allows multiple occurrences of the same identifier. However, the implementation of address resolution in the EULER machine is different from that of the previous machines in that no symbol table is maintained at execution time. Instead, each identifier is replaced by the reference symbol @ together with the block number (BN) of the block to which the identifier is bound and its ordinal number (ON) within that block.

@	BN	ON

The language restriction that variables must be declared before they can be used facilitates the determination of BN and ON by the one-pass compiler. This solution to the address resolution problem is similar to the usual software-implemented solution. EULER solutions to other language problems are described in Wirth and Weber [1966].

The 60-bit microprogram word used in implementing EULER contains fields that perform such basic functions as storage control, control of the data-flow registers and the arithmetic-logic unit, microprogram sequencing and branch control, and status-bit-setting control. To implement the EULER compiler, 500 microwords of 60-bit ROS and approximately 1200 bytes of main storage space were required. The total ROS space requirement for the string-language interpreter is estimated at 2500 microwords.

2.5 PL/1 Processors

Sugimoto [1969] has proposed a PL/1 processor that consists of a translator, called the PL/1 *reducer,* and a hardware interpreter consisting of several autonomous units, called the *direct processor.* The reducer is a programming system that translates PL/1 source text into a list-structured machine language, called the *Direct Processor Input Language* (DPIL). The DPIL consists of four parts:

(1) *Program structure list (PSL),* which describes the control flow of a program and the type of each statement in the program. In addition, each entry contains a pointer to the complete statement description in the SNFL [see (2) below]. The list-structured, concise form of the PSL permits easy on-line modification of the source program. It should be noted that the idea of representing an internal language in list-structured form has long been used successfully in software implementations of conversational programming systems. It would seem to be just as applicable in the case of a hardware implementation.

(2) *Statement normal form list (SNFL),* which is composed of an *instruction list* (IL) and an *auxiliary list* (AXL) and contains the semantic content of each statement in reverse-Polish form. Included with each operation descriptor is a tag field that indicates whether or not the next operation can be executed in parallel with this operation.

(3) *Attribute list (AL),* which contains the attributes of program variables.

(a) Sample PL/1 source program

```
P:    PROCEDURE OPTIONS (MAIN);
      DECLARE (A, B, I, J, L, M, N) FIXED DECIMAL (10);
      DO I = 1 TO J * L BY M/N WHILE (A ≥ B);
      A = A + I; END;
      END P;
```

(b) The PSL

Address	Type	T	V	H
1	PROCST	1	0	5
5	DCLST	2	8	—
8	DOST	3	18	12
12	ASGS	43	15	—
15	ENDST	0	0	—
18	ENDST	0	0	—

T = link address to the SNFL
V = vertical link address (within PSL)
H = horizontal link address (within PSL)

(c) The AXL

Address	Link address	
1**	0	
2**	0	
3**	1	(Initial value)
4**	23	(BY)
5**	13	(TO)
6**	33	(WHILE)

(d) The portion of the IL corresponding to A = A + I;

Address = 43

ADD   OPEIN = 2   P/S TAG * S *

		Type	Description	Address
OPRD	1	WS	AR RL FX DC	(0, 1)
OPRD	2	ID	AR RL FX DC	(2, 0)
OPRD	3	ID	AR RL FX DC	(2, 2)

Address = 50

TRN   OPEIN = 2   P/S TAG * R *

		Type	Description	Address
OPRD	1	ID	AR RL FX DC	(2, 0)
OPRD	2	WS	AR RL FX DC	(0, 1)

OPRD = operand
OPEIN = number of operands
WS = operand is in working storage
ID = operand is an identifier
AR RL FX DC = operand is a fixed decimal real arithmetic value
(i, j) = (block number, ordinal number) 2-level logical address

Fig. 6. Example of a DPIL program (adapted from Sugimoto [1969]).

(4) *Constant list (CL)*, which contains the attributes and values of program constants.

Figure 6 shows a portion of the DPIL representation of a sample PL/1 program.

The PL/1 reducer has been implemented. For typical scientific programs, the author claims that the length of the object code generated by the PL/1 reducer is shorter by a factor of 25% on the average than that which could be generated by the PL/1 compilers available at that time.

The direct processor consists of several functionally autonomous units (see Fig. 7). A brief description of the function of each of these units follows.

Together, the two *instruction stacks* (IS) and the *instruction issuing unit* (IIU) handle the decoding of instructions and issuing of control commands to the *operation unit controller* (OUC). The OUC checks whether or not an *operation unit* (OU) for the specified command is busy and takes an appropriate action. Several OUs are provided: fixed-point arithmetic units for both decimal and binary numbers, floating-point arithmetic units, logical-operation units, string-processing units, data-conversion units, and array-address-calculation units.

The *memory unit controller* (MUC) has two functions. One is runtime storage allocation and recovery. The other is address mapping: the two-level logical address specified in the SNFL is converted to a physical address

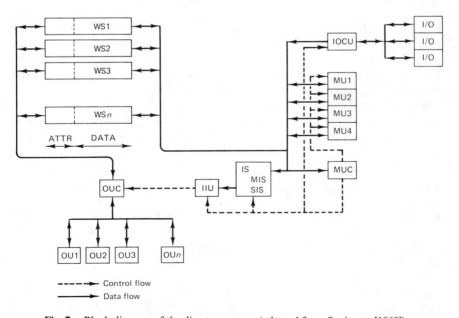

Fig. 7. Block diagram of the direct processor (adapted from Sugimoto [1969]).

by the MUC. The *memory unit* (MU) is used to store the PSL, SNFL, AL, and programmer-defined data. Finally, *working storage* (WS) is a high-speed temporary storage in which data going to or from the memory unit and temporary results from the execution of various operations are stored.

The amount of parallelism and execution efficiency achievable by the functionally autonomous units of the direct processor is not known since it has not yet been implemented in hardware. When the research was reported, only an interpreter for a subset of the DPIL had been implemented in order to validate the execution algorithms.

More recently, Wortman [1972] has also considered the design of a PL/1 machine.

2.6   ADAM Processor

Mullery *et al.* ([1963], Mullery [1964]) designed a problem-oriented symbol processor, called ADAM, and concluded that a high-level language could be implemented with a reasonable amount of hardware. They designed their own high-level language and then proposed a machine organization that would implement this language directly and yet would not impose any restrictions on the use of the language.

The most significant feature of the ADAM machine is the way in which variable-length data are structured. Special symbols are actually placed within the data for the purpose of describing the data structure (e.g., array, tree, English text). This is in contrast with conventional machines where such structure is present in the addressing portions of the object code. More recently, this concept has been extended and actually implemented in hardware as part of the SYMBOL project (Chesley and Smith [1971], Rice and Smith [1971], Rice [1972a, b], Cowart *et al.* [1971], Smith *et al.* [1971], Smith [1972], Zingg [1972], Chu [1972], Laliotis [1973], Richards and Wright [1973], Richards and Zingg [1973], Anderberg [1973], Hutchinson and Ethington [1973]).

2.7   SYMBOL Processor and the B1700

Probably the most significant event in the development of HLL computer architecture occurred in 1971 with the announcement of the construction of the SYMBOL computer system (Rice and Smith [1971]). Because so much has already been written about SYMBOL, this section will only review some of the highlights of the system.

The SYMBOL system (see Fig. 8) contains a *main memory*, onto which a virtual memory is mapped, and several hard-wired, specialized processors

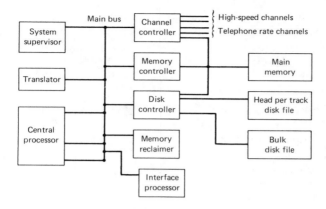

Fig. 8. SYMBOL computer system (from Smith *et al.* [1971]).

that operate as autonomous units. These processors and the functions they perform are:

(1) Central processor (39 cards)
    Polish-string processing
    Variable-length numeric and string processing
    Precision-controlled arithmetic processing
    Automatic data-type conversion
    Dynamically variable data structuring
    Structure referencing
    Direct symbolic addressing
    Variable structure assignment
(2) Translator (15 cards)
    Name-table generation
    Object-string generation
    Address linking
    Library access and linking
(3) Interface processor (8 cards)
    Buffer processing
    Information transfer to and from virtual memory
    Text editing
(4) Memory controller (15 cards)
    Page allocation
    System-address processing
    Data-string management
    Page-table management
(5) Memory reclaimer (2 cards)
    Processing of deleted space to make reusable

(6) Disk-channel processor (3 cards)
   Page-transfer control
   Page-table processing
(7) Channel controller (11 cards)
   Channel sequencing
   Buffer processing
   I/O-message control
(8) System supervisor (14 cards)
   Task-queue processing
   Interrupt processing
   Paging control
   Real-time processing
   Software communication control

The number associated with each processor indicates the number of printed circuit boards used to implement that particular unit. Each board contains from 160 to 200 integrated circuits. Approximately 18,000 integrated circuit packages were required to implement the complete machine, which puts it in the medium-scale computer range.

The SYMBOL language is a general-purpose, procedural language whose design has been strongly influenced by such languages as ALGOL, PL/1, and EULER. As indicated earlier, the hardware-implemented, one-pass translator generates a reverse-Polish representation of the source program, produces a name table, which is used during program interpretation, and performs the function of address linking.

The *central processor* (CP) is the interpretation unit for the translated language. It receives from the translator the reverse-Polish string and the nested name table. The CP has four distinct sections: the *instruction sequencer* (IS), the *reference processor* (RP), the *arithmetic processor* (AP), and the *format and string processor* (FP). The IS (1) acts as the master controller and switching unit of the CP, scanning the reverse-Polish string and accumulating items in the processing stack for the various units it supplies, (2) prepares data for assignment by the RP or output by the I/O unit, and (3) dynamically creates nested language blocks. The RP performs a number of structure-handling tasks that can be categorized as dynamically creating structures and substructures and resolving references to substructures. The AP is a serial process unit operating on variable-length data consisting of floating-point, normalized, decimal numbers. The FP unit performs several string-manipulation operations (including editing) on variable-length strings and automatic type conversion on operands requested by the IS. Determining whether or not type conversion is necessary is facilitated by the fact that type and length information is carried with the data itself.

Opinions on the significance of the SYMBOL computer system have been expressed by Rice [1972a] and Chu [1972]. Two objections to the SYMBOL project are

(1) The SYMBOL machine may not be an effective or efficient machine on which to run programs from a language that is fundamentally different from the SYMBOL language. In defense of the SYMBOL machine it should be noted that no one has investigated whether or not translation from any language X to the SYMBOL language is more difficult or inefficient than translation to the machine language of any conventional computer.

(2) Error corrections, extensions, new language elements, etc., are difficult to achieve in a language whose implementation is hard wired.

The B1700 architecture (Wilner [1972]) provides an alternative approach that claims to solve the first problem, if it really is a problem. Underlying the B1700 is a hardware machine that has been specifically designed to perform interpretation. Implemented in this machine are several firmware machines. Each firmware machine is designed for a particular application area, e.g., business data processing and numerical processing. As a result, every FORTRAN program is translated into the "machine language" of the firmware machine that most closely "resembles" the FORTRAN language. The same approach would be applied to programs written in a language such as COBOL, ALGOL, or PL/1. The only difference is that different firmware machines may be required for some of these languages. For example, languages like COBOL and RPG require a firmware machine that has been designed for business data processing instead of scientific processing.

Like the SYMBOL machine, the B1700 has abolished the idea of fixed-length word sizes and data formats, i.e., above the hardware level. Instead, the basic unit of information is the dynamically variable-length bit string. Other similarities between these two machines exist in the areas of virtual-memory management and system-level management (e.g., multiprogramming).

SYMBOL's solution to the second problem is to permit hardware interrupts at compile and execution time. These interrupts allow a breakout from the high-level language that may result in a "system program" call to perform any desired task. On conventional computers these breakouts are referred to as "programmed operators" or "extracodes."

2.8 APL Processors

APL is a compact and precise language that is better suited for handling arrays of data than such scalar-oriented languages as FORTRAN and ALGOL 60. APL has many features that distinguish it from FORTRAN and ALGOL 60, some of which are (1) the absence of type-declaration statements, (2) the absence of DIMENSION statements, (3) operators that can be applied to scalar, vector, and array operands, (4) dynamic type and dimension attributes associated with variables, (5) the inclusion of a large number of nonstandard operators such as $\lceil$ (maximum), $\lfloor$ (minimum), $\mid$ (residue), $\uparrow$, and $\downarrow$, and (6) a right-to-left operator precedence scheme for statement interpretation.

Because APL allows dynamic data types and because it is an interactive language, a number of simple functions (e.g., data-type checking, subscript checking, text editing) are performed at execution time. This, together with the inherent parallelism of various APL instructions (e.g., array operations), make it an ideal language for firmware/hardware implementation where many of these simple operations can frequently be performed in parallel rather than sequentially as in a software implementation. Thus, it comes as no surprise to learn that several APL machines have already been proposed (Abrams [1970], Zaks *et al.* [1971], Zaks [1971, 1973], Hassitt [1971, 1973], Nissen and Wallach [1973a, b], Thurber and Myrna [1970], Schroeder and Vaughn [1973], Micro Computer Machines [1974]). In fact, a compact, microprogrammed APL machine is already commercially available. Called the MCM/70 (Micro Computer Machines [1974]), this machine is reportedly APL/360 compatible. Input is achieved via a 46-key APL keyboard, and output is achieved by either a one-line plasma display unit or an impact printer. Memory includes a 2-K user work area that is expandable to 8 K and a 120-K virtual-memory cassette system. The data types available on the machine include one-byte characters, 1–8-byte integer numbers, and 8-byte decimal numbers.

Zaks *et al.* ([1971], Zaks [1971, 1973]) and Hassitt *et al.* ([1973], Hassitt [1971]) both developed APL machines that are microprogrammed extensions of existing machines, a META-4 and an IBM 360/25, respectively. No special hardware was added to either of the existing machines in order to enhance the execution of APL statements. Because of the similarity of these two efforts, only one (Hassitt *et al.* [1973]) will be described here in any detail.

In Hassitt's machine, APL source text is translated one for one into the intermediate language by a translator that is written in APL. If the intermediate text is either a function or datum, it is stored in the program memory for later use; otherwise, it is executed immediately by either a microsubroutine or an APL subroutine. All programs are translated into an internal function representation, the translator providing a standard function header to all statements that are used outside of functions. The order of the elements of a statement is reversed in the internal representation, and an end-of-statement mark is added at the end. For example, the statement

$$A \leftarrow B \times C + 3.14 \ 4 \ 2.0$$

becomes

$$3.14 \ 4 \ 2.0 + C \times B \leftarrow A \ \text{(end-of-statement mark)}$$

This is not quite correct in that identifiers such as A, B, and C are actually replaced by internal names. Unlike the way in which the previous machines have handled the problem, multiple occurrences of the same identifier are replaced by the same internal name. It is not until execution time that different variables having the same internal name are distinguished. It should also be noted that the internal form of each of the elements of an APL statement is binary-coded in such a way that the third and fourth bits of each coded element have the following meaning:

> 00 operator or separator
> 10 name of variable or function
> 11 description of literal

The internal representation of a literal or a data element begins with a descriptor field that indicates the type attribute (e.g., logical, integer, real, or character) of the element. Additional information such as the number of elements in a vector or array and the address of dimension information is included for nonscalar variables.

The interpreter consists of both microsubroutines and APL subroutines. The microsubroutines perform (1) statement scanning and syntactic analysis, (2) function calls and returns, (3) memory management, and (4) most of the mathematical and logical operations on scalars, vectors, and arrays. The APL subroutines perform (1) array compression, expansion, and reduction, and (2) most of the uncommon operations such as φ, !, $\uparrow$, $\downarrow$, etc.

A microsubroutine scans the internal program representation two bytes at a time, tests the third and fourth bits, and puts the element onto either the operator or variable stack depending on the results of the test. Next, the microsubroutine examines the top two items of the operator stack and, using their syntax types, looks in the decision table to determine what actions are necessary. Any result produced by this action is put on the stack, and the process is repeated. In performing the action mentioned above, item descriptors have to be checked. If the size, type, etc., of the items are not comformable, then an APL-written error subroutine is activated; otherwise, the appropriate action is taken.

The authors concluded that this microprogrammed APL machine is much slower than the IBM 360/25 on scalar operations but slightly faster on many vector and array operations. Since APL is generally considered to be a "good" array-handling language, the fact that the APL machine did not perform well in the scalar case can be overlooked. However, this does raise some doubts about the performance claims attributed to the firmware approach. In defense of the firmware approach, it should be noted that the vertical microcode (16-bit microinstructions) used on the IBM 360/25 was designed for the 360 instruction set, not for APL, which does limit the performance level that could be realized in the case of APL.

The remainder of the APL machines that have been proposed are similar in that their architectures all differ from that of a conventional, scalar-oriented computer. Several examples follow.

The Litton HOL computer, reported by Schroeder and Vaughn [1973], is being developed with the APL machine proposed by Abrams [1970] as the basis for their design. This computer system consists of a *master processing unit* (MPU) and one or more *satellite processing units* (SPUs) that control peripheral devices. The MPU communicates with the SPUs through a shared memory in which each processor has one or more dedicated message buffers.

Programs are executed by the MPU, which consists of four functional units, called the O, C, D, and E machines. The O machine is responsible for such functions as job scheduling, resource allocation, library maintenance, diagnostics, and system-error procedures. The C machine processes the statements written in the APL-like HLL and produces a Polish representation of them, which is passed on to the D machine. In addition, the C machine constructs a statement table that describes the control flow of a programmer-defined function. The D machine analyzes the operator–operand sequence passed to it in order to determine an optimum operator sequence. The E machine is primarily responsible for performing the individual array-processing functions, and it is the objective of the D machine to make processing by the E machine as efficient as possible. To facilitate this, the D and E machines share various registers, tables, stacks, and memory resources. Besides the location and value stacks, which are used for storing execution control information and the values of operands, respectively, the D and E machines share an *iteration stack*, which is used to control the execution of array operations. Count, direction, and conditional information are stored on this stack in order to sequence, index, and direct array operations.

As of now, only simulation studies have been conducted in order to evaluate their design.

Like the Litton HOL computer, the All Applications Digital Computer (AADC) has functional units that are similar to Abrams's D and E machines (Abrams [1970]). As reported by Nissen and Wallach [1973a, b], the AADC is being developed as a modular computer system. That is, as each application warrants, system resources such as *data processing elements* (DPEs), *channels, signal processors, random-access main memory,* etc., are attached to the main data buses in order to achieve a desired configuration. The DPE, whose instruction set includes a majority of the APL operators,

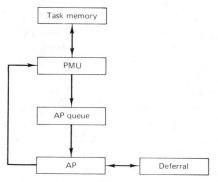

Fig. 9. AADC data processing element (Nissen and Wallach [1973b]).

normally executes all programs. As shown in Fig. 9, each DPE is composed of two computers, the *program management unit* (PMU), which is micro-program controlled, and the *arithmetic processor* (AP), which is controlled by combinational logic. The main functions of the PMU are to fetch instructions, perform effective-address calculations, support the virtual-memory addressing mechanism in microcode, take control of the AP when array operators require arithmetic processing, and issue commands to the AP to execute various control sequences during array operations. During nonarray operations, the AP is not under PMU control and simply executes instructions from the AP queue. The following list indicates some of the other significant features of the DPE.

(1) A "data insensitive arithmetic structure" is achieved by appending a data tag to every word in memory and by providing in each instruction word a bit that controls the precision of the accumulator upon completion of an operation.

(2) A precedence-based instruction-deferral-sequencing mechanism (Deerfield [1971]), called parenthetical control, is used that allows for direct execution of statements without the necessity of translation to Polish representation. Parenthetical control uses a 3-bit field of every arithmetic processor instruction to determine the sequence of execution of the instruction and consequently the control of the stack.

(3) Array-handling procedures are implemented entirely in hardware.

(4) Hardware support is provided for a virtual-addressing mechanism.

(5) Hardware facilities are provided for program debugging and performance monitoring.

(6) A pipeline architecture is provided to meet performance requirements.

In the design of the PMU microprogram, an APL simulator was utilized to functionally verify all the algorithms that it employs.

In an earlier research effort, Thurber and Myrna [1970] reported on the system design of an APL computer whose architecture is based on cellular array logic. This highly parallel, cellularly organized computer was designed to exploit the inherent parallelism of APL instructions, especially the array-handling operations.

A brief description of each of the functional units follows. The computer's memory consists of 16 identical memory arrays, each consisting of 32 × 32 words. The MLIM (matrix-logic-in-memory unit) consists of a 32 × 32 array of basic cells. In addition to storing information, each cell of the MLIM has the ability to perform certain arithmetic, logical, and relational operations on the information stored in it. The MLIM communicates with the memory arrays through the *routing logic* (RL), which routes data between the various functional units of the machine. Each of the 32 vector accumulators is capable of performing every APL reduction operation. The IMU is a read-only memory that stores all the instruction microprograms used in the computer. Finally, the preprocessing unit (PP) is a hardware/software APL metainterpreter that interprets the given APL statements and programs them into a sequence of parallel machine operations. The PP also handles storage allocation for the matrices and vectors, some elementary machine operations, and any "look ahead" features that might be incorporated into the computer.

A detailed design of the proposed computer beyond the system design level has not been completed. However, here again some of the computer's algorithms have been simulated for validation purposes.

2.9   Aerospace Processors

A frequently voiced criticism of HLL computers is that they are only effective in solving those problems for which the particular HLL that they implement has been designed. It is argued that this excludes a HLL computer from being used in a general problem-solving environment, where a multilingual computer is required. However, it does not exclude them from being used in an environment such as aerospace computing where a special-purpose, unilingual computer is required. Nielsen [1973] has reported on one such design effort. The machine that he has proposed would implement a subset of Space Programming Language (SPL), which is a derivative of JOVIAL and which contains features oriented to the aerospace programming environment. These special features include matrix- and vector-level arithmetic operations, bit-manipulation operations, and facilities for real-time control.

Like most of the machines that have been described here, Nielsen's machine assumes a software-implemented preprocessor that would convert source programs into a form that is easier to interpret. In order to determine which system functions should be handled by the interp the designers developed the following guidelines. First, the difference between source- and object-program representations should be small so that the preprocessor transformation is reversible, that is, so diagnostic information can be reported in terms of the source program. Second, a preprocessor function should be considered if it would eliminate gross inefficiencies in memory, timing, or logic requirements in the interpreter. Third, a preprocessor transformation on a statement should be considered if it would free the interpreter from performing the same transformation each time the statement is executed.

Based on these considerations, it was decided that the preprocessor would simply identify and translate the lexical elements of the language. However, syntax analysis is not even performed, which means that expressions are retained in their original infix form rather than converting them into a form that is easier to interpret, such as Polish representation.

Interpretation of preprocessed SPL programs is performed by two units: the *statement analysis unit* (SAU) and the *execution unit* (EU). The SAU simultaneously syntax-analyzes preprocessed SPL and translates it into EU commands. Architecturally, the SAU is a pushdown transducer consisting of a finite-state machine coupled with a pushdown stack. Sixteen transition tables are required to specify the SAU, representing 135 possible states and 451 legal transitions. The largest are the formula and assignment-statement tables, which represent over half the legal transitions.

The EU corresponds to the arithmetic and control units on a conventional architecture. However, operations performed by the EU are more varied and complex than those performed by these units. The EU consists of an operand stack, an operator stack, some general- and special-purpose registers, and the necessary hardware (or firmware) to implement the logic flowcharts specified for each EU command.

The author reports that the SPL interpreter requires less memory and is faster than a so-called "conventional system."

In another effort, Miller and Vandever [1973] have reported on the design of a HLL machine that supports the implementation of "block-structured programming languages." Architecturally, their machine utilizes data descriptors, a stack mechanism, and hardware display registers that facilitate the two-level addressing commonly found in block-structured programming languages.

2.10   SNOBOL **Processor**

SNOBOL 4 is used primarily for solving problems that require the manipulation of character-string information. Because the language contains facilities that are far removed from those provided in conventional computer architecture, elaborate software routines are required to bridge this gap. This means that huge amounts of memory are usually required and program execution is quite slow. This certainly provides sufficient justification for looking at alternative ways of implementing the language.

Shapiro's approach (Shapiro [1972a, b]) to implementing the language assumes a traditional von Neumann architecture as a basis and works in the direction of adding fundamental data types and operations in a multiple-accumulator environment. His intention is to provide a general-purpose machine that has a superstructure capable of efficient execution of SNOBOL because its instruction and data sets include the SNOBOL operations and data types.

Shapiro indicates that a SNOBOL-oriented machine should include the following features:

(1) The machine language should consist of a prefix string representation of the SNOBOL language.

(2) Character string and numeric-descriptor data should be included together with an appropriate set of operations that can be performed on any subfield of the descriptor. Character string descriptors should contain the memory address of the first character of a string, a character offset count (which is added to the memory address to find the first character of a substring), the string length, and a tag field. Numeric descriptors should contain numeric data and data-type information and, thus, be self-contained. The numeric data type that he suggests is designed so that conversion between a numeric value and a character string can easily be performed.

(3) Two stack mechanisms should be included for handling recursive function calls and pattern matching. In pattern matching, the stack would be used for backing up the subject string and stacking the matched portion of a string.

(4) Character string registers should be included for the purpose of improving the speed of pattern matching. Each string register would contain a string-descriptor part and a character part. The descriptor part would be used to control positioning in the character part. The character part would be a shift register that contains a fixed-length "snapshot" of the current working section of a string.

The above features form the basis for a SNOBOL machine that Shapiro calls the model 1 machine. He also describes a model 2 machine that consists of the model 1 machine together with some additional features (e.g., associative memory). Shapiro's approach is significant in that he has attempted to provide the implementor of a SNOBOL machine with a hierarchy of machines that he can choose from when deciding how to implement SNOBOL most cost-effectively.

2.11 HYDRA Processor

McFarland [1970] reported on the HYDRA computer that was designed to provide hardware support for a high-level language that he designed, called TPL. TPL is a block-structured programming language that has an extremely rich set of data structures, the control operators of EULER, and a generalization of the data operators of APL.

The logical structure of the HYDRA computer consists of four separate functional units operating in parallel:

(1) *Instruction acquisition unit* (IAU).   The IAU locates a program and reads it into fast temporary storage, called the *instruction file* (IF).

(2) *Program stream unit* (PSU).   The PSU works on the IF representation of a program and outputs a stream of executable instructions that are passed on to the *operand acquisition unit* (OAU) through an *instruction queue* (IQ). It also performs some runtime code optimization.

(3) *Operand acquisition unit* (OAU).   The OAU removes instructions from the IQ and prepares them for the *execution unit* (EU). It performs two-component (block number, ordinal number) address resolution, does type checking, executes procedure calls, etc.

(4) *Execution Unit* (EU).   The EU requests operands from main and temporary storage, breaks down complex operators not actually implemented in the OAU, executes each instruction, allocates a block of temporary storage for the result, and places the result in temporary storage.

At the time the author reported on the HYDRA processor, the design was being studied using a software simulator.

2.12   List Processors

Based on their experience with the list processing languages IPL I through IPL V, Shaw *et al.* [1958] designed an IPL computer, called IPL VI. Portions of the IPL VI machine were later implemented as a hardware extension to a conventional computer, a CDC 3600 (Hodges [1964]).

Wigington [1963] proposed a machine organization that would carry out the basic functions involved in list processing. Like IPL VI, Wigington's machine has a conventional instruction set that has been designed specifically for list processing. A similar effort was later reported by Bashkow *et al.* [1968].

2.13   Other HLL Computers

Other language-oriented processors that have been proposed include the following:

(1) Chevance [1973] describes a research project whose goal is to define a COBOL machine and a compilation machine and to implement them on a medium-scale microprogrammed computer.

(2) Wang [1969] describes his work on the design of a Compiler-Free Algorithmic Computer (COFAC), which is capable of direct execution of a high-level Scientific Algorithmic Language (SAL). SAL includes features selected from languages such as FORTRAN, ALGOL, and PL/1.

(3) Wade and Schneider [1973] describe a machine organization that is based on a set of semantic primitives that they feel adequately express the major portion of the semantics of programs written in any of the several common high-level languages (e.g., PL/1, ALGOL W).

(4) Cutts et al. [1972] proposed a machine that would implement a high-level language called ZIP, which provides the user with a set of string manipulation facilities like those of TRAC (Mooers [1966]). The machine consists of five, independent, hard-wired processors together with a shared memory, an operator-precedence table, a parse stack, and an evaluation stack. The five processors include an input processor, an output processor, a parser, an evaluator, and a storage manager. For each user, the parser and the evaluator alternatively process text (syntax analysis) and perform operations (e.g., the conventional arithmetic and string-manipulation operations).

(5) Myamlin and Smirnov [1968] describe the structure of a stack memory computer whose machine language is similar to algorithmic-type languages.

(6) Lindsey [1971] describes the construction philosophy of the MU5 machine, which is especially suited to the implementation of high-level languages. The author shows how the features of the MU5 are especially suited to ALGOL-like languages, and to ALGOL 68 in particular.

(7) Broadbent and Coulouris [1974] describe a microprogrammed machine called MEMBERS. The MEMBERS interpreter is a compromise between a full interpreter in the software sense and the limited meaning attached to microcoding of a traditional order code.

(8) Yeh [1973] presents an architectural design of a direct high-level language processor for the L6/M programming language, which is a subset of the L6 language developed at Bell Telephone Laboratories.

(9) Meggitt [1964] presents a character computer designed for high-level language interpretation.

(10) Hawryszkiewycz [1967] describes the application of microprogramming to problem-oriented languages in terms of a simulated analog system on a digital computer.

2.14   Research on Individual HLL Computer Design Problems

In addition to the HLL computer-design efforts described earlier, a number of other research efforts have been conducted relating to individual HLL computer-design problems. This section identifies these problems and some of the research that has been conducted on them.

First, research has been directed at improving the efficiency with which various language translation functions can be performed through the utilization of hardware and firmware. The functions that have been considered include lexical analysis (Roberts and Wallace [1971]), syntactic analysis (Chu [1973b]), and name resolution (Habid [1973]), i.e., determination of identifier scope.

Second, consideration has been given to the type of machine language representation to be used. Two such efforts have investigated the idea of designing a computer with a tree-structured machine language (Berkling [1971], Doran [1972]), and two others have investigated the tradeoffs in the choice of machine language representation (Lawson [1968], Broca and Merwin [1973]).

Third, Morishita *et al.* [1971] reported on the design and analysis of a device called PADEM, which is capable of parallel direct execution of FORTRAN- or ALGOL-like arithmetic statements. This device performs the syntactic analysis operation and the arithmetic operation in parallel with the aid of two pushdown stacks.

Fourth, Lesser [1971] investigates the organization of a parallel microcomputer that contains specific operators that dynamically manipulate and generate a tree-type data structure for control. This control data structure is used as a framework within which particular implementations of control concepts, such as iteration, recursion, co-routines, parallelism, interrupts, etc., can be easily expressed.

Other research efforts related to HLL computer design problems include Von Swoboda [1970], McMahan and Feustal [1973], and Welin and Henson [1973].

3.   OBSERVATIONS

In an early article, McKeeman [1967] suggested some ways in which high-level languages could exercise greater influence on the design of computer architecture. As has been noted in this chapter and elsewhere (Chu [1973a], Brooker [1970], Anderson [1971]), the feasibility of completely implementing a particular high-level language in hardware, firmware, or a combination of the two has since then been firmly established. As has also been noted, this influence has shown itself in the development of commercial as well as research HLL computers.

One of the many questions that remain is what is the "best" combination of hardware, firmware, and software for implementing a particular high-level language computer. Some of the tradeoffs to be considered in answering this question are discussed by Mandell [1972] and Broadbent [1974]. However, so far there are few tangible results to assist the HLL computer designer. From the SYMBOL project, it is reported that competitive execution times and savings in total computing costs can be realized by a hardware approach (Rice and Smith [1971]). However, the idea that it might have been better to implement at least some of the SYMBOL processors in firmware has also been suggested (Anderberg and Smith [1973]). Compared to hardwired logic, firmware clearly offers the HLL designer a more flexible implementation tool. Compared to software, the claim has been that firmware implementations would yield faster execution times. While there is some evidence to support this claim (Weber [1967], Wilner [1972]), there is also evidence to dispute it (Hassitt [1971, 1973]). Clearly, further evaluation of the tradeoffs involved is required.

Several of the HLL computers that have been proposed consist of a number of functionally autonomous processors. So far, no studies have been reported that examine the choice of processors and the configuration by which these functional units are distributed.

Another problem that needs to be considered involves the development of automatic design procedures for developing HLL computers. Much research has gone into the development of automatic procedures by which software implementations of HLLs can be achieved. The question remains how procedures such as these can be utilized to facilitate the development of HLL computers.

Finally, one needs to take a broader look at computer architecture design than has been taken in these unilingual HLL computers. SYMBOL and the B1700 have both considered the problem of developing an "operating-system-directed computer architecture," and the B1700 has considered the problem of a multilingual HLL computer. There has also been some work in the development of "data-base management-directed computer design." Thus, one long-range problem will be to consider how best to implement several HLLs, an operating system, a data-base management system, etc., through a proper combination of hardware, firmware, and software. The B1700 has given us one alternative for solving this problem.

REFERENCES

Abrams, P. [1970]. An APL machine, SLAC Report No. 114. Stanford Univ. Stanford, California.

Anderberg, J. W., and Smith, C. L. [1973]. High-level language translation in SYMBOL-2R. *Proc. Symp. High-Level Language Comput. Architecture, Univ. Maryland, Nov. 1973* 11–19.

Anderson, J. P. [1961]. A computer for direct execution of algorithmic languages, *Proc. EJCC 1961* 184–193.

Anderson, J. P. [1971]. Programming language directed machine design—problems and prospects, *Proc. Symp. Programming and Machine Organization, Lincroft, New Jersey, 1971* 39–55.

Barton, R. S. [1961]. A new approach to the functional design of a digital computer, *Proc. WJCC, 1961* 393–396.

Barton, R. S. [1971]. *In* "Software Engineering" (J. T. Tou, ed.). Academic Press, New York.

Bashkow, T. R., Sasson, A., and Kronfeld, A. [1967]. System design of a FORTRAN machine, *IEEE Trans. Electron. Comput.* August, 485–499.

Bashkow, T. R., Kroft, D., and Sasson, A. [1968]. Study of a computer for direct execution on a list processing language, AFCRL-68-0063. Columbia University, New York.

Berkling, K. J. [1971]. A computing machine based on tree structures, *IEEE Trans. on Comput.* **C-20,** 404–418.

Bjorner, D. [1970]. On higher-level language machines. IBM Research Rep. RJ 792.

Bloom, H. M. [1970]. Design and simulation of an ALGOL computer, Tech. Rep. 70-118. Computer Sci. Center, Univ. Maryland, College Park, Maryland.

Broadbent, J. K. [1974]. Microprogramming and system architecture, *Comput. J.* **17,** 2–8.

Broadbent, J. K., and Coulouris, G. F. [1973]. MEMBERS—A microprogrammed experimental machine with a basic executive for real-time systems, *Comput. J.* **16,** 205–208.

Broca, F. R., and Merwin, R. E. [1973]. Direct microprogrammed execution of the intermediate text from a high-level language compiler, *Proc. ACM* 57–63.

Brooker, R. A. [1970]. Influence of high-level languages on computer design, *Proc. Inst. Elec. Eng.* **117,** 1219–1224.

Chesley, G. D., and Smith, W. R. [1971]. The hardware-implemented high-level machine language for SYMBOL, *Proc. SJCC, 1971* 563–573.

Chevance, R. J. [1973]. A COBOL machine, *Proc. ACM Interface Meeting Programming Languages—Microprogramming, Harriman, New York, June 1973* 139–144.

Chu, Y. [1970]. Microprogrammed allocating-loader, Technical Report 70-135. Computer Sci. Center, Univ. Maryland, College Park, Maryland.

Chu, Y. [1972]. Significance of the SYMBOL computer system, *Dig. COMPCON 72* 33–35.

Chu, Y. [1973a]. Introducing the high-level language computer architecture, Tech. Rep. TR-227. Comput. Sci. Center, Univ. Maryland, College Park, Maryland.

Chu, Y. [1973b]. Recursive microprogramming in a syntax recognizer, *Proc. Sixth Annual Workshop on Microprogramming, Univ. Maryland, Sept. 1973* 91–98.

Coulouris, G. F. [1970]. A note on programming systems and the machine interface, Report CSR17. Centre for Computing and Automation, Imperial College, London.

Cowart, B. E., Rice, R., and Lundstrom, S. F. [1971]. The physical attributes and testing aspects of the SYMBOL system, *Proc. SJCC, 1971* 589–600.

Cutts, R., *et al.* [1972]. An eclectic information processing system, *Proc. AFIPS FJCC* **41,** 473–478.

Deerfield, A. J. [1971]. Instruction deferral sequencing mechanism, *Proc. Symp. Programming and Machine Organization, Lincroft, New Jersey, 1971* 16–24.

Doran, R. W. [1972]. A computer organization with an explicitly tree-structured machine language, *Aust. Comput. J.* **4**, 21–30.

Habib, S. [1973]. Name resolutions using a microprogrammed interpretive technique, *Proc. Sixth Annual Workshop on Microprogramming, Univ. Maryland, Sept. 1973*, 99–105.

Haley, A. C. [1962]. The KDF-9 computer system, *Proc. AFIPS FJCC* **22**, 108–120.

Hamblin, C. L. [1960]. Logical design for ADM, an addressless digital machine, *Proc. Conf. of Aust. Nat. Committee on Computation and Automatic Control* C6.3.

Hassitt, A. [1971]. Microprogramming and high-level languages, *Proc. IEEE Int. Comp. Soc. Conf.* 91–92.

Hassitt, A., Lageschulte, J. W., and Lyon, L. E. [1973]. Implementation of a high-level language machine, *Commun. ACM* **16**, 199–212.

Hawryszkiewycz, I. T. [1967]. Microprogrammed control in problem oriented languages, *IEEE Trans. Electron. Comput.* **EC-16** 652.

Haynes, L. S. [1973]. Structure of a Polish string language for an ALGOL 60 language processor, *Proc. Symp. on High-Level-language Computer Architecture, Univ. Maryland, Nov. 1973* 131–140.

Hodges, D. [1964]. IPL-VC, a computer system having the IPL-V instruction set, ANL-6888. Argonne Natl. Lab., Appl. Math. Div. Argonne, Illinois.

Hopper, G. M., and Mauchly, J. W. [1953]. Influence of programming techniques on the design of computers, *Proc. IRE* October, 1250–1254.

Hutchison, P. C., and Ethington, K. [1973]. Program execution in the SYMBOL-2R computer, *Proc. Symp. High-Level-Language Computer Architecture, Univ. Maryland, Nov. 1973* 20–26.

Iliffe, J. K. [1968]. "Basic Machine Principles." Amer. Elsevier, New York.

Iliffe, J. K. [1969]. Elements of BLM, *Comput. J.* **12**, 251–258.

Laliotis, T. A. [1973]. Implementation aspects of the SYMBOL hardware compiler, *Proc. First Annual Symp. Computer Architecture, Dec. 1973* 111–115.

Lawson, H. W. [1968]. Programming-language-oriented instruction streams, *IEEE Trans. Comput.* **C-17**, 476–485.

Lesser, V. R. [1971]. An introduction to direct emulation of control structures by a parallel micro-computer, *IEEE Trans. Electron. Comput.* **C20**, 751.

Lindsey, C. H. [1971]. Making the hardware suit the language, *in* "ALGOL 68 Implementation" (J. E. L. Peck, ed.), pp. 347–365. North-Holland Publ., Amsterdam.

Lonergan, W., and King, P. [1961]. Design of the B5000 system, *Datamation* **7**, 28–32.

McFarland, C. [1970]. A language-oriented computer design, *Proc. AFIPS FJCC, 1970* **37**, 629–640.

McKeeman, W. M. [1967]. Language directed computer design, *Proc. AFIPS FJCC, 1967* 413–417.

McMahan, L. N., and Feustal, E. A. [1973]. Implementation of a tagged architecture for block structured languages, *Proc. Symp. High-Level-Language Computer Architecture, Univ. Maryland, Nov. 1973* 91–100.

Mandell, R. L. [1972]. Hardware/software trade-offs—reasons and directions, *Proc. AFIPS FJCC, 1972* **41**, 453–459.

Meggitt, J. E. [1964]. A character computer for high-level language interpretation, *IBM Syst. J.* **3**, 68–78.

Melbourne, A. J., and Pugmire, J. M. [1965]. A small computer for the direct processing of FORTRAN statements, *Comput. J.* April, 24–27.

Micro Computer Machines, Inc. [1974]. "MCM-70 Brochure." Willowdale, Ontario.

Miller, J. S., and Vandever, W. H. [1973]. Instruction architecture of an aerospace multiprocessor, *Proc. Symp. High-Level-Language Computer Architecture, Univ. Maryland, Nov. 1973* 52–60.

Mooers, C. N. [1966]. TRAC—a procedure describing language for the reactive typewriter, *Commun. ACM* **9**, 215–219.

Morishita, S., Inagaki, Y., and Fukumura, T. [1971]. System design of a parallel direct execution device for arithmetic statements, *Inform. Process. Japan* **11**, 9–16.

Mullery, A. P. [1964]. A procedure-oriented machine language, *IEEE Trans. Electron. Comput.* **C-13**, 449–455.

Mullery, A. P., Schauer, R. F., and Rice, R. [1963]. ADAM—A problem-oriented symbol processor, *Proc. AFIPS SJCC, 1963* 367–380.

Myamlin, A. N., and Smirnov, V. K. [1968]. Computer with stack memory, *Proc. IFIPS 68* 818–823.

Nielsen, W. C. [1963]. Design of an aerospace computer, *Proc. Symp. High-Level-Language Computer Architecture, Univ. Maryland, Nov. 1973* 34–42.

Nissen, S. M., and Wallach, S. J. [1973a]. An APL microprogramming structure, *Proc. Sixth Annual Workshop on Microprogramming, Univ. Maryland, Sept. 1973* 50–57.

Nissen, S. M., and Wallach, S. J. [1973b]. The all applications digital computer, *Proc. Symp. High-Level-Language Computer Architecture, Univ. Maryland, Nov. 1973* 43–51.

Organick, E. I. [1973]. "Computer System Organization: The B5700/B6700 Series." Academic Press, New York.

Rice, R. [1972a]. A project overview, *Dig. COMPCON 72* 17–20.

Rice, R. [1972b]. The hardware implementation of SYMBOL, *Dig. COMPCON 72* 27–30.

Rice, R., and Smith, W. R. [1971]. SYMBOL—A major departure from classic software dominated von Neumann computing systems, *Proc. SJCC, 1971* 575–587.

Richards, H., and Wright, C. [1973]. Introduction to the SYMBOL-2R programming language, *Proc. Symp. High-Level Language Computer Architecture, Univ. Maryland, Nov. 1973,* 27–33.

Richards, H., and Zingg, R. J. [1973]. The logical structure of the memory resource in the SYMBOL-2R computer, *Proc. Symp. High-Level Language Computer Architecture, Univ. Maryland, Nov. 1973,* 1–10.

Roberts, P. S., and Wallace, C. S. [1971]. A microprogrammed lexical processor, *IFIPS 71* 577–581.

Rosen, S. [1968]. Hardware design reflecting software requirements, *Proc. AFIPS FJCC, 1968* **33**, 1443–1449.

Schroeder, S. C., and Vaughn, L. E. [1973]. A high order language optimal execution processor, *Proc. Symp. High-Level Language Computer Architecture, Univ. Maryland, Nov. 1973,* 109–116.

Shapiro, M. D. [1972a]. A SNOBOL machine: a higher-level language processor in a conventional hardware framework, *Dig. COMPCON 72* 41–44.

Shapiro, M. D. [1972b]. A SNOBOL machine: functional architectural concepts of a string processor, Dissertation, Purdue Univ., Lafayette, Indiana.

Shaw, J. C., Newell, A., Simon, H. A., and Ellis, T. O. [1958]. A command structure for complex information processing, *Proc. WJCC* 119–128.

Signiski, T. F. [1970]. Design of an ALGOL machine, Tech. Rep. 70-131. Computer Sci. Center, Univ. Maryland, College Park, Maryland.

Smith, W. R. [1972]. System supervision algorithms for the SYMBOL computer, *Dig. COMPCON 72* 21–26.

Smith, W. R., *et al.* [1971]. SYMBOL—A large experimental system exploring major hardware replacement of software, *Proc. SJCC, 1971* 601–616.

Sugimoto, M. [1969]. PL/1 reducer and direct processor, *Proc. ACM* 519–538.

Thurber, K. J., and Myrna, J. W. [1970]. System design of a cellular APL computer, *IEEE Trans. Computers* **C-19**, 291–303.

Von Swoboda, J. [1970]. Language oriented computers-addressing problems, *Elektron. Rechenal.* **12,** 26–35.

Wade, B. W., and Schneider, V. B. [1973]. A general-purpose high-level language machine for minicomputers, *Proc. ACM Interface Meeting on Programming Languages-Microprogramming, Harriman, New York, June* **1973** 169–171.

Wang, S. C. [1969]. System design of a compiler free algorithmic computer, *Proc. 2nd Hawaii Int. Conf. Syst. Sci.* 401.

Weber, H. [1967]. A microprogrammed implementation of EULER on IBM System 360 Model 30, *Commun. ACM* **10,** 549–558.

Welin, A. M., and Henson, P. H. [1973]. The internal machine, *Proc. Symp. High-Level Language Computer Architecture, Univ. Maryland, Nov. 1973* 101–108.

Wigington, R. L. [1963]. A machine organization for a general purpose list processor, *IEEE Trans. Electron. Comput.* 707–714.

Wilner, W. T. [1972]. Design of the Burroughs B1700, *Proc. AFIPS FJCC, 1972* 489–497.

Wirth, N., and Weber, H. [1966]. EULER: a generalization of ALGOL, and its formal definition, *Commun. ACM* **9,** 13–25, 89–99.

Wortman, D. B. [1972]. A study of language directed computer design, Tech. Rep CSRG-20. Computer Syst. Res. Group, Univ. Toronto.

Yeh, J. T. C. [1973]. Architectural design of a L6/M language processor, Tech. Rep. TR-279. Computer Sci. Center, Univ. Maryland, College Park, Maryland.

Zaks, R. [1971]. Microprogrammed APL, *Proc. IEEE Int. Comput. Soc. Conf.* 193–194.

Zaks, R. [1973]. Dynamic memory management for APL-like languages, *Proc. ACM Interface Meeting on Programming Languages—Microprogramming, Harriman, New York, June 1973* 130–138.

Zaks, R., Steingart, D., and Moore, J. [1971]. A firmware APL time-sharing system, *Proc. AFIPS SJCC* **38,** 179–190.

Zingg, R. J., and Richards, H. [1972]. Operational experience with SYMBOL, *Dig. COMPCON 72* 31–32.

Architecture of Stack Machines

Robert W. Doran

Department of Computer Science
Massey University
Palmerston North, New Zealand

1. INTRODUCTION

This chapter discusses the use of stack structures in the architecture of computers. The description follows a range of uses, from very simple extensions of conventional hardware up to a whole architecture based on stack structures—what has come to be called a "stack machine."

1.1 Stack Structures

The stack or "last in–first out" data structure has been widely used by systems programmers, especially for the implementation of compilers and interpreters. Although the stack has become an essential tool for constructing overall computer systems, most computers do not have an architecture that has been built to accommodate the stack. A few computers do, to a greater or lesser extent, and it is these that we will use as examples throughout this chapter.

When a computer architecture is altered to include or facilitate some software device it is a sign that the device has become generally accepted, far past the experimental stage, as an essential feature of the computer system. In the case of the stack it is not only stack structures that have been accepted but also tree structures. Stacks and trees are always closely associated; a stack may be used as an aid when traversing a tree or to hold information belonging to the nodes of the tree (the reader is referred to Knuth [1968] for a detailed description of the relationship). The emergence of stacks as hardware devices implies the recognition of the tree-structured nature of algorithms and data.

In the succeeding sections we will discuss different uses made of stacks and how these uses interrelate. These include the use of stacks for the evaluation of expressions, for subroutine linkage, for block-structured storage allocation, and as an execution record of a task.

1.2 Simple Implementations

A stack is a memory device in which data may be stored and from which they may be retrieved in, as mentioned above, a "last in–first out" order. This mode of operation has many physical analogs, such as Yo-Yos, piles of paper, rifle magazines, and push-down, spring-loaded plate holders. The choice of the model is crucial. We could choose a model where the top of the stack is fixed and the body moves—as with the plate-holding device—or one in which the body is fixed and the top moves—as with the pile. Of course, the form of the stack we think we are using may not be the one actually implemented. For example, a fixed-top stack could be implemented using a fixed-body device. Both forms are used in computers, but it turns out that the second method is better conceptually, because we often need to refer to fixed locations within the stack. In what follows we will assume that a stack of the fixed-body sort is available and is stored in a memory "M," the top element given by a pointer "top" with the last element in the stack being M[top].

No matter which form of stack is used, the act of placing information into the stack is called "pushing" and the act of removing information "popping." A typical computer using a stack would have a pair of instructions, the first to push the contents of a memory location into the stack, the second to pop the top of the stack to some location:

$$
\begin{aligned}
\text{PUSH X:}\quad & \text{top} := \text{top}+1;\\
& M[\text{top}] := M[X];\\
\text{POP}\quad\text{X:}\quad & M[X] := M[\text{top}];\\
& \text{top} := \text{top}-1;
\end{aligned}
$$

Some computers have pushing and popping instructions but go no further towards incorporating stacks. An example is the PDP-10 (Digital Equipment Corp. [1969]), a multiregister von Neumann machine having the following instructions:

$$
\left.
\begin{aligned}
\text{PUSH } R_i \text{ X:}\quad & R_i := R_i+1;\\
& M[R_i] := M[X];\\
\text{POP}\quad R_i \text{ X:}\quad & M[X] := M[R_i];\\
& R_i := R_i-1;
\end{aligned}
\right\}
\begin{aligned}
& R_i \text{ is general}\\
& \text{register } i
\end{aligned}
$$

Thus index registers may be used to point to a stack in memory. A similar pair of instructions, PUSH and PULL, is used in the XDS Sigma 7 computer (Mendelson and England [1966]), together with another pair of instructions for pushing and popping the general registers to and from the stack. The same effect is obtained in other machines by using autoincrement and autodecrement modes of addressing.

Most simple stacks are of the moving-top variety just described, the processor containing a pointer to the top of stack somewhere in memory. The fixed-top variety is quite common in microprocessors where it is implemented as a limited-capacity shift register. The KDF.9 (Haley [1962]) uses fixed-top stacks of limited capacity, but these are more complex than those just described.

2. EXPRESSIONS

This section discusses the use made of stacks for the evaluation of expressions. If stacks are to be used directly for this purpose, the conventional computer architecture must be modified substantially.

2.1 Evaluation of Expressions

An arithmetic expression, as used in a programming language or in mathematics, possesses a tree structure that shows the order in which operations are to be performed. In the expression itself, this structure is displayed partly with parentheses and partly with implicit rules of priority and associativity among the operators. For example, the expression $(A + B) \times -(C/(D \times (E + F)))$ has the structure shown in Fig. 1.

The execution order given by an expression tree is that the operator at a node in the tree obtains a value by operating on the value(s) of the node(s) below it. For serial execution, left-to-right evaluation is to be used where

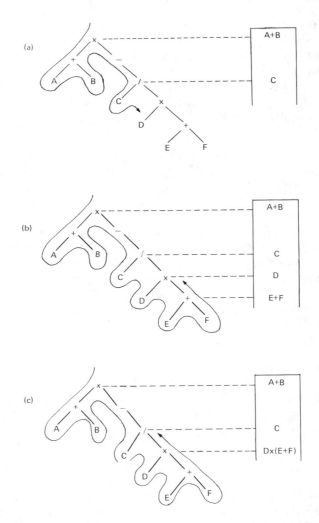

Fig. 1. Structure of expression $(A + B) \times -(C/(D \times (E + F)))$ with its associated stack at three stages in its evaluation.

possible. To evaluate an expression correctly, we, or a computer, should traverse the tree in the standard order indicated in Fig. 1, gathering partial results as we go.

Since they are associated with nodes of the tree, the partial results may be held naturally in a stack. Values are placed into the stack when either a terminal node or a nonterminal operator node is visited in the traversal. The value for the nonterminal operator node is obtained by operating on the last one or two results on the stack. The replacement of the last two stack entries by their product is shown in the transition from Fig. 1b to 1c.

To utilize this method of evaluating expressions a computer must use a stack, implemented in either hardware or software. A software stack may be disguised as a list of temporary storage locations, but it is a stack nonetheless. In hardware terms, it must be possible to PUSH values into the stack and to POP them from it; but a more important property is that arithmetic instructions must be able to operate on the top elements in the stack. For example, an ADD operation must add the top two elements together and replace them with their sum. Let us represent this as:

$$\text{ADD:} \quad M[top-1] := M[top-1] + M[top];$$
$$top := top-1;$$

Now we may execute simple assignment statements, e.g.,

$$
\begin{array}{ll}
A := B + C: & \text{PUSH} \quad B \\
& \text{PUSH} \quad C \\
& \text{ADD} \\
& \text{POP} \quad A
\end{array}
$$

Every operator must find its operands in the stack as ADD did (such instructions are sometimes called "addressless"). Let us assume that we have SUB, MPY, and DIV, and that for the unary minus we have

$$\text{NEG:} \quad M[top] := -M[top];$$

If we write from the tree structure of an expression the order in which the operations must be performed, we obtain a list in which the operators follow the values. For example, for

$$(A + B) \times -(C/(D \times (E + F)))$$

we obtain

$$A \; B + C \; D \; E \; F + \times / - \times$$

This is called a "reverse-Polish" representation of the expression (after the Polish logician Lukasiewicz who first used this notation). The instructions for a computer with an arithmetic stack appear in reverse-Polish form, e.g., the code for $(A + B) \times -(C/(D \times (E + F)))$ is as shown in Fig. 2.

```
PUSH  A  ⎫
PUSH  B  ⎬ A+B
ADD      ⎭
PUSH  C
PUSH  D
PUSH  E  ⎫
PUSH  F  ⎬ E+F
ADD      ⎭
MPY
DIV
NEG
MPY
```

Fig. 2.   Code for $(A + B) \times -(C/(D \times (E + F)))$.

That is all that is needed for a simple stack computer to evaluate arithmetic expressions. Some machines do include some extra stack-manipulation instructions to reduce the number of PUSH operations and make the stack serve the role played by high-speed general registers. Typical instructions would be DUP to duplicate the top of stack and SWAP to swap the two top items in the stack; e.g., $(A + B) \times (D/(A + B))$ could be programmed as

```
PUSH  A
PUSH  B
ADD
DUP
PUSH  D
SWAP
DIV
MPY
```

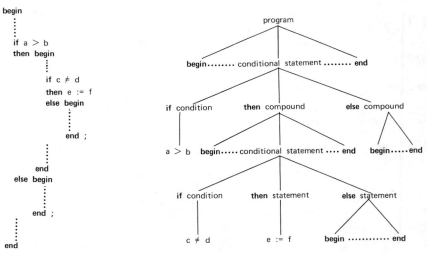

Fig. 3.   A program and its associated tree structure.

2.2 Algorithms as Expressions

A program or algorithm has a structure similar to that of an expression. This structure is particularly evident in a program written in a language defined using a phrase-structure grammar and with no **go to** instructions. For example, a program and its structure are given in Fig. 3.

As with an expression, when a computer executes a program it must traverse the structure of the program. However, not all of the program's structure needs to be traversed (for example, within a conditional statement) and some parts (such as loops) may be traversed more than once. The structure is not usually presented as such to the computer, but by using branch instructions the computer is informed how to perform the traversal. Note that, as with expressions, the task of discovering the structure is usually performed by the compiler; the computer does not have to consider the structure when executing the program. Some interpreters, however, do work directly on an explicitly structured program.

In order to make conditional branching fit the stack concept, values are chosen to represent true and false (e.g. 1 and 0) and the branch condition is determined by whether the value of the top of stack is in fact true or false. In the examples that follow we will use the instruction mnemonics B for "branch" and BF for "branch if false." To create the truth values on top of the stack some operators are needed that, like arithmetic operators, use the top elements as operands, but that compare the operands and give a true or false result. We will use GT for $>$ and NE for $\neq$, e.g.,

$$\text{GT:}\quad M[top-1] := (M[top-1] > M[top]);$$
$$top := top-1;$$

Operators such as "and," "or," and "not," which manipulate logical values, may also be necessary, but we will not use them in what follows.

Using a plain **POP** to rid the stack of an unwanted value, we can program simple statements such as **if** a > b **then** c := d **else** e := f:

```
              PUSH   a
              PUSH   b
              GT
              BF      ELSE
              POP
              PUSH   d
              POP     c
              B       OVER
      ELSE    POP
              PUSH   f
              POP     e
      OVER     ⋮
```

Since a conditional branch almost always leaves an unwanted value on the stack, most machines include an automatic POP as part of each branch.

Another difference between expressions and programs is that the former possess a value while the latter do not. Many expressions have a statement-like aspect, so this distinction between statements and expressions can be quite a nuisance when describing languages. As a consequence, some modern languages ignore the distinction and insist that every statement have a value (though the value that is given often has no real meaning). Even with ALGOL 60 there are some statementlike expressions, e.g.,

$$x := y \times (\textbf{if } b > c \textbf{ then } c \textbf{ else } b)$$

where the conditional expression can be treated as a conditional statement with a value:

```
        PUSH  y
        PUSH  b
        PUSH  c
        GT
        BF    ELSE
        POP
        PUSH  c
        B     OUT
ELSE    POP
        PUSH  b
OUT     MPY
        POP   x
```

A similar situation in ALGOL, where a statement is treated as an expression giving a value, is the case of multiple assignments. a := b := c can be thought of as a := (b := c), where b := c is a statement having a value, in this case c. Some computers implement assignment as an operator having a side effect. Since we will regard statements as expressions throughout this chapter, we need two new instructions:

PUSHADDR x: top := top + 1;
               M[top] := x;

STORE: M[M[top − 1]] := M[top − 1] := M[top];
               top := top − 1;

Now we can translate a := b := c as

```
        PUSHADDR   a
        PUSHADDR   b
        PUSH       c
```

STORE
STORE

With assignments having a value, statements such as $x := (y := z) \times t$ immediately become intelligible and even useful; e.g., in the above definition of PUSHADDR we could have written $M[top := top + 1] := x$. Now $x := (y := z) \times t$ translates to

PUSHADDR	x
PUSHADDR	y
PUSH	z
STORE	
PUSH	t
MPY	
STORE	

2.3 Data Structures

We have seen in the last two sections that algorithms have an underlying tree structure. Because of this, stacks are a useful aid when executing programs. Just as algorithms have structures, data structures imply or require algorithms for their manipulation. Not surprisingly, computers with stacks are well suited for manipulating structures that may be regarded as trees.

Figure 4a is a diagram of an ordered tree structure. By "ordered" we mean that the left to right sequence of nodes on a given level is significant

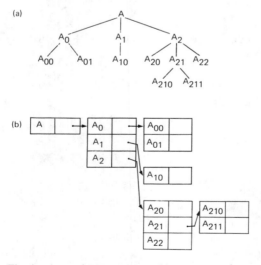

Fig. 4. A tree data structure and its representation.

(we will always deal with ordered trees). This natural order may be preserved in a computer's memory by placing the nodes in, say, an ascending sequence of memory addresses. Such a representation is given in Fig. 4b, where each node is represented by a memory cell, adjacent cells are in adjacent memory locations, and the cell for a nonterminal node contains the address of the sequence below it.

The words for nonterminal nodes are called *descriptors*. They point to a sequence of data items in memory and may also describe such properties of the sequence as its length and type. Given the descriptor of a sequence, we must have access to the address of any member of the sequence if we wish to manipulate the structure. Assuming that a descriptor and a constant are at the top of a stack, we can use INDEX to get the next address. For example,

A_2	address A_{20}

INDEXed by 1 gives address A_{21}.

INDEX is thus basically an addition operation, but it may involve other operations such as checking that the constant is less than the length of the sequence. If we have another operator, PUSHCNST, to push a constant into the stack, we can find the address of A_2 by

$$\begin{array}{ll} \text{PUSH} & \text{A} \\ \text{PUSHCNST} & 2 \\ \text{INDEX} & \end{array}$$

This leaves an address on top of the stack. To continue down the tree we need another operator:

$$\text{FETCH:} \quad \text{M[top]} := \text{M[M[top]]};$$

Now we can obtain the address A_{211} with

$$\begin{array}{ll} \text{PUSH} & \text{A} \\ \text{PUSHCNST} & 2 \\ \text{INDEX; FETCH} & \\ \text{PUSHCNST} & 1 \\ \text{INDEX; FETCH} & \\ \text{PUSHCNST} & 1 \\ \text{INDEX} & \end{array}$$

These few extra instructions enable a stack machine to manipulate general tree structures. For example, an array such as A[0:2,0:2] may be

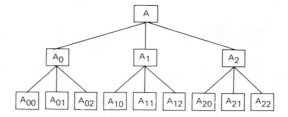

Fig. 5. An array represented as a tree.

regarded as a tree as in Fig. 5. We may then perform calculations involving arrays. For example, x := A[i, j] translates to

```
PUSHADDR   x
PUSH       A
PUSH       i
INDEX; FETCH
PUSH       j
INDEX; FETCH
STORE
```

Similarly, A[1,0] := A[1,1] := x; translates to

```
PUSH       A
PUSHCNST   1
INDEX; FETCH
DUP
PUSHCNST   0
INDEX
SWAP
PUSHCNST   1
INDEX
PUSH       x
STORE
STORE
```

By treating arrays as trees, a computer with a stack can handle random references to array elements as efficiently as a conventional computer. However, for calculations involving stepping through the rows and columns of matrices, a computer needs extra facilities to be really viable. von Neumann computers have index registers, and a computer with a stack needs these or their equivalent to be competitive. For example, the HP3000 (Hewlett Packard [1972]) and KDF.9 provide index registers, and the

Burroughs B6700 (Burroughs Corp. [1969]) has some loop control instructions as a standard feature and a special mode of operation, called vector-mode, as an option.

2.4 Implementations of Expression Stacks

Computers usually have centralized arithmetic units; operands must be obtained from where they are stored and presented to the arithmetic units. This applies to computers with stacks as much as it does to von Neumann machines. If a machine has a fixed-top stack, the operands are always in the same physical location so there is no problem in obtaining them. For variable-top stacks, however, the operands must be fetched from memory by the *central processing unit* (CPU) and the result stored.

In smaller computers this sequence of operations may be performed for each stack operation. The PDP-11 (Digital Equipment Corp. [1971]) has a very interesting method of forming effective addresses. Its addressing modes include indexing and autoincrement indexing. One form of the two-address ADD instruction is ADD $(R_i)+$, $@R_i$ where R_i is an index register. This performs

$$\text{temp} := M[R_i];$$
$$R_i := R_i + 1;$$
$$M[R_i] := M[R_i] + \text{temp};$$

The net effect, if R_i is regarded as a pointer to an "upside-down" stack, is that of a stack addition. Other instructions may be used to perform the other standard stack operations, providing the PDP-11 with arithmetic stack capabilities.

The PDP-11 type of stack instruction takes a number of memory references for each arithmetic operation. For example, the sequence

$$\text{PUSH} \quad x;$$
$$\text{PUSH} \quad y;$$
$$\text{ADD}$$

could take seven references. This is unacceptable on larger computers, so some method of decreasing memory references is needed. One method, adopted by the Burroughs B5500 (Burroughs Corp. [1964]), is to make use of high-speed registers in the local store to hold part of the stack, although most of the stack is held in memory.

In the Burroughs computers the top two words of the stack may be held in two special registers, A and B as shown in Fig. 6. All arithmetic operations are performed on these two registers, leaving the result in register B. The top of the stack in memory is pointed to by register S. The

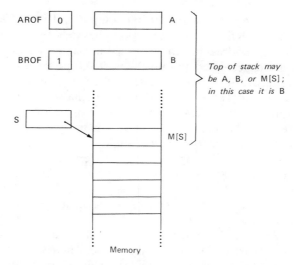

Fig. 6. Stack registers for the Burroughs B5500 computer.

actual top of the stack may be register A, register B, or M[S]. Flip/flops AROF and BROF, if on, indicate that registers A and B, respectively, are part of the stack. The machine hardware checks AROF and BROF before executing an instruction and, if necessary, adjusts the stack to fill registers A and B. No memory references are made unless they are essential.

Assuming that AROF and BROF are false (0) initially (thus indicating that A and B are both empty), then the code and stack states to execute x := (y + z) × t are given in Table I. The sequence of stack states shown

TABLE I

Sequence of Instructions and Stack Changes to Execute x := (y + z) × t

Instruction[a]		AROF	A	BROF	B	S	M[S]
initial state		0	—	0	—	?	!
PUSHADDR	x	1	address x	0	—	?	!
PUSH	y	1	y	1	address x	?	!
PUSH	z	1	z	1	y	? + 1	address x
ADD		0	—	1	y + z	? + 1	address x
PUSH	t	1	t	1	y + z	? + 1	address x
MPY		0	—	1	(y + z) × t	? + 1	address x
STORE[b]		1	(y + z) × t	1	address x	?	!
		1	address x	1	(y + z) × t	?	!
		0	—	1	(y + z) × t	?	!

[a] The mnemonics are not those used by Burroughs.
[b] STORE causes a sequence of three changes in the stack [it also stores (y + z) × t in x].

in Table I is the one used on the B6700 computer. The B5500 is similar except that the STORE instructions expect the address and the value to be reversed, i.e., the address has to be pushed into the stack after the value. This is the order expected by the B6700 as well, but since the B6700 can distinguish between values and addresses, either order is acceptable. If, in the example shown in Table I, the address was pushed into the stack immediately before the execution of the STORE operator, there would be no transfers required between register B and memory.

Other computers with stacks use the same technique to reduce storage references, but have more top-of-stack registers and thus fewer stack adjustments. The HP3000 has four such registers and the Burroughs B7700 (Burroughs Corp. [1973]) has as many as 32. The MU5 (Kilburn *et al.* [1968]) and the B7700 use an associative buffer memory to keep references to main memory to a minimum.

The stack computers mentioned so far include a large collection of operators in their instruction sets to make them more efficient. Many of these involve condensing a frequently used set of instructions into one instruction, or a large instruction into a shorter instruction. The Burroughs B6700 has instructions ZERO (PUSHCNST 0), ONE (PUSHCNST 1), NXLV (INDEX;FETCH), and STOD (STORE;POP).

The MU5 has a different approach to using a stack for arithmetic. It is best considered as a single-accumulator von Neumann machine with a stack available for temporary storage. Transfers into the stack from the accumulator must be programmed rather than automatic (as with a Burroughs type of stack mechanism). Thus, arithmetic instructions normally use one address. For example, the ADD operator is of form ADD x and performs, in our notation, PUSH x;ADD, though without any stack movements. The LOAD instruction normally loads into the accumulator, performing the equivalent of POP;PUSH x. However, an ordinary PUSH instruction is available. The top of the stack in memory may also be referenced as an autodecrement address by the arithmetic operators, thus giving our standard stack instructions. The operands are reversed, though, and special inverted instructions are provided for noncommutative operators.

The MU5 approach is intended to result in machine code that is efficient in terms of its compactness and the number of stack/memory transfers it causes. There are, in fact, five accumulators in the MU5 of different sizes and intended for different types of operands. Each register may be pushed into the single stack, although if the MU5 is being programmed as a stack machine, one will not usually get the effect of more than one top-of-stack register since the accumulators must be stacked in a predetermined sequence. In terms of minimizing stack/memory transfers, optimized MU5 code is the most efficient that can be produced. How great the actual savings are compared to the Burroughs method depends on the programs being executed; in fact, at the extremes of very simple and very complicated expressions, they cause the same number of transfers.

The MU5 approach is also difficult to evaluate in terms of code compactness. Although it uses fewer instructions than a Burroughs machine, more of its instructions use addresses; therefore the average instruction length is greater than would otherwise be the case. If instructions are coded as variable-length syllables, then there may be little or no advantage. For example, the instruction $A := B + C$ takes five instructions totaling 64 bits with the B6700 and three instructions totaling 48 bits with the MU5. However, the B6700 uses 22 bits for the operation codes compared to 21 for the MU5, implying that the difference is really due to the longer addresses in the B6700. Incidentally, neither machine needs any stack/memory transfers for the above expression.†

3. SUBROUTINE LINKAGE

Any computer that is to be used for program development must provide some means of facilitating subroutine linkage. There must be a method of returning from a subroutine to different points of call and some way of communicating parameters to (and results from) the subroutine. We will now see how stacks may help provide these functions.

3.1 Return Addresses

A set of subroutines or procedures that call one another defines a tree structure of possible calls. The tree may be finite, as in the three FORTRAN routines in Fig. 7a. However, in more advanced programming languages a subroutine may use itself, either directly or through some intermediate stages. This is called a *recursive* use of a subroutine. By including a routine used recursively (as in Fig. 7b) the tree of possible calls becomes infinite.

In both cases, finite and infinite, execution of the program will involve a traversal of the tree, although the whole tree is not necessarily traversed (in the infinite case, necessarily not). The tree may be traversed if, at each node, a record is kept of where in the calling program to continue the traversal, i.e., the return address. These return addresses may, of course, be kept in a stack.

---

† These figures assume typical situations; a valid comparison of the merit of the two approaches would require simulation of an appropriate program mix.

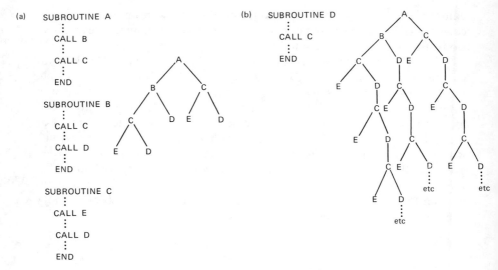

Fig. 7. Subroutines and associated trees of possible calls.

The simplest use of a stack for return addresses is as found in the KDF.9, which has a fixed-top stack (capable of containing sixteen return addresses) and two instructions of the form:

$$\text{CALL SUB:} \quad M[\text{top} := \text{top}+1] := IC;$$
$$IC := SUB;$$
$$\text{RETURN:} \quad IC := M[\text{top}];$$
$$\text{top} := \text{top}-1;$$

(where IC is the *instruction counter* that points to the next instruction to be executed). A large number of microcomputers have small return address stacks of this form.

The PDP-10 has a similar pair of instructions, PUSHJ R_i, L and POPJ R_i, which use a stack in memory pointed to by general register R_i. The Sigma 7 also has an instruction pair of this form.

3.2 Parameters

From one point of view, the return address can be considered to be one of the parameters passed to a subroutine. Whether it is or not, the other parameters can be placed into the stack, where they can be obtained by the subroutine. Since there may be more than one parameter, there must be some method of addressing stack elements other than the top one.

For a stack that is held in memory, the top-of-stack pointer is available for relative addressing, e.g., if R_i is being used as top pointer then CALL P(A,B) could be coded on the PDP-10 as:

$$\begin{array}{lll}
\text{PUSH} & R_i & A \\
\text{PUSH} & R_i & B \\
\text{PUSHJ} & R_i & P \\
\text{POP} & R_i & \\
\text{POP} & R_i & \\
\end{array}$$

and, inside P, the parameters would be at addresses -1(B) and -2(A) relative to R_i (as long as R_i does not change).

With this setup the calling routine inserts the parameters into the stack and then has to remove them when control returns. A more elegant method is to remove all the parameters at once. This may be performed by a modified RETURN instruction that "knows" the number of parameters. The number of parameters could be specified as part of the RETURN instruction or placed into the stack by the CALL.

The B5500, HP3000, and PDP-11 all place the return address into the stack after the parameters and access parameters relative to the return address (although this is not the top of the stack). The HP3000 includes the number of parameters in its return instruction; the B5500 includes a pointer to the location before the parameters; and the PDP-11 places a special instruction, including the number of parameters, in the stack.

A variant to discuss at this point is the Burroughs B2500 series (Burroughs Corp. [1966]), which uses a stack for return addresses and parameters only. The NTR instruction includes the number of parameters that are actually placed after the NTR in the program. The NTR places into the stack the parameters, the return address, and the contents of index register X3, which is then set to point to the new parameters. The top of the stack is pointed to by memory location 40. This is a low-speed location, but it does not matter because high-speed register X3 is used for addressing the parameters. A return instruction EXT uses X3 to reset location 40, and X3 itself, to their values before entry.

3.3 Multiple Use of Stacks

So far we have assumed that the subroutine stack is different from the arithmetic stack. The KDF.9 does have two stacks, but this is unusual; with many computers a single stack is used for both purposes. This is possible because, in most programming languages, expressions and subroutines are mutually well nested.

It is hard to see what advantage is obtained by having just one stack. There is some utility in that a function can leave its value on the stack and thus be immediately available for use in arithmetic; also, there is only one stack memory area to manage. This small gain is paid for with an increase in complexity. Top-of-stack relative addressing is no longer valid for subroutine parameters since the top of the stack will vary as the subroutine proceeds. To overcome this, a pointer to the position of the top of the subroutine stack within the expression stack must be available for relative addressing, as shown in Fig. 8.

The "top-sub" pointer must be maintained at all times. To reset the pointer when returning from a subroutine, the value of top-sub must be saved in the stack when the subroutine is called. Usually this is done in the same word as the return address, the combined word being termed a *return control word,* or, as we will call it, a *return constant.*

As shown in Fig. 8, a "snapshot" of the stack at any time will show a chain of return constants linked together with saved top-sub pointers. Another way of describing this situation is to say that the arithmetic stack

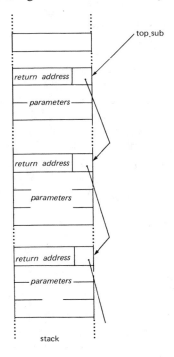

Fig. 8.   Combined subroutine and arithmetic stacks.

is defined by memory contiguity but the subroutine stack is given by an explicitly linked list (the top-sub pointers are sometimes called *dynamic links*).

The B5500, HP3000, and PDP-11 (more expensive models only) have stacks that correspond to this level of development. They all differ, as described before, in the way they remove parameters from the stack. Another difference is how the value is returned from a function subroutine. The B5500 takes the current top of the stack as the value and moves it down; the HP3000 uses the bottom-most parameter as the value; and the PDP-11 provides no built-in mechanism for returning a value. The three computers all provide extra features beyond the two-purpose stack, but basically they follow the model just outlined.

4. BLOCK STRUCTURE

This section outlines a method of allocating storage for variables while a program is executing. The method is based on the block-structure concept of ALGOL.

The technique of dividing a program into blocks relative to which declarations are made gives identifiers a restricted scope and implies locality of storage allocation. The storage allocation aspect of the ALGOL block structure was really designed for computers with fixed-size memories. Modern computer systems with virtual memories make explicit overlaying of storage unnecessary. However, block structure is part of most advanced programming languages and must still be accommodated.

4.1 Data Stacks and Displays

A program may be thought of as a tree from the point of view of its block structure. The structure is exhibited in a fully parenthesised form, with a **begin** as the left parenthesis and an **end** as the right parenthesis. A sample program and its structure are given in Figs. 9a and 9b.

Since the tree structure is traversed as the program is executed, a stack may be used to hold the data storage allocated for each block as long as the size of the data area is known at the start of the block. The contents of the stack while executing each block of the sample program are given in Fig. 9c.

The storage allocation scheme just described is quite adequate for simple variables because each variable has a storage location that is fixed in the stack and whose address can be determined when the program is compiled.

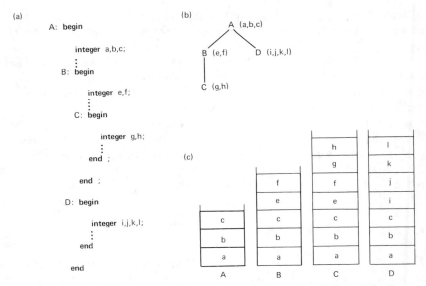

Fig. 9. Block structured program with associated tree and stack "snapshots."

However, consider the following program:

> **begin**
>> **integer** n;
>> read (n);
>> **begin**
>>> **integer array** A[0:n];
>>> **begin**
>>>> **integer** b;

If space is allocated in the stack for b after it has been allocated for A, then the position of b will vary as n varies. The location of b is not determinable at compile time (even if arrays are not held in the stack, using the stack for the other purposes will have the same effect, as discussed below).

The general method of handling a variable data address as the program runs is not to change each instruction that uses that address, but rather to compile each instruction with a constant address that is used indirectly in some manner.

This technique will work here too. Let us allocate one word in the stack for each name declared in a block (e.g., n, A, and b) and allocate all subsequent storage to elements that are not named simply (e.g., the array elements). Then each named item has a fixed address relative to the other named items declared in a block. If the blocks are assigned level numbers in the normal way for trees, then an address may be given as an *address pair* (level number, position on that level). This may be translated into an absolute address if the address of the first item with that level number is known. In the program in Fig. 9, a–*l* are (0,1), (0,2), (0,3), (1,1), (1,2), (2,1), (2,2), (1,1), (1,2), (1,3), and (1,4), respectively.

We now need some mechanism for translating each address pair into an absolute stack address. This amounts to knowing the address of the start of the storage area for each block. Such a list of addresses is called a *display* and may be held in high-speed *display registers*. The stack address represented by the pair (level, position) may be calculated as display [level] + position. The display setup for the program of Fig. 9 within block C is given in Fig. 10.

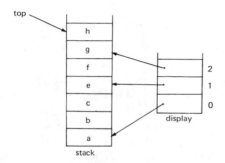

Fig. 10.   Data stack with display registers inside block C of the program of Fig. 9.

As with subroutines, the use of blocks is well nested with respect to expressions, and the same stack may be used for both purposes. A pointer to the top of the data stack must be kept in the processor and the combined stack must contain a linked chain of addresses defining the data stack. The link word is usually called a *block marker* and is the zeroth word of each addressing level. Along with the address of the previous block marker (sometimes called a *static link,* we will include the level number in one of the fields of the block marker, which becomes a compound word of the form

level	previous_ block _marker

If the pointer to the last block marker in the stack is held in register "top_ block," the stack state of Fig. 10 is modified to that of Fig. 11 (the "ground" symbol represents a null pointer).†

†At present, the setup we have developed is redundant. The level fields, in fact, render the display registers unnecessary for evaluating an address pair.

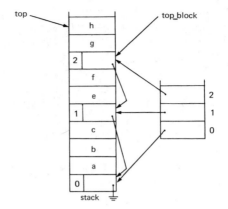

Fig. 11. Combined stack for data and expressions, same state as Fig. 10.

A stack machine needs some specific instructions to handle the block markers. All instructions with addresses that we have examined so far need to be extended to handle address couples by using the display registers. In particular, as we will see later, PUSHADDR (level, position) must use the display to evaluate (level, position) as a stack address before placing it on the stack. Also required are two instructions, one to be used on entering a block, another to be used on leaving. These will be called BLOCK size and UNBLOCK, respectively. BLOCK has the field, size, which gives the size of the stack area to be reserved for this block. We will assume that a block leaves a value on top of the stack.

In the following definitions of BLOCK and UNBLOCK we will use the operator "of" to obtain a subfield of a word.†

> BLOCK size: top := top + 1;
> level of stack[top] := level of stack[top_block] + 1;
> display[level of stack[top]] := top;
> previous_block_marker of stack[top] := top_block;
> top_block := top;
> top := top + size;

> UNBLOCK: p := top_block;
> top_block := previous_block_marker of stack[p];
> stack[p] := stack[top];
> top := p;

A nonsense program and its translation into stack code are given in Fig. 12.

† Note that we have not specified how the values of the pointers are initialized for the zeroth level. This could be allowed for in the definition, but most likely in practice the pointers and possibly the zero-level block marker would be initialized by the operating system. We do not wish to go into this matter here but ask the reader to bear with incomplete algorithms.

```
begin
    integer i,j,k ;              BLOCK         3
         i :=                    PUSHADDR     (0,1)
         begin
             integer e,f ;       BLOCK         2
             e := 6 ;            PUSHADDR     (1,1)
                                 PUSHCNST      6
                                 STORE
             f := e-k            POP
                                 PUSHADDR     (1,2)
                                 PUSH         (1,1)
                                 PUSH         (0,3)
                                 SUB
                                 STORE
         end                     UNBLOCK
         x j                     PUSH         (0,2)
                                 MPY
                                 STORE
    end                          UNBLOCK
```

Fig. 12. Block-structured program and corresponding stack code.

4.2 Environments and Procedure Constants

We have now seen how a stack may be used for subroutines and arithmetic or for data storage and arithmetic. This section describes the extensions needed to tie all three uses together in the same stack.

A simple combination of the stack of Section 4.1 with that of Section 3.3 will be adequate for languages such as APL, where a subroutine may use variables declared globally from where it is called. However, most programming languages are designed so that a procedure may be translated directly from where it is declared. Hence, the global variables that may be used by a procedure are those valid where the procedure is declared. For example, the ALGOL program of Fig. 13a will print out 3 (rather than 9 or

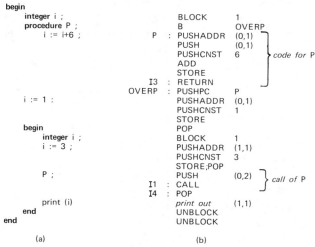

(a)   (b)

Fig. 13. ALGOL program using a parameterless procedure.

7) because P operates on the i at level zero, while it is the i at level one that is printed.

The set of identifiers that may be used at a point in a program is called the *environment* of that point. For the stack setup of Section 4.1 the identifiers that may be used are those whose stack addresses may be found via the display registers. Thus the display registers define the current environment. There is a permanent copy of the display registers in the block-marker chain and this is pointed to by top_block. Hence the top_block pointer completely defines the current environment.

When calling a procedure the display registers must be reset to what they were when the procedure was declared; when returning they must be reset to what they were before the procedure was called. Since the environment is determined by the top_block pointer, the pointer should be saved when the procedure is declared and when it is called. We will save it, when declared, in *procedure constant* (PC) and, when called, in *return constant* (RC) (see Fig. 13b). Both words have a special two-field form:

environment	program_address

We will use the instruction PUSHPC P, where P is a program address, to create a PC and place it in the stack:

PUSHPC P: top := top+1;
            environment of stack[top] := top_block;
            program_address of stack[top] := P;

A procedure declaration will be like any other declaration in that a stack location will be allocated for it. However, the stack location will be initialized to contain the PC for the procedure.

Another instruction is required for branching to a procedure and changing the display while saving the old environment in an RC. Assuming that the top of the stack contains the PC of the procedure, the following will do the job:†

CALL: reset_display_from(environment of stack[top]);
        swap(top_block, environment of stack[top]);
        swap(IC, program_address of stack[top]);

Yet another instruction is needed for returning from a procedure. We will assume that procedures always have values. When the RETURN instruction below is executed, top-of-stack should contain the value and next to top-of-stack the RC:

† IC is the address of the next instruction to be executed.

RETURN: reset_display_from(environment of stack[top − 1]);
           top_block := (environment of stack[top − 1]);
           IC := (program_address of stack[top − 1]);
           stack[top − 1] := stack[top];
           top := top − 1;

Both CALL and RETURN use the same microprogram to reset the display registers. This could simply reset all the registers as follows:

```
procedure reset_display_from(t);
  value t; integer t;
  begin
              integer level;
  loop:   level := level of stack[t];
          if level = 0 then go to exit;
          display[level] := t;
          t := previous_block_marker of stack[t];
          go to loop;
      exit:
  end;
```

Some display registers may, in fact, contain valid pointers, so a more complicated algorithm, which only resets registers as far as necessary, may be used:

```
procedure reset_display_from(t);
  value t; integer t;
  begin
              integer oldlevel, level;
              oldlevel := level of stack[top_block];
  loop:   level := level of stack[t];
          if level ≤ oldlevel ∧ display[level] = t then go to exit;
          display[level] := t;
          t := previous_block_marker of stack[t];
          go to loop;
      exit:
  end;
```

Figure 13b shows a translation into stack code of the program of Fig. 13a. Figure 14 gives the stack states before the execution of instructions I1, P, I3, and I4. Note that some stack locations associated with a block are allocated by using a BLOCK size instruction, others by placing a value directly on the stack.

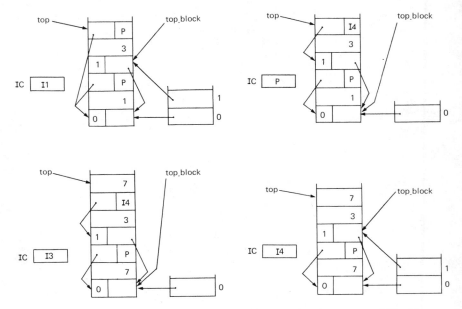

Fig. 14.   The stack state at four stages when executing the program of Fig. 13.

4.3   Subroutine Linkage Combined with Block Structure

The extension to the stack mechanism made in the last section was necessary to make the stack suitable for block-structured languages. We have not specified how parameters are to be handled, but presumably a technique such as that of Section 3.3 could be incorporated on "top" of the block structure mechanism. This would then give us a combined stack with three pointers, top, top_block, and top_sub, which give the tops of the stacks "within." The change in the stack setup discussed in this section will effect an economy, merging the uses of the stack for subroutines, parameters, and block structures.

When, in Section 3.2, we dealt with subroutine parameters, we really considered only one type of parameter, the ALGOL "call by value" used in the program shown in Fig. 15.

Inside a procedure, such as SUM in Fig. 15, value parameters i and j are treated like locations for ordinary variables. When the procedure is called [e.g., by sum(16, k + 3)] the actual parameters are evaluated, their values are placed in the locations reserved for the formal parameters, and the procedure is called.

In essence, a procedure is like a block. When it is called, locations are reserved for each of the parameters, and when it returns the locations are

```
begin                             BLOCK      0
    integer procedure             B          OVRSUM
        sum(i,j) ;        SUM  :  BLOCK      2      recover parameters
        value i,j ;       A2   :  PUSH       (1,1)
        integer i,j ;             PUSH       (1,2)
        sum := i+j ;              ADD
                                  UNBLOCK
                                  RETURN
                          OVRSUM :  PUSHPC   SUM
    begin
        integer k ;               BLOCK      1

        k :=                      PUSHADDR   (1,1)
            1 +                   PUSHCNST   1
            sum(16,k+3) ;         PUSH       (0,1)   PC for sum
                                  PUSH               space for blockmarker
                                  PUSHCNST   16      1st parameter
                                  PUSH       (1,1)
                                  PUSHCNST   3       2nd parameter
                                  ADD
                          A1   :  CALL       2
                          A3   :  ADD
                                  STORE

        end                       UNBLOCK
    end                           UNBLOCK
```

Fig. 15.   ALGOL program using a procedure with value parameters.

lost. The only difference is that for a procedure the locations must be initialized to the values of the actual parameters before the procedure is called. If we consider the procedure as starting with a BLOCK instruction and ending with an UNBLOCK instruction, the procedure will execute correctly if we arrange for the parameter stack locations to be preinitialized to the correct values. Then we need only alter CALL as follows:

CALL size: **if** size > 0 **then** top $:=$ top $-$ (size $+ 1$);
                  CALL as before;

Figure 15 shows the stack code for a sample nonsense program and Fig. 16 the stack status just before executing instructions A1, SUM, A2, and A3. The reader should follow the example through to the **end** to see how the return from the procedure works.

Although the example is rather trivial the mechanism is quite powerful. It is adequate for handling all value parameter situations, including procedure constants passed as values. No one would suggest using this method of subroutine linkage because it is not sound to lose values off the top of the stack and then recover them. However, this does illustrate the principles involved and it is a straightforward task to extend the instruction set so that the top pointer is not altered during the procedure-calling sequence.

When discussing procedure parameters in Section 3 we noted the need for storing in the stack the number of parameters passed to a procedure so that they could be removed on returning from the procedure. As the parameters are now above a block marker, the UNBLOCK operator does

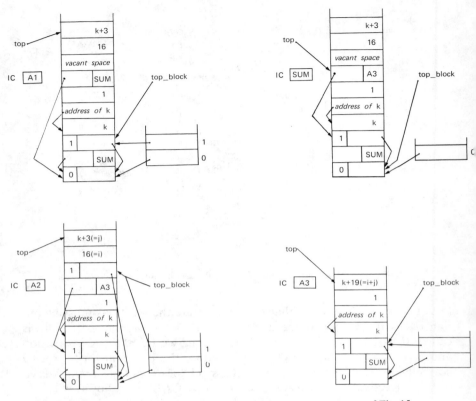

Fig. 16. The stack state at four stages of executing the program of Fig. 15.

the job for us. However, there are situations where knowledge of the number of parameters is necessary. Consider the following program segment:

```
begin
      ⋮
      a := b × begin
                    integer i, j;
                    ⋮
                    ⋮
                    if tog then go to 1;
                    ⋮
                    ⋮
               end ;
      1: ⋮
end
```

Here the **go to** must rid the stack of all storage that is reserved for blocks more deeply nested than the destination label and any other unnecessary items in the stack. This must also be done in the more practical jump from within a procedure to a global label. We will not extend our sample stack mechanism to handle this situation, but we could do so by including a "number-of-parameters" field in the block markers. The B6700 system places a special marker in the stack above the parameters and uses a subroutine to search for the marker and cut the stack back.

4.4 Some Implementations

The stack mechanism just described has only been fully implemented in one commercially available computer system, the Burroughs B6700/B7700 series. This is not too surprising; up till now, the most widely used programming languages do not use block structure. FORTRAN, for example, can make do with just two levels of addressing, one for common and one for local variables. In fact, most programs use only two levels; well-written program modules should be too small to need block structure. This is not to say that block structure is useless; on the contrary, it is very useful, especially in large systems programs for handling procedures declared local to other procedures.

However, much useful work may be accomplished with two levels of addressing, and two computers, the B5500 and HP3000, implement a two-level scheme. We will consider these first and then consider the B6700.

4.4.1 *The B5500 and HP3000*

In both machines addressing relative to a top_sub pointer may be both positive and negative (as it could be with the PDP-11). Procedure linkage takes place in three stages: parameters are placed in the stack, the procedure is called, and space is allocated in the stack for variables local to the procedure. While a procedure is executing it may obtain its parameters with negative addressing relative to top_sub and its local variables with positive addressing relative to top_sub. In this scheme there are procedures, but no blocks as such; a block must be treated as a procedure that is called from where it is defined.

Both computers use other forms of addressing, including one that allows constants to be obtained from within a program and another that may be used to give access to global variables. The HP3000 mechanism is illustrated in Fig. 17. The global variables are held in the stack and are addressed relative to the DB register, which serves as display[0]. The machine allows positive and negative addressing relative to both register Q and the top-of-

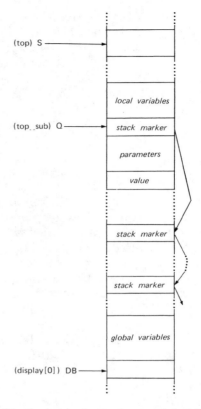

(top) S

local variables

(top._sub) Q — stack marker

parameters

value

stack marker

stack marker

global variables

(display[0]) DB

Fig. 17. Stack setup for Hewlett Packard HP3000.

stack register S. The number of parameters to be removed from below a block marker (called a *stack marker* and, in fact, four words long) is given in the RETURN instruction. The value, if there is one, is the bottommost parameter and is not removed on return.

The B5500 stack is shown in Fig. 18. In this case global variables are assigned, not in the stack, but in another memory area called the *program reference table* and pointed to by register R. Links are placed in the stack before and after the subroutine parameters, thus enabling the RETURN instructions to remove them. The value of a procedure is on top of the stack when the procedure returns; it can usually be equated with the topmost local variable and is thus addressable. When the link below the parameters is placed into the stack, a copy is also placed in location $R+7$ of the previous return constant. Since this register may be used as an indirect address, there are really three levels, although $R+7$ relative addressing is

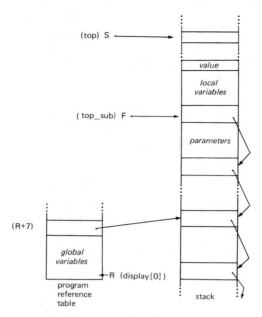

Fig. 18.   Stack setup for Burroughs B5500.

intended to facilitate the implementation of parameters called by name (see Section 5.2).

4.4.2   *The B6700*

The B6700 implements the scheme we have described but makes a number of changes. The machine follows Randell and Russell [1964] in that it treats all blocks as procedures and all procedures as blocks, placing a double word, consisting of a *mark-stack control word* (MSCW) and a *return control word* (RCW), into the stack. The two words contain the same information as our block marker and return constant did, but distribute it differently. The general stack setup is given in Fig. 19.

In the B6700, program constants (called *program control words* or PCWs) give an address relative to a segment table. The relative address is so large that there is not enough room in the PCW for an environment pointer. Because of this, program constants can not be transferred around in the stack but, once created, must stay above the block marker (MSCW) that defines the environment. Thus, the calling sequence is: push a MSCW into the stack, then push a pointer to the PCW, then push the parameters, and finally call the procedure (using the operator ENTR). In the simple case where the procedure being called is in the current environment, the PCW

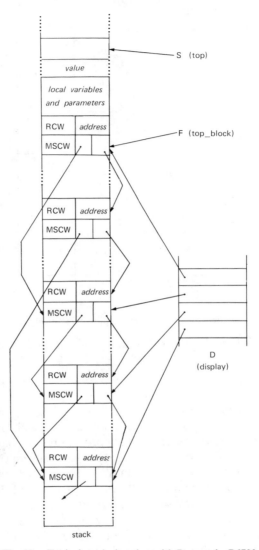

Fig. 19.   Typical stack situation with Burroughs B6700.

is directly pointed to by an address pair (an *indirect reference word* or IRW) and the display does not have to be updated. This situation (before executing the ENTR operator) is given in Fig. 20a. When the procedure being called is not in the current environment, it is pointed to by an IRW, which points to a different type of address word (a *stuffed indirect reference word* or

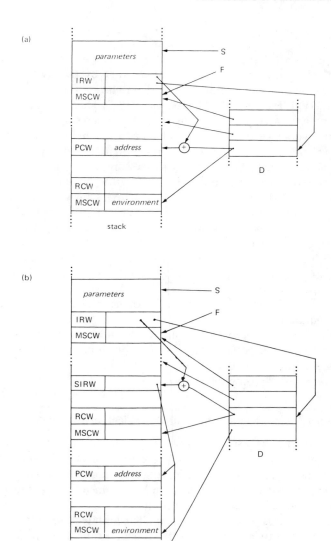

Fig. 20. The B6700 stack before calling a procedure. (a) Procedure in current environment; (b) procedure not in current environment.

SIRW), which gives a block marker address, and thus defines the environment and the PCW relative to that block marker. This is illustrated in Fig. 20b. In both cases the return operator is the same—a combination of UNBLOCK and RETURN.

5. EXTENSIONS

The computers we have been using as examples fall into two categories, those that extend a von Neumann architecture by the use of stacks and those whose whole architecture is based on stacks. Of the latter we have only the KDF.9, HP3000, B5500, and B6700/B7700 computers. Computers of this type are worthy of the title *stack machines* since they represent a significant divergence from the von Neumann machine.

However, the stack architecture is inadequate for many purposes. For example, as mentioned before, array processing takes an excessive number of memory references. The HP3000 and KDF.9 include index registers in their designs and the B5500 provides a few extra instructions; these help, but do not solve the problem. The B6700 has similar instructions but also provides a special *mode* of operation where the character of the computer completely changes from a stack machine to a vector processing machine. (The B5500 and B6700 both use the same change-of-mode technique to facilitate string processing.) Either by extending the machine itself or by including more than one machine under the same "cabinet," the stack architecture can be made just as viable for general computing as a more conventional architecture.

All computers are used for a number of different purposes, the stack architecture being especially suitable for program development. In the following sections we will see how a stack machine fits in with other extensions required of computers nowadays.

5.1 Tagged Memories and Operand-Dependent Instructions

When a computer is used for multiprogramming it is essential that the operating system and user tasks be protected from the ravages of a rogue program. The memory of a classic von Neumann machine consists of a linear array of words that have no inherent meaning to the processor. Any word may be an instruction, a number, or some characters, etc., depending on how it is used by a program. The architecture must be extended in some way to provide protection from a program that mistakes instructions for data, or data for instructions.

There are numerous ways of making the memory a more complex device and providing some measure of protection. Usually these methods involve splitting the memory space into areas that can only be accessed by the process that "owns" that area and prohibiting the overwriting of information in areas known to contain programs. These methods would be of some help for stack machines, but they do not solve a further protection problem, that of protecting a process from itself. This, if it could be done, would facilitate debugging. If one takes the realistic attitude that large programs, such as those used in operating systems, are never completely error free, some sort of protection seems essential. The complication with stack machines is that, unlike other computers, their data area contains control information, such as block markers and return constants. Hence, protection must be provided down the level of individual words.

To enable a computer to distinguish control words from data it is necessary that some bits of each word be dedicated to that purpose. The bits that are used for protection, and are therefore unavailable for use as data, are called the *tag*. Tagged memories are not used widely, partly because of the loss of memory space involved and partly because protection by areas is adequate for conventional machines (for a design based on tags see Iliffe [1968]). It is not suprising, though, to find stack machines using tags. The B5500 does not provide pure tags as it cannot distinguish between program words and stack words (they use different areas). However, words held in the stack have one bit, the "flag" bit, used as a tag to distinguish data from control words. By the use of further bits the B5500 can distinguish three classes of control words—descriptors of arrays, descriptors of programs, and others.

The B6700 uses a tag of three bits appended to each of its 48-bit words and thus can distinguish eight classes of words directly. Some of these classes are further divided by the use of other bits. For example, arrays may be of 4-, 6-, 8-, 48-, or 96-bit elements, the type being given by bits in the array descriptor. As in the B5500, integer numbers are a subset of floating-point numbers and thus may be distinguished by the hardware.

Once a computer is given a tagged memory the design of the whole machine will change to take advantage of the tags. An instruction can then tell what sort of object it is operating on and may take different actions for different data—instructions become *operand dependent*. Let us take two examples from the repertoire of the B6700.

First, two of the tag classes used by the B6700 are for single and double-precision data. Each top-of-stack register is duplicated. Thus the processor can handle mixed single- and double-precision data and make the necessary conversions automatically. This, combined with the fact that integers are a subset of other numbers, means that the B6700 has just one instruction for the basic arithmetic operations—just one ADD compared with, for example, the fourteen addition instructions of the IBM 360. (To be fair, the B6700 ADD must be followed by conversion instructions, such as "integerize" or "convert to decimal" to obtain the same effect as some IBM 360 instructions.)

Second, the B6700 INDEX instruction expects to find on top of the stack a number and an array descriptor in *either order*. It then *rounds* the number to an integer before performing the INDEX operation, *checking* that the index is not negative and is not greater than the extent of the array. In the B6700 a long linear array may be segmented, that is, broken into smaller arrays of length 256 (similar to paging). If the array is segmented, the descriptor points to an array of descriptors, in which case the INDEX instruction *fetches* the appropriate descriptor and *indexes* that, taking into account the number of data items that may be stored in a word (i.e., ½, 1, 6, 8, or 12).

5.2   Parameter "Call by Name"

In Section 4.3 our discussion of subroutine parameters was restricted to those transmitting a value. This type of parameter is adequate for most purposes since it accounts for the passing of procedure constants. However, since value parameters are inconvenient in many situations, other parameter forms are in common use. We postponed our discussion of other parameter *disciplines* until we had equipped the stack machine with tags, since they simplify matters considerably.

One simple parameter discipline, which is used to implement FORTRAN, is "call by reference." In "call by reference," an actual parameter is evaluated to give either an operand or an address, which is then passed to the subroutine. For example, if

> SUBROUTINE TEST (I, J)
> I = J
> RETURN
> END

was invoked by CALL TEST (A(N), M) or by CALL TEST (A(3), 5), then TEST would be passed the addresses of A(N) and M or the address of A(3) and the value 5, which would be used, at different times, for I and J. To do this efficiently, stack locations for I and J would be initialized to the actual parameters. If the parameter was an address it would be accessed indirectly, while a value would be obtained directly from the parameter location.

The question is: How does the computer know whether an address or a value has been passed to it? A conventional computer cannot tell and thus locations in the calling area must be reserved for actual parameters that are values, the address of these temporary locations being passed to the subroutine. Also, all parameters must be accessed indirectly. On the other hand, if the computer has a tagged memory, then the instructions to PUSH a value or an address onto the stack can be extended to make indirect references only if they are necessary.

The same question arises with the ALGOL parameter discipline of "call by name." The ALGOL 60 language designers seemed loathe to introduce the concept of an address or reference into the language, perhaps because of hard-to-handle situations such as a reference into a block being used after the block has been exited. They managed to avoid mentioning addresses entirely by using a different discipline, which is delightfully simple to describe.

The idea is contained in this rule: To obtain a statement with the same effect as a procedure call, replace the call with a copy of the procedure body, having substituted actual parameters for the formal parameters throughout.

Within TEST in the above example, I = J would be treated as A(N) = M for CALL TEST (A(N), M) and as A(3) = 5 for CALL TEST (A(3), 5). (If the names of variables local to the procedure conflict with those of the parameters, the local names are to be systematically changed.)

How is this to be implemented? Actually, applying the above rule is ruled out by efficiency considerations. In fact, the effect inside the called procedure is that when a formal parameter is used, a call is made to a little routine that evaluates the name parameter. These little routines have come to be called *thunks* (Ingerman [1961]).

With a conventional computer, all references to name parameters would be treated as thunks, but with a tagged memory the PUSH instructions can be extended further so as to cause thunks only when they are necessary. To handle "call by reference" and "call by name," the processor must be able to distinguish words describing thunks, references, and values. As values include ordinary program constants and addresses, it is necessary to introduce special words for thunks and references—a *thunk constant* and a *reference*. These are similar to program constants and addresses but with a special bit set to indicate that they are to be evaluated when accessed.

The machine can distinguish the different types of words by examining their tag fields. We will indicate this ability by the use of the predicates (Boolean procedures) *value, reference,* and *thunk*. To convert an address to a reference and a procedure constant to a thunk constant, we will use a new instruction, NAME.

The mechanism for calling a procedure is the same as that discussed for value parameters. The only difference is that the compiler, having knowledge of the procedure declaration, does not evaluate name parameters but, instead, passes a reference or thunk constant. For example, for

procedure P(i);
value i;
integer i;

the use P(m + n) translates to

```
PUSH    P (i.e. a location containing the PC for P)
PUSH
PUSH    m
PUSH    n
ADD
CALL    1
```

but for

procedure P(i);
integer i;

P(m + n) translates to

```
             PUSH        P
             PUSH
             B           OVERTH
TH:          PUSH        m
             PUSH        n
             ADD
             RETURN
OVERTH:      PUSHPC      TH
             NAME
             CALL        1
```

P(3) translates to

```
PUSH        P
PUSH
PUSHCNST    3
CALL        1
```

and P(m) becomes

```
PUSH        P
PUSH
PUSHADDR    m
NAME
CALL        1
```

The inside of procedure P, whatever it does, would be the same in all the above cases. Some extra instructions are needed, however, to evaluate thunks and chase references. To replace PUSH we will use GETVAL and to replace PUSHADDR we will use GETADDR, as follows:†

    GETVAL (level, position):
    PUSHADDR (level, position);
    repeat:
        stack[top] := M[stack[top]];
        if value(stack[top]) **then go to** fin
        else if reference(stack[top]) **then go to** repeat
        else if thunk(stack[top]) **then** CALL* 0
        else error;
    fin: . . .

    GETADDR (level, position):
    PUSHADDR (level, position);
    repeat:
        loc := stack[top]; (*converted to an address if a reference*)
        stack[top] := M[stack[top]];
        if value(stack[top]) **then** stack[top] := loc
        else if reference(stack[top]) **then go to** repeat
        else if thunk(stack[top]) **then** CALL* 0
        else error;

The same thunk procedure may be required to return an address or a value depending on whether it is used by GETVAL or GETADDR. To ensure that it does, the thunk procedure should always return a reference if possible. The CALL on the thunk (indicated by CALL*) should use as a return address the program address of the GETVAL or GETADDR. The return constant should have a bit set that indicates that the address in the instruction returned to should be ignored, since the instruction is to operate on the top of the stack (in the preceding programs, reexecution should start from the label "repeat"). Reexecution of the instruction that caused the thunk assures that the correct type is returned from the thunk. (Another way of looking at this is that CALL returns to the microaddress repeat.)

An example of a procedure using thunks is given in Fig. 21a. Figure 21b shows the stack at its largest point—inside the procedure TWICE called

---

† Note that PUSHADDR places an absolute address in the stack, not an address pair.

from the thunk caused by GETADDR inside P. The code for the complete program is

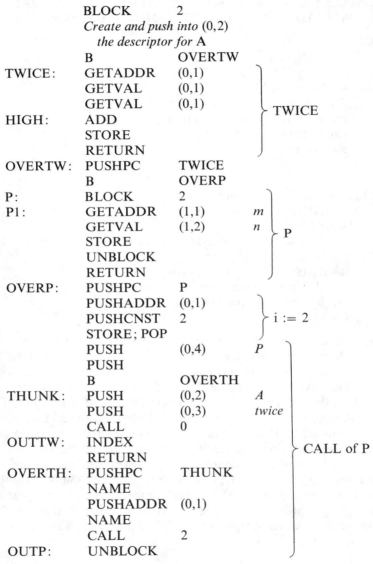

	BLOCK	2	
	Create and push into (0,2)		
	the descriptor for **A**		
	B	OVERTW	
TWICE:	GETADDR	(0,1)	
	GETVAL	(0,1)	
	GETVAL	(0,1)	TWICE
HIGH:	ADD		
	STORE		
	RETURN		
OVERTW:	PUSHPC	TWICE	
	B	OVERP	
P:	BLOCK	2	
P1:	GETADDR	(1,1)	*m*
	GETVAL	(1,2)	*n* P
	STORE		
	UNBLOCK		
	RETURN		
OVERP:	PUSHPC	P	
	PUSHADDR	(0,1)	
	PUSHCNST	2	*i := 2*
	STORE; POP		
	PUSH	(0,4)	*P*
	PUSH		
	B	OVERTH	
THUNK:	PUSH	(0,2)	*A*
	PUSH	(0,3)	*twice*
	CALL	0	
OUTTW:	INDEX		
	RETURN		CALL of P
OVERTH:	PUSHPC	THUNK	
	NAME		
	PUSHADDR	(0,1)	
	NAME		
	CALL	2	
OUTP:	UNBLOCK		

Although tags and automatic thunks are not necessarily confined to stack machines, they are particularly compatible. The two machines that we mentioned as using tags both provide instructions for handling name

(a)

```
begin
    integer i ;
    integer array A[0:4] ;
    integer procedure twice ;
        twice := i := i + i ;
    procedure P(m,n) ;
        integer m,n ;
        m := n ;
    i := 2 ;
    P(A[twice], i) ;
    comment here i = 4 = A[4] ;
end
```

(b)

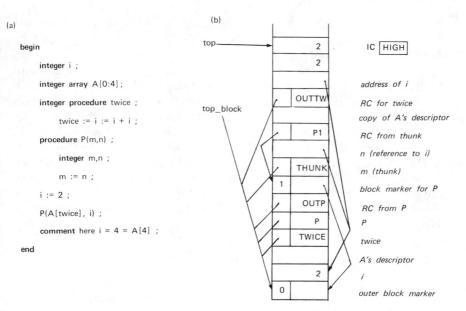

Fig. 21. A program using "call-by-name" parameters and the stack at its largest point while executing the program.

parameters. In fact, with the earlier B5500 all procedure calls had to be made using a GETVAL type of instruction. The B6700 implements a scheme much as we have described but with significant differences to increase efficiency and to accomodate ALGOL 60. We will not consider the B6700 in depth, but a few of the differences may be of interest.

Because ALGOL does not use addresses as values and restricts the use of procedures as values, special words for thunks and references are unnecessary. Procedure constants are never shifted from the block marker where they are declared; instead, a reference is passed as a parameter where we would expect a PC. References are always evaluated by the "pushing" operator VALC (if an address has to be passed to a procedure it is necessary to first convert it to a constant). Again, because PCs are never shifted, a thunk is not created where it is used but is treated as an ordinary procedure declared in the immediately surrounding block.

The B6700 has no ordinary PUSH operator but uses the operator VALC, which is very like our GETVAL. Rather than have a GETADDR operator, which is somewhat inefficient since it always looks one memory cell ahead for a value, the B6700 NAMC operator pushes an address couple (an IRW) into the stack, leaving the evaluation of the address to the store operator STON. Since the memory of the B6700 is a standard two-cycle core, the

STON operator can use split-cycle operation to look ahead with no loss of efficiency. Thus our GETADDR; GETVAL; STORE is replaced by NAMC; VALC; STON.†

To get side effects from thunks the correct way around, the effect of GETADDR is obtained by using EVAL; i.e., NAMC; EVAL is used in place of GETADDR. An address couple may be converted to a base-of-stack relative address by the use of the operator STFF (*stuff environment*), which converts an IRW to a SIRW (which defines an environment). In particular, PUSHADDR is replaced by NAMC;STFF. The operators VALC, EVAL, and STON handle two varieties of addresses: the within-stack references IRW and SIRW and, for addresses outside the stack, indexed array descriptors. Any address on top of the stack may be loaded from its value using the operator LOAD; thus our PUSH is replaced by NAMC;LOAD.

5.3   The Stack as an Execution Record

With tags and other standard protection schemes the stack machine is as ready as any other to receive an operating system and to be used for multi-programming. A multiprogramming system is one that has more than one *task* (or *process*) resident in the logical memory, where a task is defined as a program plus an *execution record* (i.e., all variables and other information used by the executing program). Tasks are considered to be more fundamental than programs because two or more tasks may share the same program as long as the program does not modify itself. We may think of tasks as executing simultaneously, although unless there is more than one processor this will not actually happen.

The Burroughs Corp. has demonstrated with the development of operating systems for the B5500, and more recently the B6700, that stack machines are well suited to this purpose. One of the main reasons lies with the identification of a stack with the execution record of a task. All information necessary to restart the task, apart from a few special registers, is contained in the stack or, as is the case with the Burroughs computers, is accessed via the stack. Hence a task is a program plus a stack.

Switching a processor from one task to another is greatly facilitated by the mechanism available for subroutine linkage. The current display-register contents are defined by the top_block pointer, which may be saved in the stack, along with the current instruction counter, by a slightly modified CALL instruction. Similarly, when reinitiating a task's execution

---

† VALC; NAMC; STON is also acceptable and is the more usual sequence. Since ALGOL does not make extensive use of statements with values, the operator STOD, equivalent to STORE and POP, is used more often than STON.

on a processor, a RETURN operator may be used to reset the display and instruction counter.

The B6700 develops the idea of a stack as a task by basing the operating system on the stack concepts of block structure and displays. For a full description we refer the reader to Organick [1973]; we can give only the briefest outline here.

If a procedure is initiated as a subtask of a given task, then the procedure must use as its environment part of the execution record of the parent. This leads to a tree-structured stack or *cactus stack* as it is called by Burroughs. At the lowest level in the cactus is the stack containing variables and descriptors for the MCP (*Master Control Program*, i.e., operating system) pointed to by the level zero display register. At level one is a table of information about the program, including the equivalent of a page table. The stacks of user tasks start at level two. A typical situation of the cactus stack, where two tasks are using the same program and another task is processing a subtask, is shown in Fig. 22.

5.4 Observations

We have seen the various uses that have been made of stacks in computers up to the present. There are only a few computers that include stacks in their hardware. These computers have demonstrated that stack machines are successful, but give us no basis for predicting the future of hardware

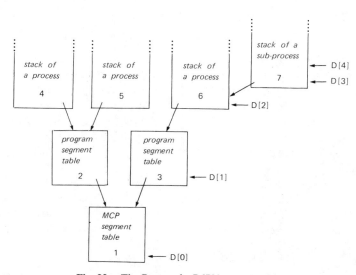

Fig. 22.   The Burroughs B6700 *cactus stack*.

stacks. In order to forecast trends in design we must look at other aspects of computing systems.

Hardware, in general, does change to meet the needs of software. Stacks are widely used in software, but most computers lack hardware stacks. The reason for this contradiction is that most manufacturers of small- and medium-scale computers have experienced a period of retrenchment in architectural innovations since the early sixties. Perhaps because of the inertia of the investment in software, the old architectures have been made faster, but not altered significantly. When the current product lines were conceived the importance of stacks, or for that matter, software as a whole, had not fully been grasped by the designers. Most of the computers discussed here are of a later period and perhaps do indicate a trend towards stack machines or a greater use of stacks.

One software trend that makes this very likely is the use of high-level languages such as PL/s for systems programming. Of all programmers, the systems designers have the greatest opportunity to influence the hardware design and if they are using recursive, block-structured languages they will be demanding stacks.

Another trend that encourages the use of stack architectures is the incorporation by microprogramming of multiple (and not completely fixed) architectures in one system. This gives the system designers a much freer reign to make the emulators suit their purposes (see Wilner [1974] for such an architecture that uses explicitly tree-structured programs). The techniques we have considered will most likely be incorporated into future firmware architectures, which will also be extended to cover other software techniques, such as expression translation, that we have not even discussed.

Note added in proof

On October 24th, 1974, International Computers Ltd. announced their new range of computers as the ICL 2900 series. As this is the first general-purpose architecture introduced in some years it deserves a careful analysis, especially since it is only the second commercial system to be dedicated to high-level language programming. There is only space here for a brief discussion of the stack; this is unfortunate as other features of the architecture are very interesting.

With regard to the arithmetic aspects of its stack, the ICL 2900 follows the MU5. The only difference is that it has three top-of-stack registers rather than five; however, the accumulator operates in three sizes. The subroutine mechanism is fairly standard and encompasses the use of the stack for data storage. The architecture also follows the MU5 in not dealing completely with displays; display registers are provided for local and global variables only. Another register may be set to give access to intervening addressing levels, but maintenance of the display is the responsibility of software. Provision is made for automatic entry into thunks, the action being called an *escape*.

The new architecture does not make use of a tagged memory. The obvious results of this are that the instruction set consists of a large number of simple operations and, more seriously, there is no protection of control words within the stack. Protection is applied to segments as a whole and an interesting multiple-level protection feature is built into the hardware. Although a process could contaminate its own stack, the operating system is protected by being held in areas with a safer level of protection. Protection is further maintained by making an automatic switch to a new stack whenever a procedure calls another on a less-trusted level.

As with the Burroughs B6700, the ICL system is built around the concept of making a stack the execution record of a task. The main differences lie in the virtual memory system and in the fielding of interrupts. The ICL 2900 uses a clean, two-level, storage management scheme that does not involve the stacks in the manner of the B6700. Interrupts logically belonging to a task are treated as subroutine calls in the task's stack. Interrupts that are more properly the business of the operating system cause an automatic switch to an "alter ego" stack, which is maintained for each task (in fact, in the next virtual segment from the first stack).

In summary, the ICL 2900 is a well-designed integration of stack, virtual memory, and string-processing architecture. It confirms the trend towards the use of stacks in hardware, but does not go as far in this direction as some other machines.

Acknowledgment

I would like to thank Mr. Donald McCrea of Burroughs Corp., Goleta, California, and Ted Drawneck, Lloyd Thomas, and Ian Thompson of Massey University for help in the preparation and proofreading of this paper.

I would also like to thank ICL (New Zealand) Ltd. for giving me access to the literature on their new computers (International Computers [1974]).

REFERENCES

Burroughs Corp. [1964]. "Burroughs B5500 Reference Manual."
Burroughs Corp. [1966]. "Burroughs B2500 and B3500 Systems Characteristics Manual."
Burroughs Corp. [1969]. "Burroughs B6700 Systems Reference Manual."
Burroughs Corp. [1973]. "Burroughs B7700 Systems Reference Manual."
Digital Equipment Corp. [1969]. "PDP-10 Reference Handbook."
Digital Equipment Corp. [1971]. "PDP-11/45 Processor Handbook."
Haley, A. C. D. [1962]. The KDF.9 computer system, *Proc. AFIPS FJCC* **21,** 108–120.
Hewlett Packard Co. [1972]. "HP3000 Computer System Reference Manual."

Iliffe, J. K. [1968]. "Basic Machine Principles." MacDonald, London.
Ingermann, P. [1961]. Thunks, *Commun. ACM* **4,** 55–58.
International Computers [1974]. "ICL 2900 Technical Overview Brochure."
Kilburn, T., Morris, D., Rohl, J. S., and Sumner, F. H. [1968]. A system design proposal, *Int. Fed. Inform. Process. Soc. Congr.* 806–811.
Knuth, D. E. [1968]. "The Art of Computer Programming," Vol. I, Fundamental Algorithms. Addison-Wesley, Reading, Massachusetts.
Mendelson, M. J., and England, A. W. [1966]. The SDS Sigma 7: a realtime time-sharing computer. *Proc. AFIPS FJCC* **29,** 51–64.
Organick, E. I. [1973]. "Computer System Organization—The B5700/B6700 Series." Academic Press, New York.
Randell, B., and Russell, L. J. [1964]. "ALGOL-60 Implementation." Academic Press, New York.
Wilner, W. T. [1974]. Structured programs, arcadian machines, and the Burroughs B1700. *Lecture Notes in Computer Sci.* **7,** 139–142.

Architecture of the SYMBOL

Computer System

Theodore A. Laliotis

Systems Technology Division
Fairchild Camera and Instrument Corporation
Palo Alto, California

1. SYSTEM OVERVIEW

1.1 Historical Background

The preliminary work that led to the development of SYMBOL began during the mid-sixties at the Digital Systems Research Department of the Fairchild Camera and Instrument Corporation under the leadership of R. Rice and W. R. Smith. The machine was operational by 1970 and was delivered in January 1971 to Iowa State University under the sponsorship of the National Science Foundation. It is presently being used as a working computer and as a research tool.

The 1950s was the first decade of serious developments in the digital computer field. The von Neumann architecture and transistor technology dominated the field during that decade. As we entered the 1960s a considerable wealth of computer science had been accumulated, the new technological era of integrated circuits was beginning to emerge, and economic conditions were very healthy. The SYMBOL design team recognized the existence of these conditions and decided that this was the perfect time to design a machine with the user in mind. Until that time, digital computers were designed by engineers and technologists mainly as a technological challenge with very little consideration for the users. On the other hand, the users had grown sophisticated and very demanding of the capabilities of their machines. They had to resort to large amounts of software in order to serve their needs. Software became costly and the adequacy of some aspects of the von Neumann architecture was being questioned. SYMBOL represents a major departure from the von Neumann architecture, which is still considered the conventional architecture. SYMBOL was primarily a research project. Its prime objective was to demonstrate, with a working system, that a high-level, indirectly executable language, a large portion of the time-sharing operating system, and an automatic, virtual-memory management system could be implemented directly in hardware, resulting in a more efficient system. A large portion of that hardware, however, had to be invented.

By the time the SYMBOL hardware was functional (in the late 1960s), the economic conditions of the whole electronic industry had deteriorated. Thus, even though the experimental objectives of SYMBOL had been accomplished, it was impossible to continue the development of the system with a marketable version.

It is very interesting to notice that many of the features pioneered by SYMBOL are slowly appearing in new machines.

1.2   Overall System Description

1.2.1   *SYMBOL from the User's Viewpoint*

The features that distinguish SYMBOL from all other machines are the following.

a. The Language.   The SYMBOL language is a high-level procedural and artifact-free language. The format is free; procedures can simply be called by name and the size and attributes of fields, strings, and structures are free of any hardware or software constraints such as declarations. All the powerful features found in most popular languages, such as FORTRAN, ALGOL, and PL/1, are incorporated in SYMBOL. The FORMAT and MASK operators make it very easy to manipulate numeric and alphanumeric strings by simply applying a pictorial string against the operand. Other features associated with the language will be discussed in detail in Section 2.

b. The Lack of Machine Language.   A reader accustomed to conventional computer literature would now expect a description of the instruction set and the instruction word format of the machine language, usually given in the form of a data word with op-code and operand address fields. Such information is essential for writing system software control programs and for debugging programs in the machine language. An instruction set and instruction word format do not exist in SYMBOL. This is perhaps SYMBOL's most striking departure from conventional computers. The high-level SYMBOL language is also the machine language. There is only one level of transformation that a SYMBOL program undergoes before execution (indirect execution architecture). That transformation is performed by the hardware compiler, which generates a reverse Polish string of operation codes and operand addresses ready for execution by the *central processor* (CP).

c. Automatic Virtual Memory Management.   The SYMBOL main memory facility features a virtual memory system. Memory is allocated automatically by the hardware memory controller in small increments as required during the various stages of processing. Also, memory space gets automatically reclaimed and is returned to the available space when no longer needed. Thus, the user is totally free of any memory-management tasks such as keeping track of addresses and overlays. Actually, the amount of memory allocated to a program varies dynamically, like a rubber band, during the various phases of processing, but the user has no need to know about it since it is managed automatically by the hardware. Direct automatic memory allocation and reclamation in small increments by the hardware is perhaps the second most striking characteristic of SYMBOL.

d.   Text-Editing Capability.   This feature allows for on-line program editing in the source language through the *interface processor* by using a special terminal without the use of the *central processing unit* (CPU) resource.

e.   System Library of Procedures.   A library of system procedures in source language is available to the user. The user is required only to call the procedure by name in his program. The procedure is then compiled along with his program as if it were a part of it. This is done, independent of the CPU, by the *compiler processing unit.*

f.   Time-Sharing Efficiency.   SYMBOL is a time-sharing system. However, only 32 channels were designed in the system since it was meant to be only a research vehicle. Its efficiency as a time-sharing system should be higher than others due to the multiprocessor architecture that will be discussed in the next section and due to the hardware implementation of many functions traditionally done in software. In general, hardware implementation yields higher speed.

1.2.2   SYMBOL from the Architectural Viewpoint

a.   Multiprocessor Architecture.   One of the objectives of SYMBOL's architecture is to maximize the efficiency of the system's resources by minimizing idle time. Having the other sections of a system lay idle while waiting for a specific section to finish its processing task is a waste of the system's resources, especially in a time-sharing environment. Various solutions to this problem have been implemented in the industry and they are all based on various forms of parallelism. SYMBOL achieves parallelism and execution efficiency through multiprogramming and multiprocessing by means of seven autonomous processors operating simultaneously and sharing a common virtual memory. These processors are totally heterogeneous and each is dedicated to a specific task. They are interconnected via a common bus structure. The overall block diagram of SYMBOL is shown in Fig. 1. A user's program gets passed from one processor to another during the various stages of processing, but it can never be in two processors at the same time. With the exception of the *memory controller* (MC), the *memory reclaimer* (MR), and the *system supervisor* (SS), which are service

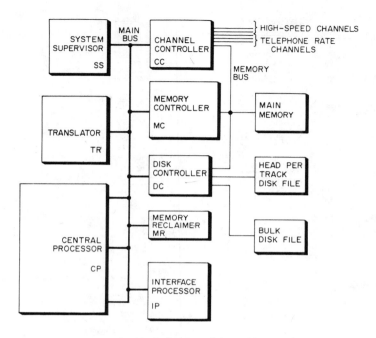

Fig. 1. Gross block diagram of the SYMBOL system.

processors, each of the other four units, i.e., the *channel controller* (CC), the *interface processor* (IP), the *translator* (TR), and the *central processor* (CP), may be processing a different program at any given time. Thus, four programs can be processed simultaneously. A maximum of 32 programs (32 channels maximum) can be active simultaneously at the queues of the various processing units. Each unit has a queue of active programs waiting for service. The queues are maintained by the hardware supervisor. The channel controller acts as a traffic controller for the input/output activities of the 32 channels with their I/O buffers. The interface processor carries out the bidirectional data transfers between I/O buffers and virtual memory. It also manages the text editing. The translator, or compiler, translates the program to a reverse-Polish-string form suitable for execution. The central processor performs the execution of the complied program. The system supervisor controls the transfer of programs from processor to processor, maintains the queues, and controls the paging activity. The memory re-claimer returns the storage space that is no longer needed to the available space list for use by other programs. The disk controller, although shown in Fig. 1 as a separate processor, is actually a part of the memory controller because it does not have its own system communication facilities. It is

PROCESSING FUNCTIONS   SERVICE FUNCTIONS

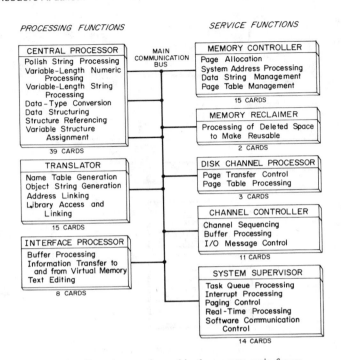

Fig. 2. Functions performed in the SYMBOL main frame.

shown separately, however, in order to separate the bulk-memory path from the main memory. Its function is to perform the page swapping between main memory and disk.

Figure 2 depicts a summary of the functions performed by each processing unit. The number below each box gives the number of 12 × 17-in. printed-circuit cards used for the implementation of each processor. Each card contains 160–200 integrated-circuit packages.

Figure 3 shows, in sequential order, the task flow of a user's program during the various stages of processing. Beginning with step 1, the program data is entered from the terminal through the CC directly into the I/O buffers in main memory through step 2. The CC is the only processor that is allowed direct access to memory. All other units must go through the MC. Input control information is communicated from the CC to the SS at step 3. Thus the SS transfers control to the IP when a buffer has been filled (step 4). The IP empties the buffer into the *transient working area* (TWA) of virtual memory and returns control to the SS (step 5). Steps 1–5 are repeated many times until the program input is complete. Text editing may also occur in steps 1–5, 12, and 13. When the user is satisfied with his pro-

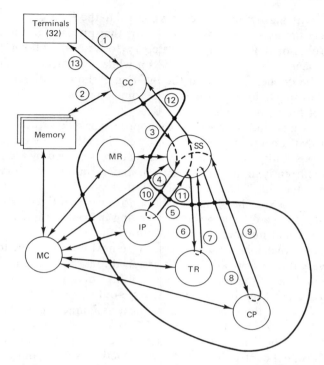

Fig. 3. Idealized task flow for processing a source program in SYMBOL. All interprocessor communications take place through the common bus (shown in heavy lines).

gram, he presses the RUN button (or types in the command RUN). The SS transfers control to the TR and supplies it with all the pertinent information, such as the beginning address of the source program in TWA and the beginning address that the TR is to use for depositing the object code of the program being compiled. The TR returns control to the SS at step 7 after the program has been complied. At that point, the SS transfers control to the CP in step 8, again supplying the pertinent address information. During execution, the CP initiates any necessary I/O by notifying the SS through step 9. The SS then goes back to the IP through step 10 (same as step 4). The IP loads the I/O buffers and returns control to the SS through step 11 (same as step 5), which in turn goes to the CC for communication with the user through steps 12 and 13.

The sequence described above is oversimplified because it ignores time-sharing, memory interaction, and scheduled or unscheduled program interrupts. In order to accommodate time-sharing, the SS maintains an active waiting list (queue) of jobs for each processor. When a processor has finished with a program and returns control to the SS (e.g., step 7 of TR), the SS enters the user's terminal number for that program in the queue of the next processor (CP's queue after step 7). Jobs are then taken from the top of the queue and given to the processor while new jobs are added to the bottom of the queue. Thus, even though Fig. 3 shows a direct transition from step 7 to step 8, it may actually take some time for the job to percolate to the top of the CP's queue.

Memory access and storage by each processor takes place indirectly through the MC on a priority basis. However, since this is a virtual memory system, the possibility exists that the virtual address needed by the processor may not be currently in main memory, but may be in bulk memory instead, causing a "page-out." The processor at that point saves its status and returns control to SS. The SS marks the control word of the user's terminal number with a page-out bit without removing it from the queue. It enters the user's terminal number at the bottom of the MC's queue for paging, and assigns another job to the processor (the next one from the top of the queue). Every time a new task is to be assigned to a processor, the SS scans the queue and skips the users that are waiting for a page from the disk. After the page has been brought in, the page-out mark is removed and the job is reassigned to the processor at the next assignment pass. Queue manipulation for program interrupts and I/O requirements during execution is handled similarly. That is, the SS initiates the necessary action and marks the user's terminal control header. No other action is taken until that mark has been cleared.

b. Interprocessor Communication.   The multiprocessor architecture that facilitates time-sharing and multiprogramming is implemented through the main or common bus, which ties all the processors together forming a global communication path. The bus consists of 111 signals. The usage and allocation of the bus is shown in Appendix 8. There are basically two types of uses for the main bus. One type is a memory data transfer between the MC and one of the other processors. The second type is a control exchange cycle between the SS and one of the other processors, including the MC. Usage of the bus is priority oriented; that is, each possible use is assigned a certain priority as defined in Appendix 8 by the signals MP (1–9) where MP1 has the highest priority and MP9 the lowest. All processors are continuously monitoring the MP (1–9) bus. When a processor needs to use the bus, it raises its priority line and, if there are no higher priorities active on the bus, proceeds to use the bus during the next cycle or clock period. However, if there are others higher, it honors their priority and waits until after they have been serviced. Thus, the honor system is observed by all bus users. Lines MP5 and MP7 are controlled by the

MC. MP7 is used to indicate that the memory is free and available. If MP7 is not true, no processor can use the bus for a memory cycle because the MC is busy performing another operation. However, control exchange cycles (MP6) can occur while MP7 is down since memory operations take many cycles (see Fig. 4). Therefore, control exchange cycles do not have to wait more than two clock periods to be granted. Statistically, control exchange cycles are granted immediately most of the time since the core memory's cycle time is 2.5 μsec and the clock period is 180 nsec. As the MC finishes the current operation, it raises MP5 to warn all others that the next cycle will be used by MC in order to announce the results of its current operation. A timing diagram of a typical bus usage situation is shown in Fig. 4. As indicated, the MP2 request rises during clock period $t1$ while MP7 and MP2 drop to indicate the start of MP2 processing. MP5 rises for the first time during $t(n + 2)$ to indicate that during $t(n + 3)$ the bus will be used to return data from the operation requested by MP2. Thus, MP7 rises during $t(n + 3)$ to indicate that the memory controller is free. However since MP4 has been waiting for service, MP7 and MP4 drop immediately after $t(n + 3)$ to indicate that the MC has begun servicing the MP4 request. MP5 rises at $t(m + 1)$ to indicate that during $t(m + 2)$ the bus will be busy with data for the MP4 request. MP7 rises again at $t(m + 2)$, but since MP8 is high, MP7 drops at the end of $t(m + 2)$ to start servicing MP8. A control exchange cycle (MP6) can be granted during any

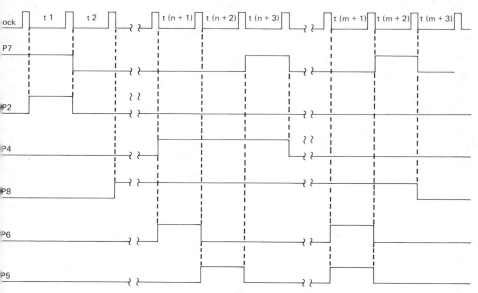

Fig. 4. Timing diagram of typical bus-usage situations in SYMBOL.

clock period except the one immediately following an MP5. This is indicated in Fig. 4 by showing MP6 and MP5 being high simultaneously during
$t(m + 1)$ and MP6 being high while MP7 is down during $t(n + 1)$.

The MC (0–5) lines are used by the processors to define one out of 15
possible memory operations to be performed by the MC. In addition, the
same lines are used by the MC to report the results of the operation back
to the requesting processor at the end of the cycle (see Appendix 8).

The MP6 line is universal. It signifies a request for a *control exchange
cycle* (CEC) by any processor. During a CEC, any or all processors may
put control information on the bus according to the assignment of the
main data bus bits shown in Appendix 4.

Another section of the main bus used for interprocessor communication
is the *terminal number bus*. The terminal number, indicated by lines MT
(0–4) in Appendix 8, is always transmitted with either type of bus cycle.
It is the key to user identification and is needed by the system supervisor

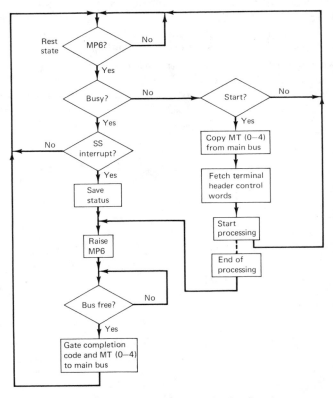

Fig. 5.   Processor to SS communication flowchart.

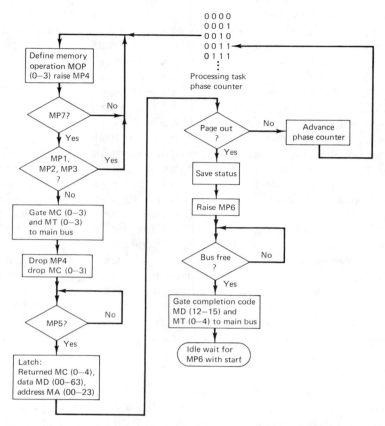

Fig. 6. Processor to MC communication flowchart for a typical processor (TR).

in order to manage the queues and the time-sharing supervision, including the virtual-memory management (paging).

The MD (00–63) and MA (00–23) shown in Appendix 8 are the *data* and *address* buses, respectively.

Each processor's hardware includes a section for SS communication and a section for MC communication. Typical flowcharts describing the actions of the hardware are shown in Figs. 5 and 6. Figure 5 shows that the processor–SS communication hardware for a given processor is constantly monitoring the MP6 line (top of figure). When an MP6 appears, control data for this processor may or may not be on the bus. If there are data on the bus they can only be either start signals or interrupt signals from the SS. If the processor is busy, only the interrupt signal is meaningful. If it is not busy, only the start signal is meaningful. Thus, there are two main branches in the flowchart. One branch is for initialization, the other for shutdown. The shut-down branch is also entered after the normal completion of a task (end of processing). During the last phases of the shut-down branch, the processor requests a control exchange cycle by raising MP6. When the bus is free, the processor gates a completion code, which is received and interpreted by the SS, onto the appropriate bits of the data bus. Appendix 4 indicates the completion codes for the various processors. Figure 6 is a flowchart describing, as an example, the functions of the MC communication hardware of the TR. It shows a typical task phase counter currently in state (0001), which is a memory operation phase. The phase defines the memory operation by forcing the MOP (0–3) lines to the appropriate binary combination for one out of the fifteen possible memory operations. It also raises the MP4 line, which is the TR's memory priority line. When memory is free (MP7) and there is no higher priority on the bus (MP1, MP2, or MP3), service of MP4 begins and MP4 drops. The TR hardware then waits for an MP5, which signifies that the results of its memory operation will be on the bus during the next clock period. If the MC completion code at that point indicates a successful operation (no page-out occurred), the hardware latches the returned address and data and signals the task phase counter to proceed to the next state (0010). If a page-out had occurred, however, the processor would save its status and transmit a page-out completion code to the SS.

1.2.3 *Implementation of SYMBOL*

Figure 7 is a picture of SYMBOL's main frame. The core memory, the disk file, and the terminals are physically separate boxes. The packaging technology developed for SYMBOL is as innovative and interesting as the architecture of the system itself. The amount of hardware that was used to build SYMBOL was large compared with other machines built about that time. Approximately eighteen thousand SSI *dual-in-line packages* (DIP) were used. With this much hardware, the cost and complexity of interconnections would have been prohibitive if conventional techniques were used. To take advantage of SSI, large (12 × 17 in.) single-layer printed-circuit (PC) boards were used. The single-layer PC boards consist of copper on both sides with a single layer of insulation between them. Such boards have the advantages of being fast and inexpensive to implement as well as easy to alter, important requirements for a research project. An average of 160 to 200 DIPs were placed on each board. With so many circuits on a PC board, a relatively large number of pins was needed to get signals in and out. In order to accommodate the pins and eliminate the problems of backplane wire wrapping, a cam-operated spring-contact system, which also allowed for zero insertion force, was invented. Thus, each PC board has

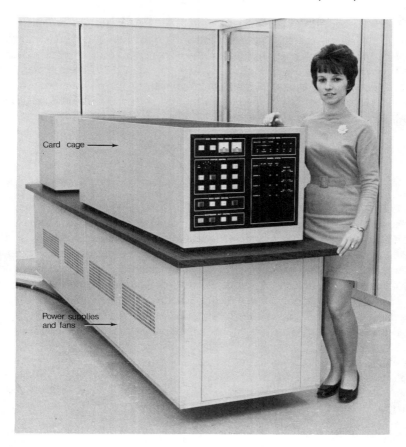

Fig. 7. SYMBOL main frame.

100 contact pads at each of the 17-in. sides for a total of 200 signal I/O pins. Before inserting a board into the machine, four cam rods (two on each side) are turned in order to open the contact springs that are soldered on the mother board. The board is then freely (zero force) lowered from the top into the slot. The cam rods are turned again and the board is locked in place. Approximately one hundred such boards were used in the system.

The boards are spaced at half-inch intervals. Figure 2 shows the number of boards (cards) that comprise each processor.

The system is air-cooled by forced convection through a set of fans directly under the card cage. No special air-conditioning or cooling is needed. Each board requires about 8 A at 6.7 V for a total power of approximately 5000 VA for the system. The power supplies occupy the space under the card cage.

The circuit family used for implementing SYMBOL is the *complementary transistor micrologic* (CTμL). CTμL is a positive-logic, nonsaturating, high-speed (5 nsec typical propagation delay) family, with wired-OR capability. The wired-OR capability is very significant for the implementation of the common bus and for reducing the hardware on each board. The system clock period is 180 nsec. For more details on the physical, electrical, and testing aspects of SYMBOL see Rice and Smith [1971].

2. THE LANGUAGE

Before we proceed with the detailed description of the language, the interrelationship between the system architecture and the language should be pointed out. The most significant feature of the language is the fact that declarations of size and type are not needed; data size and type can vary dynamically without any special attention on the part of the programmer. This feature was made possible through the dynamic variable-length dataspace management provided by the *memory controller* (MC) and through the type conversion capability provided by the *central processor* (CP). The MC arranges data in linked lists of small quanta that are not necessarily contiguous in the physical layout of the memory. Additions, deletions, or modifications of data can thus be made by the MC at any point in the links. Since SYMBOL is a multiprocessor system and this service of the MC is available to all processors in the system (IP, TR, and CP), dynamic variations in the data can take place at any phase of processing (input, compilation, or execution).

2.1   Description of the Language Elements

2.1.1   *Reserved Characters*

Reserved characters in the SYMBOL programming language (SPL) are graphic symbols having a unique interpretation to the system. They are used as operators, separators, and control characters. They can be categorized as follows:

Break characters:	space CR TAB
Grouping:	( ) [ ] ⟨ ⟩
Separators:	, | ; : ≠
Operators:	* + − / =

The specific meaning of these characters is given in the syntax (see Appendix 13).

2.1.2   Reserved Names

Reserved names are contiguous strings of alphabetic characters having a specific meaning to the system. Each is interpreted as a single entity by the hardware compiler, which recognizes them and inserts their equivalent internal code in the reverse-Polish object string to be executed by the CP. Reserved names can be grouped functionally as follows:

Operators:	GREATER, GTE, EQUALS, NEQ, LTE, LESS, BEFORE, SAME, AFTER, AND, OR, NOT, ABS, JOIN
Statements:	INPUT, OUTPUT, GO, IF, LOOP, BLOCK, GLOBAL, PROCEDURE, RETURN, ON, ENABLE, DISABLE
Statement Clauses:	LINK, TO, FROM, THEN, ELSE, END, INTERRUPT, FOR, WHILE, BY, THRU

2.1.3   Identifiers

Identifiers are alphanumeric strings starting with an alphabetic character. They are isolated by reserved characters or reserved names and may contain embedded spaces allowing multiword names. They are used to identify variables and procedures and to label transfer points in the program.

2.1.4   String Literals

A string of characters enclosed in vertical bars ("|"), known as field marks, is a string literal. String literals are interpreted as data rather than as references to data. Numerical data that satisfy the syntax rules for numbers (see Appendix 13) do not have to be enclosed in field marks even though they are string literals.

Two examples of string literals are

$$A \leftarrow |\text{Jim Jones, 123 First St.}|, \quad \text{and} \quad B = 1234.5678$$

Both data fields A and B are string literals.

2.1.5   Expressions

Expressions are language elements that are used to generate or to modify data, as opposed to the elements in the two previous sections, which are used to reference data. Expressions can be made out of various combinations of the following types of elements: reserved character operators, reserved name operators, variable operands, string literal operands, numeric literal operands, and parentheses.

2.2 Language Examples

In this section some details of the language will be presented by using partial SPL programs. The material consists of verbatim sections from Richards and Wright [1973, pp. 27–33].

2.2.1 *Scalar Values, Operators, and Expressions*

A scalar value in SPL is simply a string of zero or more characters. There exist, in SPL, twenty-two operators defined on scalar operands and yielding in all cases, scalar results. The examples in this section are intended to illustrate these operators and to give some idea of the character-processing capabilities of SPL. It is assumed that the use of the assignment operator ("←"), prior to its treatment in Section 3, will be self explanatory.

$$x \leftarrow 12345.67;$$
$$y \leftarrow |abCD12\uparrow?*\$|;$$
$$x \leftarrow x \text{ join } y;$$
$$\text{OUTPUT } x;$$

result:

$$12345.67abCD12\uparrow?*\$$$

Literal scalars, or constants, are enclosed in vertical bars ("|"). These vertical bars are optional for literal scalars that conform to the syntax of numbers.

String relational operators yield either "1" or "0", depending upon the lexicographic order of their operands. There are three such operators, whose effects are illustrated by the following example.

$$\text{alpha} \leftarrow |abcde|; \text{ beta} \leftarrow |xyz|;$$
$$\text{gamma} \leftarrow 1234;$$
$$\text{OUTPUT alpha BEFORE beta,}$$
$$\text{gamma SAME } 1234.0,$$
$$\text{beta AFTER } |xy|;$$

result:

1

0

1

Boolean operators are defined on strings containing only 1's and 0's.

$$\text{OUTPUT } 0011 \text{ AND } 1010,$$
$$0011 \text{ OR } 1010,$$
$$\text{NOT } 0011010001;$$

result:

> 0010
> 1011
> 1100101110

There is also a string-editing operator, MASK, which constructs an edited version of its preoperand under the direction of its postoperand. The following example gives an idea of MASK's capabilities.

> pre ← |abcdefgh|; post1 ← |sissississi|;
> post2 ← |ssbs/4s'123'bs'4'|;
> OUTPUT pre MASK post1, pre MASK post2;
> OUTPUT pre MASK |'length = 'fc' characters'|;

result:

> acdfg
> ab c
> defg123 h4
>
> length = 0008 characters

SPL's numeric operators are defined on the scalars that conform to the syntax of numbers. The following are examples of such numerical scalars:

123	486,725.448	$-925.72_{10} + 27$
.7	$_{10}53$	3.14159EM

A number's mantissa may contain as many as 99 digits (this is the only restriction on the length of scalar values in SYMBOL). Its exponent, if any, contains one or two digits, preceded by the character "$_{10}$" and an optional sign. The significance of the suffix "EM" is explained below.

SPL offers the usual four dyadic arithmetic operators (signified by $+$, $-$, $*$, and $/$), as well as three monadic ones ($+$, $-$, and ABS). Exponentiation is not included. The result of one of these operations is expressed in exponential notation whenever its magnitude is nonzero and outside the interval $[10^{-10}, 10^{+10}]$.

Because SPL imposes no general restrictions (such as commonly derived from a computer's word length) upon the length of scalar values, there arises a need to control the length of arithmetic results, if only to define the results of operations such as "1/3". The method chosen for SYMBOL is an entity named "LIMIT". Although not a variable in the strict sense, LIMIT may be assigned any integer value in the interval [1,99] (its default value is 9); its value is accessible and alterable as if it were a variable. The function of LIMIT is to provide an upper bound on the number of significant mantissa digits generated by any arithmetic operation. The following example demonstrates this function.

$$\text{LIMIT} \leftarrow 2; \text{ } x \leftarrow 1/3;$$
$$\text{LIMIT} \leftarrow \text{LIMIT} + 6; \text{ } y \leftarrow 2/3;$$
$$z \leftarrow 1 + 3; \text{ OUTPUT } x,y,z;$$

result:

.33EM
.66666667EM
4.

As the example shows, results longer than LIMIT permits are rounded off and tagged with the suffix "EM" (for "empirical"), which signifies the number's limited precision.

Whenever a number bearing the "EM" suffix is used as an operand in an arithmetic operation, its length, in conjunction with LIMIT, restricts the length of the result. As the following example shows, the effect of an empirical operand in addition or subtraction is dependent upon the decimal weight of its least significant digit, whereas in multiplication or division, it is the number of significant digits in the operand that is important.

$$A \leftarrow 3.2; \text{ } B \leftarrow |0.0001\text{EM}|; \text{ } C \leftarrow |3.2\text{EM}|;$$
$$\text{output } A + B, \text{ } B + C, \text{ } A + B - C, \text{ } A*B;$$

result:

3.2001EM
3.2EM
0.0
.0003EM

A zero result loses the "EM" suffix.

SPL provides a full set of numeric relational operators whose results, like those of the string relational operators, are "1" or "0" as their operands do or do not stand in the indicated relationship to one another. The following example illustrates their use.

$$x \leftarrow 25.37; \text{ } y \leftarrow -25.37;$$
$$\text{OUTPUT } x = y, \text{ } x \text{ LTE } y, \text{ } x \text{ NEQ } y,$$
$$x \text{ GREATER } y, \text{ } x = (\text{ABS } y);$$
$$\text{OUTPUT } x \text{ SAME } (\text{ABS } y);$$

result:

$$0$$
$$0$$
$$1$$
$$1$$
$$1$$

$$0$$

To facilitate the use of I/O devices (such as TTYs) whose character sets are limited, each of the numerical relational operators has an alphabetic synonym (e.g., NEQ, EQUAL, GET). The last expression in the example above illustrates clearly the distinction between string and numeric relational operators.

The last operator to be described is FORMAT. Superficially similar to MASK, FORMAT provides a distinct number-editing function, as illustrated in the following example:

n ← − 1234.56; f1 ← |6d.4d|; f2 ← |4i.4d|;
f3 ← |6d|; f4 ← |−8z|; f5 ← |−d.4d$_{10}$−dd|;
OUTPUT n FORMAT f1, n FORMAT f2, n FORMAT f3,
        n FORMAT f4, n FORMAT f5;

result:

001234.5600
.5600
001234
      − 1234
− 1.2345$_{10}$ 03

Expressions in SPL are constructed, in the usual manner, of subexpressions, operators, and parentheses. The following examples are fairly representative.

z ← (a + b)(c − d) MASK r;
z ← (x FORMAT fmt1)JOIN(y FORMAT rst)FORMAT q;
x ← (a LESS b and r AFTER s) OR pq;
bc ← arthur[j + t, x]/(x[a, k]*sin(x + y));

2.2.2 Structured Values

In addition to the scalar values described above, SPL provides for structured data values called structures. A structure is an ordered list, each of whose components is either a scalar or another structure. Thus, structures may be of arbitrary size and shape. The components of a structure value are denoted conventionally, by subscript lists, as in the following example:

$$y \leftarrow x[3] + x[2,4]; \quad w \leftarrow x;$$

In the above partial program, the variable y is assigned the value of the sum of the third component of the structure x and the fourth component of the second component of the structure x. The addition operator requires that the variable x have as its value a structure whose third component is a number, and whose second component is a structure whose fourth component is a number. Finally, the variable w is assigned a copy of the structure x.

The size and shape of structures may vary according to program demands, and it is only necessary to access a component in order to bring it into existence and, conversely, a structure-valued component (or, for that matter, an entire structure) can be replaced at any time by a scalar value. Accordingly, structures are not declared as to their size and shape, and no limit (other than that derived from the aggregate amount of available storage) is placed on the number or size of a structure's components.

Individual subscript expressions are subject only to the restriction that, when evaluated, each expression must yield a numerical value not less than 1 (fractional parts of subscript values are disregarded). As was mentioned above, any reference to a non-existent structural component automatically causes the structure to be appropriately modified to contain that component.

$$z[1] \leftarrow 1;$$
$$x[i + j, k, 5] \leftarrow 3*(a + b);$$
$$z[3, 2] \leftarrow 5;$$

For example, in the above partial program, the third assignment causes the variable z to take as its value a structure with three components, the third component of which is itself a structure having two components. The second component of the third component of z has value 5, and the first component of z still has value 1. $z[2]$ and $z[3, 1]$ both have null values.

Although a structure responds to ordinary accesses by expansion as necessary, it is nevertheless possible to interrogate a structure value to determine its extent. The means provided for this purpose is the "IN-reference," which consists of a subscripted variable name preceded by the reserved word "IN." For example, the statement

$$A \leftarrow IN \; x[3, 2];$$

assigns to A the value "1" if the indicated component of x exists, and "0" otherwise.

Finally, SPL provides a means for indicating the shape of structures explicitly within programs. The convention for doing so is as follows:

(a) Each structure is enclosed in angular brackets "⟨" and "⟩".
(b) Neighboring scalar components are separated by a vertical bar "|".

For example, ⟨12|13⟨15|16⟩⟩ indicates a structure consisting of three components, the third of which is another structure.

Such explicit structures are used in initial-value statements, assignment statements, and in representing structures on external media for purposes of input and output. These uses will be discussed more fully in the remaining sections.

2.2.3 Specification of Variable Values: Initial Value, Assignment, and I/O Statements

In an SPL program, a variable may take on any value, scalar, or structure, with no practical restrictions as to its size, length, or shape, without declarations of any sort, and regardless of the variable's previous value (if any). This high degree of flexibility is unusual in general-purpose languages, and imposes a considerable burden on the system's memory-management facilities.

In SPL, variables may receive values by initial-value statements, assignment statements, or input statements. Initial-value statements are, in effect, compile-time statements, and are disregarded during execution. (Actually, they are "executed" at the time of first reference to the initialized variable, but this is a detail of implementation invisible to the user.) The following are examples:

$$x|2|;\qquad pi|3.1415927EM|;$$
$$alphabet|abcdefghijklmnopqrstuvwxyz|;$$

$$greeks⟨alpha|beta|gamma|delta⟩;$$
$$family⟨mother|father⟨son|daughter⟩⟨dog|cat⟩⟩;$$

$$SWITCH\ nextstep⟨step\ a|step\ b|step\ c|step\ d⟩;$$

The statements in the first group above specify scalar initial values for the variables x, pi, and alphabet. Those in the second group specify structure initial values for greeks and family. In such statements, the characters that appear between the structure marks are interpreted to be the values of the scalar components of the structure value. In the last statement above, which is qualified by the reserved word "SWITCH," the characters between the structure marks are interpreted as label identifiers (to be dealt with in Section 4).

Every variable that is not explicitly initialized has the same initial value, namely, a null scalar.

Assignment statements come in two varieties:

(a) Simple assignment statements, e.g.,

$$x \leftarrow a + b; \quad y \leftarrow c;$$

The first of these assigns to x a value that is necessarily scalar (due to the presence of the operator "$+$"), whereas the second can assign to x either a scalar value or a structure, depending on the value of c.

(b) Structure-assignment statements, e.g.,

$$x \leftarrow \langle a + b | r | z \text{ JOIN } p \langle x[a, b] | x | 3 \rangle \rangle;$$

In this type of statement, the characters appearing between the structure marks are interpreted not as literal values (as they would be in an initial-value statement), but as expressions. The computer executes a structure-assignment statement by evaluating each of the constituent expressions, assembling the resulting values into a structure of the indicated configuration, and finally assigning the structure value to x. Note that the structure configuration explicitly represented is not necessarily identical to that of the assigned value, for certain of the explicit structure's components (in the example above, [2], [4, 1] and [4, 2]) may themselves be structure valued.

Assignment statements can specify the value of a component of a structue-valued variable, as in

$$x[a + b, c] \leftarrow m \text{ JOIN } n;$$
$$array[i, j] \leftarrow \langle 3(a - ab/c) | z | q \rangle;$$

Finally, assignment statements allow multiple entries on the lefthand side, e.g.,

$$x, a[i, j], y \leftarrow x + 1;$$

The remaining device by which a variable's value can be specified is the input statement. (For convenience, we also discuss output statements here, not because they specify variables' values, but because of their relationship to input statements.) The conventionally messy area of input, output, and the conversions between "internal" values and their external representations, is greatly simplified by SPL's stipulation that all values are character strings. Further simplification results from SPL's treatment of all I/O devices as sources (or sinks) of single dimensional character streams, notwithstanding the fact that these streams may be mapped into two dimensions by such artifices as carriage-return characters and the like.

Input statements can be as simple as

INPUT x;

which will accept any number of consecutive characters from the currently selected input device up to the next end-of-record character, and assign that character string as a scalar value to x. Should the input record contain structure marks, the record will be interpreted as a literal structure, and a structure value will be assigned to x. The following statement

INPUT x, b[r, s], t;

will read the next three records, and assign corresponding values to the respective destinations specified in the list.

The interpretation of records containing structure marks as structure values can be suppressed by the inclusion of the qualifier "STRING," as in

INPUT STRING x;

Such a statement always results in a scalar value being assigned to x.

The source of input records can also be specified, as in

INPUT FROM 7, e, f;   INPUT STRING FROM n + 2, y;

in which the integer value of the expression following "FROM" specifies, in the case of a multidevice user terminal, which input device (or which of several input modes) is to be selected.

Output statements are very much like input statements, as the following examples illustrate.

OUTPUT x, y, g;
OUTPUT a + b, x mask m, y format r;
OUTPUT to m + n, 4, (j + 7);
OUTPUT string to 7, p, q, r;

In output statements, it is permissible to include expressions in the output list. "TO" replaces "FROM" in the device-designation clause. The qualifier "STRING" has a somewhat different meaning here: in its absence, the system inserts a carriage-return character before the first value output, and after each value in the list, so that each value appears on a new line on the output medium. The qualifier "STRING" simply suppresses this formatting.

2.2.4 *Control of Program Execution*

SPL contains a generally standard set of constructs for the purpose of controlling program execution, namely conditional statements, transfer statements, procedures, and on-blocks. No iteration statement is currently included in the language.

Conditional statements have two forms:

> IF expression   THEN statements   END
> IF expression   THEN statements
>   ELSE statements   END

Execution of such a statement begins with the evaluation of the expression following "IF." If the resulting value is "1," then the statements following "THEN" are executed, and the statements following "ELSE" (if any) are skipped. If the value is "0," the "THEN" branch is skipped, and the "ELSE" branch (if any) is executed (a value that is neither "1" nor "0" results in an execution error). The statements within the conditional branches are subject to no restrictions whatever. Some typical conditional statements follow:

> IF a less b THEN a ← a + r; ELSE r ← r − 1; END

> IF p THEN q; END

> IF alpha before x and (y or z)
> THEN z ← x + y; fff ← cotan(g/h);
> ELSE output lambda;
> END

> IF not(alpha before x and (y or z))
> THEN output alpha;
> END

The "END" that closes the conditional statement is SPL's solution to the "dangling ELSE" problem.

Transfer statements have the following form:

> GO TO x;

where x is an identifier that is declared as a label. A label "declaration" consists simply of an identifier followed by a colon, as in

> label: y ← x + 3;

A transfer statement can also refer to a subscripted identifier, as in, e.g.,

> GO TO a[b + c, d];

provided that the identifier has been declared as a label structure by a switch statement such as

> SWITCH destination⟨f|s⟨t1|t2⟩⟩;

In a switch statement, the characters between structure marks are interpreted as labels.

A procedure in SPL is a compound statement having one of the following forms:

PROCEDURE identifier (formal parameter list);
statements END

or simply

PROCEDURE identifier; statements END

Procedure statements are ignored when encountered in line.

A procedure-call may be either freestanding, as a call statement, or embedded within a statement, as in the following examples.

proc(x, y);
CALL proc(x, y);
a ← b + 4*proc(x, y) − 7;
GO TO proc(x, y);
proc(x, y) ← b + 4(a);

The number of actual parameters in a procedure-call must equal the number of formal parameters in the procedure's declaration. SPL procedures employ a single parameter linkage mechanism, namely, call-by-name (or substitution). The effect is as if each actual parameter were to be inserted into the procedure body, in place of the corresponding formal parameter, at every instance of the latter. The following example demonstrates this.

PROCEDURE f(x, y);
   output y;
   x ← x + 1;
   output y;
END

a ← 1; b ← 2; f(a, a + b);

result:

3.
4.

In the example above, the expression that constitutes the second actual parameter is evaluated twice (once at each encounter of the formal parameter y), and the intervening assignment statement alters the value of one of the operands of the expression.

Control returns from the procedure body to the calling point in one of several ways. A procedure called from an embedded calling point must return an appropriate value, label, or assignment recipient by means of a RETURN statement such as

$$\text{RETURN x; RETURN a} + \text{b/c};$$

whereas one called from a call statement would terminate by a statement such as

$$\text{RETURN};$$

or simply by reaching the END that closes the procedure.

Recursive procedure-calls are prohibited in SPL (though provisions have been included in the hardware for eventual handling of recursion by software). This rules out not only calls to a procedure from within itself, but also, because of the parameter linkage mechanism employed by SPL, such constructions as

$$y \leftarrow b + f(a, f(c, d));$$

An on-statement is also a compound statement. The following are examples:

$$\text{ON x;} \qquad \text{END}$$
$$\text{ON x, y, j;} \qquad \text{END}$$
$$\text{ON INTERRUPT, r;} \qquad \text{END}$$

On-statements resemble procedure statements except for the manner in which they are called. Whereas procedures are called by explicit procedure-calls, on-statements are executed in response to certain events which we will call on-events. The on-header consists of a list of one or more identifiers, which specify on-events in the following way:

1. If an identifier is a variable, the on-statement will be executed immediately following any assignment to the variable.

2. If an identifier is a label or a procedure name, the on-statement will be executed immediately preceding a GOTO or a procedure-call to the label or procedure.

An on-header that includes the reserved word "INTERRUPT" denotes an on-statement to be executed in response to external intervention by the user (pressing a key at his terminal). Such an on-statement is executed at the completion of the statement being executed at the instant of the external intervention.

Execution of an on-statement terminates when control reaches either a RETURN statement or the END of the on-statement. In either eventuality, control then returns to the point at which execution had been interrupted by the on-event.

The connection between a particular identifier and its on-statement is temporarily suspended by statements such as

$$\text{DISABLE x; DISABLE y, z;}$$

and restored by

$$\text{ENABLE x; ENABLE y, z, c;}$$

INTERRUPT can also be DISABLED and ENABLED; it is, moreover, automatically disabled while its on-statement is in execution.

2.2.5   *Block Structure and Scope of Identifiers*

Like ALGOL 60 and PL/1, among contemporary languages, SPL employs a nested block structure, which creates a hierarchy of contexts that determine the meanings of identifiers enclosed within them. Procedures, on-statements, and entire programs define such contexts, as does the BLOCK statement (which has only this function). For purposes of this paper we will refer to the above context-defining compound statements together under the term "block."

As in ALGOL and PL/1, an identifier within a block is not necessarily synonymous with the same identifier outside the block. In contrast to the standard languages, however, in which the meanings are the same unless a declaration is made to the contrary, the SPL convention is that all identifiers not specified otherwise are strictly local to the block in which they appear. The following example illustrates this principle:

$$i \leftarrow 1;$$
$$\text{BLOCK}$$
$$\quad i \leftarrow 2; \text{ output i;}$$
$$\text{END}$$
$$\text{output i;}$$

result:

$$2$$
$$1$$

The example above contains two variables. Though they have the same

identifier, namely, "i," they are in different blocks, and are therefore un-
related.

An identifier can be specified to be synonymous in two nested blocks by
means of a GLOBAL "declaration" statement in the inner block. For
example, in the following program

```
i ← 1;
BLOCK
       GLOBAL i; i ← 2; output i;
END
output i;
```

result:

$$2$$
$$2$$

the GLOBAL statement in the inner block makes the innermost "i" synonymous with the outermost "i."

To make an identifier synonymous in several nested blocks, GLOBAL
statements must be inserted into all but the outermost block, as in the
following example.

```
x ← 3;
BLOCK
     GLOBAL x; output x; x ← 2;
     BLOCK
          GLOBAL x; output x; x ← 1;
          BLOCK
               GLOBAL x; x ← 0;
          END
     END
END
x ← −1;
BLOCK
     GLOBAL x; output x;
END
output x;
```

result:

3
2
−1.
−1.

Certain uses of identifiers are incompatible with their inclusion in a GLOBAL statement in the same block. These are as follows:

1. An identifier cannot be declared GLOBAL to a block in which it labels a statement (jumps into the interior of enclosed blocks are thus prevented).

2. Nor can an identifier be declared GLOBAL in a block in which it is initialized; initial-value statements must appear in the outermost block of the initialized variable's scope.

3. Procedure-names cannot be declared GLOBAL to the blocks in which they are defined. A procedure must be defined in the outermost of all the blocks in which it is called.

4. A procedure that possesses a parameter list is automatically accessible not only from the block in which it is defined, but also from all blocks enclosed by that block.

5. Formal parameters cannot be declared GLOBAL to their procedures.†

3. MEMORY STRUCTURE AND ORGANIZATION

3.1 Storage Space Organization and Linking

An overview of the storage facilities of SYMBOL is shown in Fig. 8. The user sees a virtual memory system (in the conventional meaning of the term), which is well described in the literature. However, the major difference between SYMBOL and conventional systems is the way that storage space is organized, allocated, and accessed. The following material will point out how the storage space organization in SYMBOL differs from conventional systems.

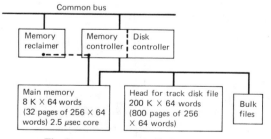

Fig. 8. SYMBOL storage facilities.

†From "Introduction to the SYMBOL 2R Programing Language." *Proc. Symp. High-Level Language Computer Architecture.* (Copyrighted by IEEE.)

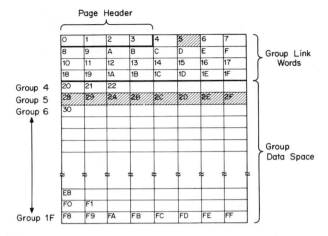

Fig. 9. Page organization showing group and link word layout where addresses are given in HEX notation.

In conventional systems data storage is organized in physically contiguous memory cells, which are allocated in fairly large blocks as requested by the user or dictated by the system. Storage and retrieval in conventional systems takes place via two basic commands (Store and Fetch) and via an incrementable counter used as the address generator to step through the desired contiguous memory cells.

In SYMBOL, data storage is organized in logically contiguous memory cells, which are not necessarily physically contiguous. They are logically contiguous because they are linked together by using a small portion of the storage space itself as pointers (links). Thus, a section of data storage in SYMBOL can be traversed by following the links rather than by counting. Figure 9 shows the organization of a storage space quantum called a page. A page consists of 16 K bits of storage and it is divided into 32 smaller quanta called groups. Each group consists of 256 bits of storage organized as 8 words of 64 bits per word. Even though the smallest addressable portion of memory is a word, the smallest quantum of automatic memory allocation is the group. Groups within a page are linked together in an arbitrary sequence (depending upon the availability at the time of the assignment) to provide contiguous strings of information of variable size as shown in Fig. 10. The first four groups of each page are reserved for use as links. Thus, there are 28 groups available for storage of program data. Twenty-eight words out of the 32 of the first four groups are called *group link words*. The remaining 4 words are called *page header words* and are used for linking pages together in groups of pages known as page lists to

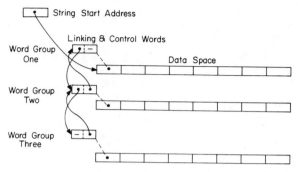

Fig. 10. Structure of a typically linked storage space portion comprising a variable-length string.

serve users with requirements of more than one page. The format of the group link words and the page header words is shown in Appendix 5.

Figure 11 shows an example of various page lists. List processing will be discussed in the next section.

The address field consists of 24 bits and it is used as follows: 16 bits (0–15) are used for the virtual page number (BCD coding) and 8 bits are used to address one of the 256 words in each page. The 16 bits for the page are used to access the associative memory, which in turn translates it into a current page address in main memory (Fig. 12). The associative memory consists of one register for each page in the main memory. The paging-disk memory has a fixed assignment for page number locations (Fig. 13). A page is brought into any available location in main memory upon demand. When it is purged back to the disk, it is returned to its original location on disk. (The return transfer is omitted if the page was not changed while in main memory.) The core memory organization is shown in Fig. 14. The first page is used for system tables. This includes a reserved-word table for the hardware compiler, a software-call table, and the control words for memory allocation and queuing. The next set of pages is used for storing

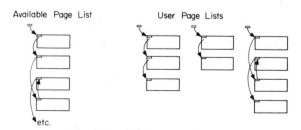

Fig. 11. Simplified page list structure within the virtual memory.

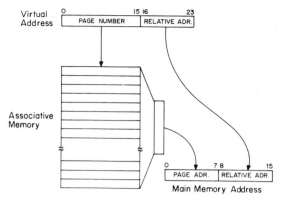

Fig. 12.   The simple two-level addressing structure for the virtual memory.

the control words of the various terminals (users) on the system. Each active terminal has 24 words of control information in these four pages.

The input/output buffers for the various active channels are held in the next 1–2 pages of core. The buffers require 16 words (two groups) per active channel. Variable buffer sizes, although possible, were not implemented.

The remainder of main memory is available for virtual-memory buffering. Paging is managed by the hardware with the page selection for purging under the control of the system supervisor. The algorithm is a very flexible parameterized process that allows most conventional algorithms to be

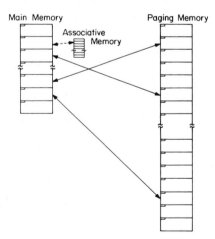

Fig. 13.   Virtual-memory organization showing the fixed location of pages in the paging memory.

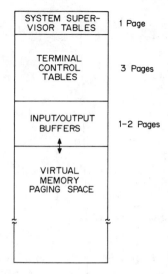

SYSTEM SUPER-VISOR TABLES	1 Page
TERMINAL CONTROL TABLES	3 Pages
INPUT/OUTPUT BUFFERS	1-2 Pages
VIRTUAL MEMORY PAGING SPACE	

Fig. 14.   Layout of main memory.

executed. Parameters are maintained for each terminal so that the paging dynamics can be tailored on a terminal basis.

3.2   Storage Space Allocation and Access

In contrast to the simple READ/WRITE commands of conventional systems, the *memory controller* (MC) of SYMBOL has a set of memory operation commands that are available to all processors in the system. Those commands form the basis for automatic memory allocation and linking. The complete set of commands is shown in Appendix 9.

When a processor needs to store a vector of data fields, an *assign group* (AG) command is sent to the MC along with a tag specifying a page list with which the string is to be associated. The MC then selects an available group from that page list and returns its address to the requesting processor. When the processor is ready to store a word, it transmits the data and the address to the MC along with the *store-and-assign* (SA) command. The MC stores the word and generates the address of the next available word, which it returns to the processor. When the end of the group is reached, the MC assigns another group and links it automatically into the string.

In the string-storing process, the requesting processor receives addresses from the MC and resubmits them to the MC at a later time for future extension of the string. All address arithmetic is done by the MC. Consider

TABLE I

Simplified Example of a Memory Usage Sequence

Mnemonic	Operation	Address to MC	Return address	Data to MC	Return data
AG	Assign group	—	a	—	—
SA	Store and assign	a	b	A	—
SA	Store and assign	b	c	B	—
SA	Store and assign	c	d	C	—
SA	Store and assign	d	e	D	—
FF	Fetch and follow	a	b	—	A
FF	Fetch and follow	b	c	—	B
FF	Fetch and follow	c	d	—	C
FF	Fetch and follow	d	—	—	D
DS	Delete string	a	—	—	—

the example in Table I. The first five commands result in the words A, B, C, and D being stored in a string beginning with word A. To reaccess the string, the original start address A is submitted to the MC with the *fetch-and-follow* (FF) command. The data in cell A are returned along with the next word address in the string. When the string is no longer needed, a *delete string* (DS) command, along with the string starting address, is submitted to the MC. The entire string is then placed on a space reclamation list. The memory reclaimer processor scans the space reclamation lists of the various page lists during idle memory time and makes groups of the deleted strings reassignable.

One of the MC commands, not used in the example of Table I, is *fetch-and-reverse-follow* (FR). It fetches the data at the given present address and returns the address of the previous word in the string. Thus, by using FRs and following the back links as shown in Fig. 10, a string can be traversed in the reverse direction. This feature is very useful in text-editing and searching tasks.

3.3   List Processing

The linking approach to storage space results in sets of links referred to as lists. It is the processing of these lists that gives the system its dynamically variable memory allocation. There are basically two types of lists, *page lists* and *group lists*.

3.3.1   *Page Lists*

The basic mechanism for allocating multiple pages of storage space to users is by linking pages together to form page lists. In order to keep the paging

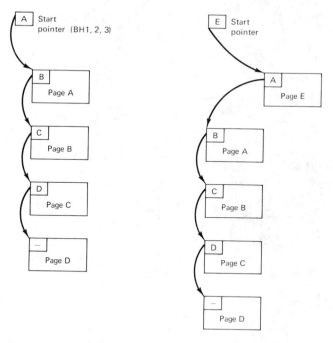

Fig. 15. Typical user page list before and after adding page E.

activity to a minimum, different page lists are assigned to a given user during the various phases of processing (input, compilation, and other common functions).

The method of processing these page lists (adding or removing pages) is very significant to the system dynamics. One of the important considerations is that the number of memory references should be minimized during list maintenance. Also, the risk of running into a page-out (a needed page not in core) must be minimized. With these considerations in mind, page lists are modified by adding or removing pages from the top of the list after the current page. Thus, as shown in Fig. 15, if a page is added to the top of the list, the contents of the page-list-start pointer must be moved to the link word in the new page and the address of the new page must be entered in the pointer. The start pointer is held in the nonpageable portion of the memory and the page being added is already in core. Therefore, there is no possibility for a page-out to occur. The same holds true in the case of adding the new page after the current page.

There are four types of page lists.

a. Available Page List (APL).   There is only one APL for the whole system. It is made up of a tree of page lists as shown in Fig. 16. This is the

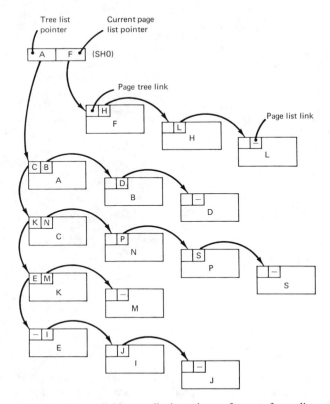

Fig. 16. The available page list is made up of a tree of page lists.

supply and sink for user page lists. The tree structure is necessary so that entire user lists can be added to the APL by simply adding one pointer. Thus, additions and deletions take place at the top of the list and the linking can be described as a forward-linked tree. The tree pointer and current list pointer shown in Fig. 16 are kept at the *system header area* (SH0) as shown in Appendix 7.

b.   User Page Lists.   User page lists are limited to a maximum of four pages for each function. The linking is simply forward linking as shown in Fig. 15. Additions are done either at the top or after the current page. Removals do not occur one page at a time. Instead, when the list is no longer needed, the entire list is transferred to the available page list. Each of the 32 users (terminals) is assigned a different page list for each of the following functions: input (transient working area), object string (compiler output), and name table (compiler output). The start pointers for those lists are kept by the system in the *terminal header area* (BH1–BH3) as shown in Appendix 2.

The actual links on each page are kept at the *page header area* as shown in Appendix 5.

c.   *Space Available Lists* (SAL).   The space available list is a subpage list within a user page list. It links together those pages within a given page list that have unused space available for assignment. By maintaining this sublist, it is not necessary to search the entire user page list in order to find space when it is needed. The SAL pointers are maintained in the same terminal header words as the user page list (BH1–BH3).

d.   *In-Core List* (ICL)   The ICL links together the entire 28 virtual pages that can possibly reside in core. They are linked in a simple forward-linking scheme with the top and bottom pointers kept at SH2. The links are held at PH2. The ICL is used during the paging-control tasks.

3.3.2   *Group Lists*

There are three types of group lists.

a.   *User Strings.*   These are the strings making up the variable-field-length data for user programs. The linking and generation of these strings has been described previously in this section.

b.   *Available Group List* (AGL).   This is a list of the groups within a page that are available for assignment. There are two mechanisms for assigning a new group, the *initial group assignment counter* (IGAC) and the *available group list.* When a new page is added to the list, all groups are available and assignment occurs by simply incrementing the IGAC counter until all groups have been assigned. However, as various groups are reclaimed by the reclamation processor, they are linked into the AGL. After the IGAC runs out, its active flag is cleared and thereafter groups are assigned from the AGL. The AGL start pointer and the IGAC are kept in the page header of each page (see Appendix 5).

c.   *Space Reclamation Group List* (SRGL).   During certain phases of processing (compilation and execution mainly), the processors notify the memory controller, using the reclamation commands, that certain groups are not needed anymore. Thus, a list of groups is formed to be processed by the *memory reclamation* processor (MR). The SRGL is a tree-structured list because of the need to add entire strings to the list.

3.4   Space Reclamation

Space reclamation in SYMBOL is necessary because of the assignment approach, which is done by linking. Thus, when a section of storage space is no longer needed, it must be cleaned up and freed of any residual linking and control information that may hinder future use. Such residual linking may be mistaken for valid address linking. After this cleanup process has been completed, the reclaimed space is returned to the available page list. There are two types of reclamation activities. One is at the page list level and the other at the group list level. Group list reclamation is a continuous background operation performed by the memory reclamation processor using the space reclamation group list without interference from the system supervisor. By constantly recycling groups within the user's current page list, the number of pages needed in a page list is kept to a minimum. Figure 17 shows the overall flow of group lists.

Page list reclamation takes place at the system level and involves the system supervisor. When a task (input, compilation, or execution) is com-

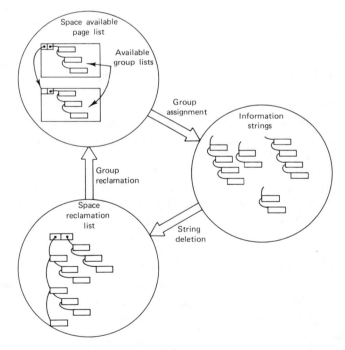

Fig. 17.   Strings are created from the available group lists. After being used, they are moved to the space reclamation group lists. Finally, they are returned to the available group lists for future assignment.

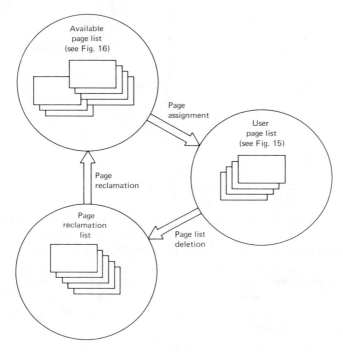

Fig. 18.   Page list cycling through usage and reclamation.

pleted, the SS puts the entire list on the MR's queue for reclamation. The MR scans all groups and words in the page list looking for certain types of residual data that must be cleaned up before moving the entire page list to the system's available page list. Figure 18 shows the overall flow of page lists through the cycle of reclamation.

Space reclamation information is maintained for each of the 32 users (terminals) in the terminal header area (BH1–BH3, BH6) as shown in Appendix 2.

4.   SYSTEM SUPERVISOR

The system supervisor (SS) of the SYMBOL system controls all activities in the system. All the other processors can be viewed as slaves to the SS. They take their assignments from the SS and they report the results of their work back to the SS. The communication between the SS and the other processors takes place through the common bus during control-exchange cycles. Figure 19 depicts the relationship between the SS and the other processors.

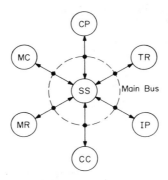

Fig. 19. Use of the main bus for control-exchange cycles.

The SS is basically an interrupt-driven processor. It recognizes interrupts from the various processors or from external sources (such as the operator's console) and it services those interrupts either by assigning them to the processors or by performing the necessary system tasks. It maintains an active queue of jobs for each processor and it manages the virtual-memory traffic. It also maintains a number of control tables (terminal headers and system headers) that contain information needed during the servicing of the various interrupts.

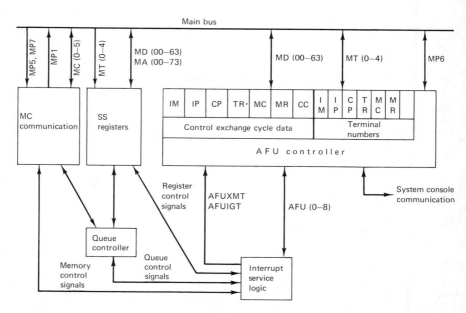

Fig. 20. System supervisor block diagram.

As shown in Fig. 20 the SS consists of four major parts. We will now examine the various sections of the SS individually and describe some of the most interesting operations.

4.1 AFU Controller

The acronym AFU (*autonomous functional unit*), as used in SYMBOL literature is synonymous with the word "processor." The AFU controller is a buffer that is used to hold interrupt and status information for the various processors. It consists of a number of small autonomous controllers (one for each processor) and a priority-resolution network.

Interrupts from the various processors occur asynchronously, but the SS can process only one interrupt at a time. During the time that one interrupt is being serviced by the SS, a number of other processor interrupts may occur. The corresponding buffers of the AFU controller will save the interrupt information, and at the end of the current service the interrupt with the highest priority will be selected to be serviced next.

The AFU controller has three basic modes of operation: the service mode, the transmit mode, and the interrogate mode. The service mode is used during the servicing of an interrupt. The transmit mode is entered when a message is to be transmitted to a processor. The interrogate mode is entered when information about the status of a processor is needed. A local bidirectional bus AFU (0–8) is used for communication between the AFU controller and the various interrupt service routines. AFU (0–2) are used to define eight groups of interrupts and their relative priorities as follows:

AFU (0–2)	Interrupt service group
000	IM Immediate interrupts (highest priority)
001	CC Channel controller
010	MC Memory controller
011	IP Interface processor
100	CP Control processor
101	TR Compiler
110	MR Memory reclaimer
111	JC Miscellaneous system interrupts (lowest priority)

Each group of interrupts relates to either a single processor or to a common function.

The IM interrupts are tasks that need immediate attention such as page-out returns from memory or warnings of forced system shutdowns. The IM interrupt service will be discussed later.

The miscellaneous system interrupts (lowest priority) include real-time accounting functions and system-console switch commands. Each of the remaining interrupt groups is associated with one of the processors.

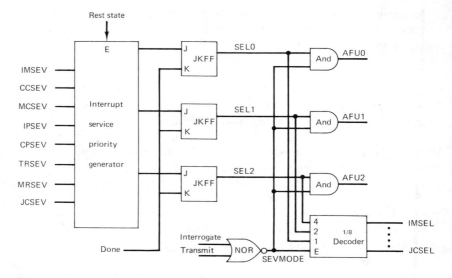

Fig. 21.   AFU main controller.

Figure 21 shows the logic functions of the main AFU controller. The main AFU controller is the master for all the other AFU controllers. At the end of an interrupt servicing, the signal DONE clears the SEL (0–2) register and puts the SS in the rest state. This activates the interrupt-service priority generator, whose outputs get loaded in the SEL (0–2) flip/flops. The SS is in the service mode (SEVMODE) by default at that point since the other two modes can only be forced by the service logic. The SEVMODE signal activates the one-out-of-eight decoder, which decodes the selected group interrupt (IMSEL–JCSEL) and gates the AFU (0–2) on the bus. The decoded select signal (IMSEL–JCSEL) then gates the completion code of the selected processor onto the AFU (3–6) bus as shown in Fig. 22, which shows the AFU controller for the compiler (TR) as a typical example. The particular interrupt service routine that matches the AFU (0–2) and AFU (3–6) code becomes active at that point and starts servicing the interrupt. The AFU controller remains at that state until the interrupt servicing is complete (DONE). At that point it returns to the rest state.

Interrupt service processing is halted if an IM interrupt occurs. After the IM interrupt has been serviced, the halted processing is allowed to continue.

The functions of each AFU controller as exemplified in Fig. 22 by the TR AFU controller are threefold: (a) to latch the completion code, to raise the service request (TRSEV), and to display the completion code when

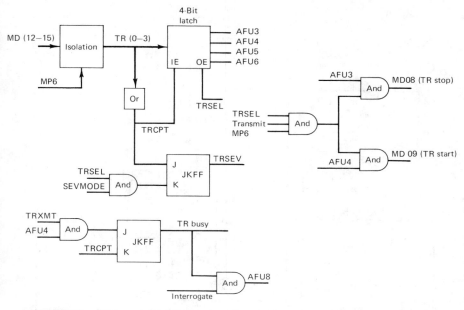

Fig. 22. The AFU controller for the compiler (TR) shown here is typical of the AFU controllers for the various processors.

selected; (b) to transmit the START and STOP commands to the TR; and (c) to present the status of the processor (TRBUSY) when interrogated.

In another section of the AFU controller are the terminal-number registers (Fig. 23). A five-bit register is maintained for each of the six processors. The register is loaded when a START command is given to the processor. Thus, the contents of the register identify the user (one of thirty-two) whose program is being worked on by a given processor at a given time. The contents of the terminal-number register are displayed during the interrogate mode (IGTMODE) or the interrupt service mode (SEVMODE), during which they are used to generate the addresses of the terminal header control words, which are manipulated during the interrupt service. Also, part of the AFU main controller is the control-exchange-cycle-request logic, which gets activated during the XMTMODE in order to initiate a control-exchange cycle by the SS.

4.2 SS Registers

The overall structure of the SS registers is shown in Fig. 23. This very flexible network of registers provides content-manipulation capability at

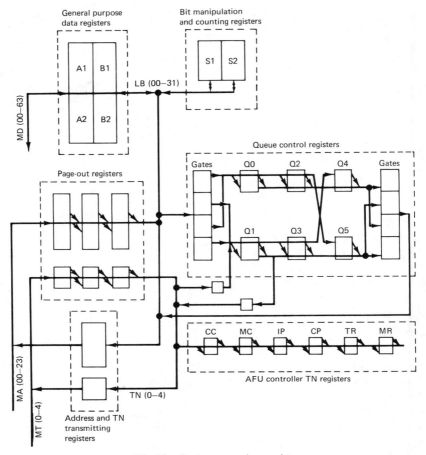

Fig. 23. System supervisor registers.

the bit, character, half-word, and full-word levels. The general-purpose data registers (**A** and **B**) are 64-bit registers used to receive and transmit data from and to memory. They are latch-type registers with half- or full-word load and unload capability. After data have been received, they can be moved around one half-word at a time over the local data bus LB (00–31).

The S1 and S2 registers are 32-bit registers made up of individual JKFFs. Thus, individual bits can be set or cleared. They are also connected as binary down counters for the purpose of setting initial values and counting them down to zero. Such manipulations are useful for maintaining the system- and terminal-control tables.

The page-out address and terminal-number registers provide double buffering to accommodate the case where a second page-out occurs while the first is being serviced. Not more than two page-outs can occur since the IM takes over immediately after the first one and raises its MP1, which is the highest-priority memory request.

The queue-control-register network is a flexible, multipath character network suitable for transposing 8-bit characters in order to accommodate the shifting of queue links in the various character positions of the control words that indicate relative position in the queue.

The AFU controller's terminal-number registers are also tied in to the local TN (0–4) bus for communication purposes.

The address MA (00–23) and terminal-number TN (0–4) transmitting registers are used for communicating with memory.

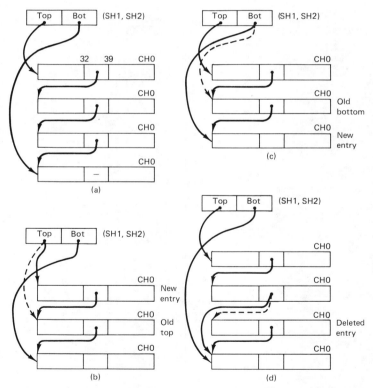

Fig. 24. Typical examples of queues and queue manipulation: (a) basic queue form; (b) add to top; (c) add to bottom; (d) delete entry.

4.3   Queue Controller

The queue controller is a hardware-service subroutine available to all the interrupt-service routines. It has the capability to add an entry to the top of a queue, to add an entry to the bottom of the queue, or to delete an entry from a queue. The queues consist of lists of terminal numbers maintained

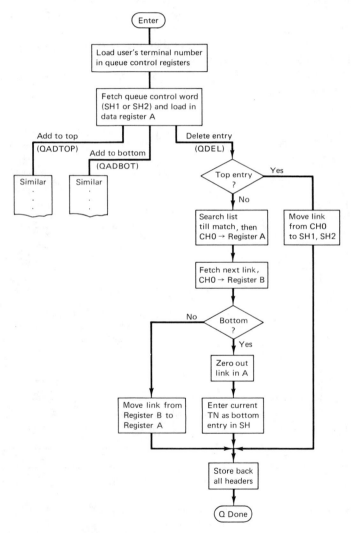

Fig. 25.   Typical queue controller task flowchart.

in the control table's area. Figure 24 shows the basic form of a queue. The top and bottom pointers for each processor's queue are kept at system headers SH1 or SH2 (see Appendix 7). The pointer to the next entry in the queue is kept at terminal header CH0 (bits 32–39) of each terminal in the list (see Appendix 3). Figure 24b–d shows the three typical mechanisms for queue modification. The dotted lines indicate the link before the modification has occurred.

The queue controller service is invoked during a given state of an interrupt-service task (usually at the end of the task) by raising certain control lines that define the queue operation to be performed. The queue controller becomes activated at that point and begins processing while the requesting-service task halts at that state. With the service task halted, there is no other activity taking place in the SS other than the queue controller, which has, therefore, exclusive use of all the overhead facilities of the SS, such as the memory communication section and the registers. At the end of its processing, the queue controller raises a signal QDONE, which allows the requesting-task logic to move on to the next state and continue with the rest of the interrupt-service task.

A simplified flowchart of a typical queue controller task is shown in Fig. 25 for the case of deleting an entry from the queue.

4.4   Paging Control

The paging activities needed to support the virtual-memory capability of SYMBOL are performed by the *memory controller* (MC) under the control of the SS. The paging-control tasks are included in the interrupt-service logic block of Fig. 20 since they are interrupt driven.

There are four different tasks involved in the paging-control function of the SS as shown in Fig. 26. They occur in the sequence shown but they are not necessarily chronologically contiguous. The first task is performed under the control of the IM section of the AFU controller as shown in Fig. 27. The SS watches all MC completion codes regardless of who the requesting processor may be. When the SS recognizes a page-out or a new page assignment it halts its current activity and performs the functions shown in Fig. 27. The halted activity is allowed to continue after the IM task is completed. The branch of the IM task for new page assignments (Fig. 27) is necessary whenever a new page is allocated to a user to ensure that the user does not exceed the maximum number of pages he is allowed. The maximum initial value is placed at CH2 during system-setup time. Each time a new page is added, the value is counted down by one. This mechanism protects the system against perpetuating programs that can run away and occupy unduly large amounts of storage.

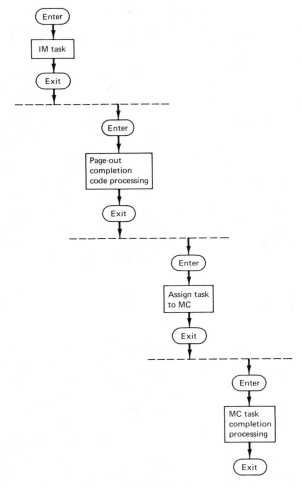

Fig. 26. Paging-control tasks performed by the SS.

The second paging-control task is that of processing the page-out completion code of the processor (AFU) that received the page-out. A simplified flow chart of this task is shown in Fig. 28. The first part of the task is to select a page to be PUSHed from core to disk in order to make room for the new page. The paging dynamics of the system center around the selection of the page to be PUSHed. The selection is based upon the following parameters: (1) the usage priority of the requested page kept in CH0; (2) the relative priority of the requesting processor; (3) the paging threshold field

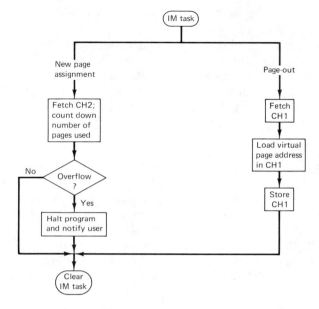

Fig. 27.   IM task flowchart.

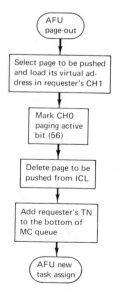

Fig. 28.   AFU page-out completion processing.

of the user (established by the system and kept in CH0); and (4) a simple first in–first out algorithm (Smith [1972]).

It should be mentioned that even though the requester's TN is added to the MC queue at the end of the task as shown in Fig. 28, it is not deleted from the queue of the processor that got the page-out. The TN is left at the same relative position in the processor's queue, but its CH0 is marked with the paging active bit (bit 56). Thus, during the AFU new-task-assignment process, the paging active bit is recognized and the SS skips over to the next entry in the queue for assignment.

The third paging-control task is that of transmitting the proper command to the disk controller through the MC in order to perform the core-to-disk or disk-to-core transfer. Figure 29 shows a simplified flowchart. The disk is divided physically into four quadrants. Each page is contained totally in one quadrant. Part of the virtual-page address is used to identify the quadrant and track in which the page resides. As the disk turns continuously, it informs the disk controller which quadrant has just passed under the magnetic heads and which quadrant is coming up next. This information is passed from the MC to the SS, which proceeds as shown in

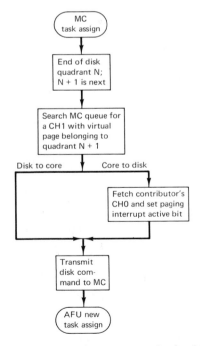

Fig. 29. Paging assignment transmitted to MC.

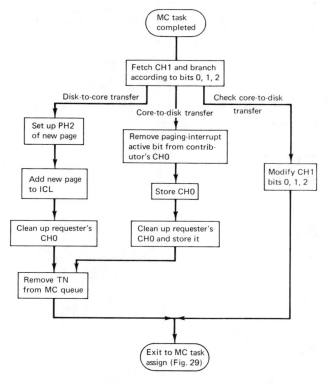

Fig. 30. Disk controller completion-code processing.

Fig. 29. It should be noted that three passes are needed to complete the task of PUSHing a page out and bringing a new page in. The first pass is to transfer the PUSHed page from core to disk. The second pass is to check the core-to-disk transfer for possible errors during the transfer. The third pass is to bring the new page in at the space previously occupied by the PUSHed page. After each pass the TN remains on the MC queue but bits 0, 1, and 2 of its CH1 are modified appropriately. The term "contributor" is used in Figs. 29 and 30 to signify the TN that uses the selected page (it contributes the page to be PUSHed). The term "requester" is used to signify the TN that received the page-out (it requests the new page to be brought into core).

The fourth paging-control task comprises the necessary activities after the completion of each of the three passes mentioned in the previous paragraph. Figure 30 shows a simplified flowchart of these activities. This task is entered at the completion of a quadrant assignment. Note, however, that this task always exits to the MC task assign in order to check if there is any work for the upcoming quadrant.

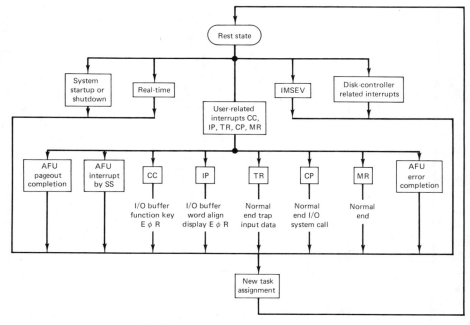

Fig. 31.   Interrupt-service block diagram.

4.5   Interrupt-Service-Logic Tasks

Figure 31 shows all the interrupt-service-logic tasks performed by the SS. They can be classified into two categories: system-related interrupts and user-related interrupts. The system-related interrupts are shown in the top half of the figure. The IMSEV and the disk controller tasks were covered in the previous section (paging control). The real-time interrupt is initiated by a timing oscillator that issues a pulse at prearranged time intervals (adjustable from 0.1 sec to 1 msec). The real-time interrupt-service logic is the basis for the time-sharing capability of the system. Two time values are maintained in order to allocate the system resources: accumulated processor time and top queue time. All processors are subject to a maximum limit of accumulated processor time on each program. However, the CP is in addition subject to a maximum limit on top queue time. The maximum limits are kept in the CH3 of each user and can vary from one user to another according to their needs and priorities. Control word CH2 gets initialized at the beginning of the task by copying the limits from CH3. At every occurrence of a real-time interrupt, the values in CH2 are counted down. When zero is reached, an interrupt is issued to the processor and the user's TN is moved to the bottom of the queue. The time-limit values are also reinitialized at that point.

The time limits for each terminal are controlled by the system software through the system operator. Besides system control and guarding against abuse of valuable system resources by inexperienced users, the mechanisms described above provide an excellent tool for studying the dynamics of the system under various conditions.

The functions of the startup and shutdown interrupts are obvious. The user-related interrupts are shown in the middle of Fig. 31. There are three interrupts that are serviced by the same routine for all processors: the page-out, the SS interrupt, and the error completion. The SS interrupt is sent to the various processors by the SS when situations such as exceeding the time limit occur. The processor, after recognizing the SS-interrupt signal, saves its status in the appropriate A-header control words (AH0–AH7) and transmits an SS-interrupt completion code to the SS, which processes it and takes the necessary action. The AFU error completion is sent to the SS by the various processors if an error is detected during processing. The SS examines the status information saved in AH0–AH7 and relates it to a table of messages located in groups 21–31 of core page zero (Appendix 6). The proper error message is then transmitted to the user via the IP and the CC.

The remaining five classes of user interrupts are associated with the five processors as indicated in Fig. 31. Their primary functions are to modify the control words and the queues appropriately as the program gets moved from processor to processor, or to perform functions related to the user during the various steps of normal program processing.

The new-task-assignment function shown at the bottom of Fig. 31 is not an interrupt in itself. It is a subroutine to which the SS branches after servicing any interrupt and just before returning to the rest state. In most cases, at the end of an interrupt service the processor queues are modified. Therefore, there is a good probability that a processor is free and needs a new assignment.

5. I/O SECTION

Input/output activities in the SYMBOL system are carried out through five major sections of the hardware:

> The terminals
> The channel controller (CC)
> The interface processor (IP)
> The system supervisor (SS)
> The central processor (CP)

The terminals are at the user's location. The other four are part of the main frame hardware.

5.1 The Terminals

There are two basic types of terminals used with SYMBOL. The first is a teletype or a CRT-type of terminal commonly used as an I/O device in computer equipment. It is referred to as the type I terminal in the SYMBOL literature and it is used locally by connecting it to the main frame via a single twisted pair of wires or remotely by connecting it to the main frame via a telephone line. The second type of terminal is a special terminal designed as part of the SYMBOL system and is referred to as the type II terminal. There are two important differences between the type I and type II terminals. The first difference is that the type I terminal lacks any special function keys and, therefore, requires additional system software in order to interpret the various I/O commands. Text editing also requires additional system software.

The type II terminal gives the user the full on-line editing capability of the system and also provides some off-line data preparation and copying capability. The second difference is that the type II terminal can support a variety of I/O devices such as punched-card, magnetic-tape, and paper-tape equipment, whereas the type I cannot support such devices.

The SYMBOL system is designed for two modes of data transmission. The communications mode passes one character to a terminal or accepts one character from a terminal each time that terminal is polled. The block

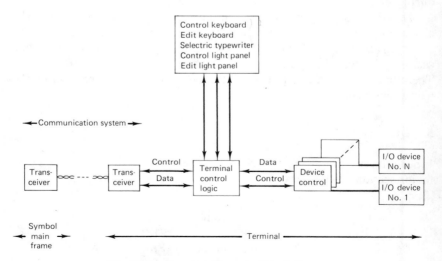

Fig. 32. SYMBOL type II terminal block diagram.

transfer mode allows exactly one page of data (2084 characters) to be transferred without interruption. The type I terminal accommodates only the single-character mode while the type II terminal accommodates both modes. The type II terminal can be functionally partitioned into three sections: the communications system section, the terminal-control-logic section, and a collection of I/O devices each with enough control logic to accommodate the peculiarities of the particular device. Figure 32 shows a block diagram of the type II terminal.

5.1.1 The Communication System

The communications system consists of two parts: the transceiver circuits located in the main frame of SYMBOL and the transceiver circuits located at the terminal itself. The two are connected via a twisted pair of wires up to one mile long. This communications system uses automatic inquiry–reply circuitry to provide

a continuous monitor on transmission integrity,
parity generation and detection circuitry,
the ability to retransmit automatically characters detected to be in error,
error flags to both the CP and the user when an unrecoverable transmission error has been detected.

5.1.2 Terminal Control Logic

The terminal control logic directs all the input/output activities that occur through the communications system between the main frame and the I/O devices. In addition, it can operate in an off-line mode with the capability of transferring information from any input device to any output device connected to the terminal.

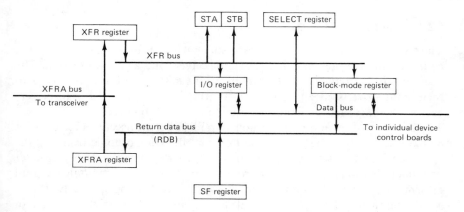

Fig. 33. Type II terminal registers and data paths.

The logic section also controls a number of registers that are employed for handling data and control. Figure 33 shows a block diagram of the registers and data paths in the terminal control logic. Each register is eight bits long and each bus is eight bits wide. The XFR register receives all the information coming to the terminal from the main frame. The XFRA register holds the next character to be transmitted to the main frame.

Status update information is moved to the STA–STB register from the XFR register. Other information coming from the main frame is moved to the I/O register or the block-mode register from the XFR register. Special function information is moved from the SF register to XFRA. Other information to be sent from the terminal to the main frame goes from the I/O register or the block-mode register to XFRA.

Either the I/O register or the block-mode register is the source of data sent to any of the I/O devices. This communication takes place via the main data bus. The SELECT register also communicates with the I/O register via the data bus. The SELECT logic directs the information to the selected device according to the device-selection code.

The contents of the keyboards are shown in Appendix 12.

5.1.3   *I/O-Device Control*

The I/O-device control is done in a modular fashion (one printed-circuit board per device control) so that the system configuration can be easily modified.

5.2.   The Main Frame I/O Facilities

Figure 34 shows the block diagram of the I/O facilities within the SYMBOL main frame.

5.2.1   *The Channel Controller (CC)*

The CC is a character-oriented processor that serves up to 32 channels in a commutating manner. It consists of transceivers and a control section. The transceivers are part of the communications system and are connected to their counterparts at the terminal. In the input mode the transceivers accumulate information from the terminals serially, one character at a time. The CC control section is continuously polling the transceivers looking for a character-ready signal. When that occurs, the control logic transfers the character into its registers and analyzes it to decide if it is a control character or a data character. If it is a control character, the CC communicates that information to the SS and modifies the system tables appropriately. If it is a data character, the CC deposits it directly in the terminal I/O buffers in

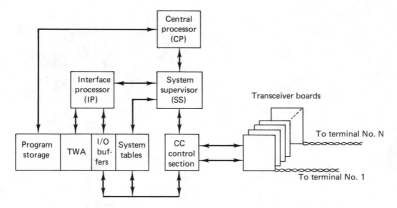

Fig. 34. SYMBOL main frame sections involved in the I/O activities.

main memory. The CC is the only processor that is allowed to communicate directly with the memory without going through the priority scheme of the memory controller. This was done in order to assure fast response to the terminals. Figure 35 shows the information flow during the LOAD mode of a terminal. Figure 36 shows a block diagram of the CC control section. The CC communicates with the SS via word BH7 of the system tables (see Appendix 2).

5.2.2   The Interface Processor

The IP is a fairly simple processor. Operating on a burst basis, the IP empties or fills I/O buffers and transfers appropriate characters to and from the

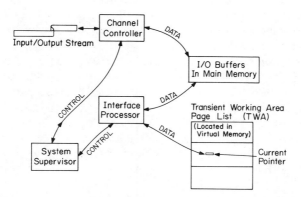

Fig. 35.   Information flow in the LOAD mode.

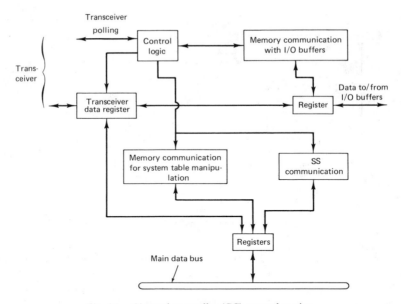

Fig. 36.   Channel controller (CC) control section.

virtual memory. The IP works with a current text pointer while performing its functions, which include basic text insertion, displaying designated text portions, deleting designated text portions, and moving the current pointer.

Part of the justification for implementing editing functions into hardware came from the desire to relieve the CP from many of the system-overhead tasks. In addition, response times would be unacceptable if the CC were to communicate with virtual memory through the MC. The IP was developed to make the basic transfers between small buffers and paging memory. Once a special processor was developed, it was found that double buffering and many editing tasks could be handled using essentially the same data-transfer hardware.

The IP is an operation-oriented processor receiving its operation codes from the SS. The SS, after interacting with the CC, sets up the proper operation code in bits 0–3 of AH7 (see Appendix 1) and the buffer current address (copied from CH7) in bits 40–63 and adds the user (terminal) to the IP's queue. Note that in CH7 (Appendix 8) the left half contains the A-buffer start address and the right half contains the B-buffer start address. Thus, each terminal is allocated two I/O buffers so that while one buffer is being filled by the CC, the other can be emptied by the IP, achieving the operation known as double buffering.

The assignment and state of the buffers are controlled by the SS, as will be explained in the next section.

The operations performed by the IP are shown in Appendix 10. It can be observed that there are two groups of operations, I/O-related operations and text-editing operations. The current pointers maintained by the IP in AH6 are used in conjunction with the edit operations. Thus, from the architectural standpoint, the IP consists of a number of hardware sub-routines for the various operations. The various steps of these subroutines control the registers, the memory communication logic, and the SS communication logic. The subroutines are called by the op-codes found in AH7, which is set up by the SS.

5.2.3 The System Supervisor

The SS plays an important role in the area of I/O during both the load mode and the execution mode. During the load mode, it performs two main functions: (a) it decodes all the control codes generated by the various control keys on the terminal and initiates the appropriate action; and (b) it manages the I/O-buffer states, thus controlling the activities of the CC and the IP. Appendix 11 shows the state diagram for the I/O-buffer-state management. The numbers in the circles represent the states (HEX notation).

The words adjacent to each state indicate the action occurring during that state. For example, IPUNLD stands for IP unload. The words along-side the transition lines between states represent the event whose occur-rence causes the transition. For example, CCBFE stands for *CC buffer full–empty;* where full or empty depends on the previous state's activity. The buffer states are maintained by the SS in bits 4–7 of CH0 (Appendix 3). A typical example would be as follows: The LOAD button at the terminal causes the SS to enter through START into state 8, which says that the CC is filling the buffer (CCFILL). When the buffer is full, a CCBFE completion code from the CC to the SS causes the SS to change the present buffer state from 8 to 9. It also signals the IP to start unloading the full buffer and the CC to start filling the second buffer. During state 9 one of three things may happen: The IP may finish unloading the buffer first (IPBFE); the CC may fill up the second buffer before the IP has finished unloading (CCBFE); or the CC may detect the end-of-record character (CCEOR). In case of IPBFE, we enter state B, where the first buffer has been emptied (EMPTY) and the second is in the process of being filled. In case of CCBFE we enter state 3, during which the IP is still unloading the first buffer (IPUNLD), but the second buffer is full. The reader should continue through this example and follow the mechanism of the buffer management. It is important to understand that each transition from one state to another is caused by an interrupt (completion code) from the CC or the IP and is handled through the AFU controller as described in Section IV.

5.2.4 *The Central Processor*

The role of the CP in I/O activity is only to handle the I/O requirements during execution. Thus, when the CP comes upon an I/O statement in the progran it sends an I/O interrupt to the SS with the string start address (in case of output) placed in the appropriate header area. The IP is notified and given the starting address. The IP then works with the CC through the SS and the buffer states as described above, until it recognizes a string end code, at which time the process is stopped and control is given back to SS, which subsequently returns control to the CP to continue executing the rest of the program.

6. PROGRAM COMPILATION

The hardware compiler of SYMBOL and the compilation process have been described elsewhere in sufficient detail (Laliotis [1973a], Anderberg [1973], Anderberg and Smith [1974]). The reader is referred to these publications for detailed information in that area. Figure 37 shows a block diagram of the total information flow during compilation. The translator is the hardware processor that performs the compilation. The transient working area is where the source program resides. During compilation the translator processes the source program by calling on the reserved-word table to

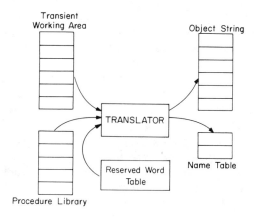

Fig. 37.   Information flow in the compile mode.

OBJECT STRING

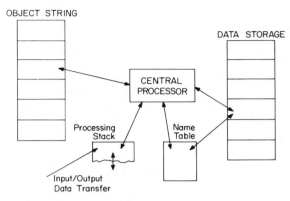

Fig. 38. Information flow during program execution.

recognize reserved words and on the procedure library when system procedures are called by name. The compiled program consists of an object string and a name table stored in virtual memory. The object string is in reverse-Polish-string form with identifier references to the name table.

7. PROGRAM EXECUTION

The execution of a program in SYMBOL is performed by the central processor (CP). After compilation, during which the source program is translated into a reverse-Polish-string object code and a nested block-structured name table, the terminal number is deleted from the TR queue. All the information needed by the CP for execution, such as the various starting addresses, is stored in the A-header of the terminal (AH0–AH7) as shown in Appendix 1.

The basic task of the CP is to evaluate expressions consisting of operands and operators stored in reverse-Polish-string form. It accomplishes that by using a last in–first out push-down stack to store operands as it scans the object string. When an operator is encountered, the proper number of operands is removed from the stack, the operation is performed, and the results are placed back on the top of the stack. Figure 38 shows a block diagram of the information flow during program execution.

The functions of the CP in SYMBOL are considerably more formidable than those of conventional-architecture CPUs. This is due to the novice language features that make the system so attractive to the user because of their added flexibility and capability. Such features include the variable length of data, the programability of the limit register for arithmetic operations, the dynamic flexibility of structures and subscripting, the nested-language block structure that allows localizing identifiers, the FORMAT and MASK operations that allow easy string manipulation, and a number of other features that the reader can appreciate by studying the language section in detail.

Perhaps it should be pointed out here that SYMBOL was implemented by defining the language features first and then designing the hardware to execute those features. Thus, it was designed giving user requirements higher priority than designer requirements.

To cope with all the program execution requirements, the CP consists of four distinct sections or subprocessors. The master of the four subprocessors is the *instruction sequencer* (IS), whose prime task is to scan the object string and accumulate items in the stack. When an operator appears, the IS calls upon one of the other three subprocessors to perform the operation.

The second subprocessor is the *arithmetic processor* (AP), which uses the limit register to perform arithmetic operations and numeric comparisons at user-specified precisions.

The third subprocessor is the *format processor* (FP), which performs all string manipulation operations, lexicographic comparisons, and necessary data-type conversions.

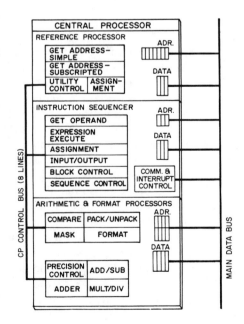

Fig. 39.   Block diagram of the central processor.

The fourth and last subprocessor is the *reference processor* (RP), whose basic task is to deal with structures. It processes and accesses data structures, initializes data variables, and handles assignment operations. In addition, the RP decodes the flag of the name table control words in order to recognize and treat appropriately such cases as label and parameter references, procedure calls, identifier indirection, and on-events occurrence.

A block diagram of the CP is shown in Fig. 39. The IS has to preserve the contents of all of its registers while waiting for the results of an operation from one of the subprocessors. Therefore, each subprocessor (RP, AP, FP) is equipped with its own address and data registers for communicating with the memory. However, there is only one set of SS and MC communication hardware for the entire CP. For example, if the RP wants to make a memory access, it uses its own address and data registers, but the loading and unloading of the registers as well as the priority and op-code lines are controlled by the communication and interrupt-control logic shown in the IS. A local control bus consisting of eight control lines is used for local communication between the IS and the other three subprocessors. Using this local bus for communication control among the subprocessors, the CP has the capability of using the main data bus to transfer data back and forth between the subprocessors on a cycle-stealing basis. Thus, during the waiting period of any processor's memory cycle, the CP can use the main data bus for local transfers as long as there is no control exchange cycle in progress (MP6). These cycles are referred to as "sneak" cycles. In fact, the CP does not even care whether a memory cycle is in progress or not. As long as the conditions (MP5*) and (MP6*) are true, it proceeds to use the next cycle as a sneak cycle if it needs to.

The detailed process of the program execution in SYMBOL has been described by Hutchison and Ethington [1973].

APPENDIXES

The following are the appendixes to which various references have been made in the text.

Bit positions: 00 — 08 — 16 — 24 — 32 — 40 — 48 — 56 — 63

CP | IP

AH0: Block Flag | Inner Block | BLOCK NUMBER (FULL WORD INIT TO ZERO BY JC) | CURRENT BREAK POINT

CURRENT BREAK POINT bit fields (top to bottom): Processing Lmted / System On / On / Rsrtr Procesng / Procedure / Unstrst'd Proc / Go To / Within Sprgrps / Prev Item=in / Input/Output / Data Type I/O / Get Name / Ind Stack Ntry / Oprnds Xchnged / 'A' Operand In / Addr. / OS 1/2 Word / Spare / Delete Local / Utility 5 / Utility 4 / Utility 3 / Sbscr Intgrzed / Operation Cpt

AH1: LIMIT COUNTER | PHASE COUNTER CONTENTS (INIT. TO ZERO) | M V E S I T B C P D H — BOARD SELECTION FOR PHASE COUNTER (INIT. TO ZERO EXCEPT FOR BIT 21 = 1) | ERROR CODE CHARACTER | CP STACK CURRENT ADDRESS

AH2: I/O OPERATION CODE (See CHO) — Exact / Empirical — Q I D S | OBJECT STRING CURRENT ADDRESS (INIT. BY JC. REMAINDER OF WORD ZERO) | UNIT NUMBER | CP TEMPORARY STACK ADDRESS

AH3: CP INTERNAL STACK ADDRESS | CP INTERNAL ADDRESS

AH4: CP INTERNAL STACK DATA | WORD (NON I/O ONLY)

AH5: CP STACK | DATA WORD

AH6: BOTTOM CHAR. ADDRESS | BOTTOM CURRENT ADDRESS | CURRENT CHAR. ADDRESS | CURRENT I/O ADDRESS

AH7: I/O OPERATION CODE (See CHO) | INTERNAL OPERATION CODE | BCD COUNTER | BUFFER CHAR. ADDRESS | BUFFER CURRENT ADDRESS

BCD COUNTER bit fields (top to bottom): Strng Strt Set / Insrt Atlwd / GP Mark Last / Field Mrk Last / Inside Sprgrp / Line Cnt Flag / Line Cnt Valid / Go to Bottom

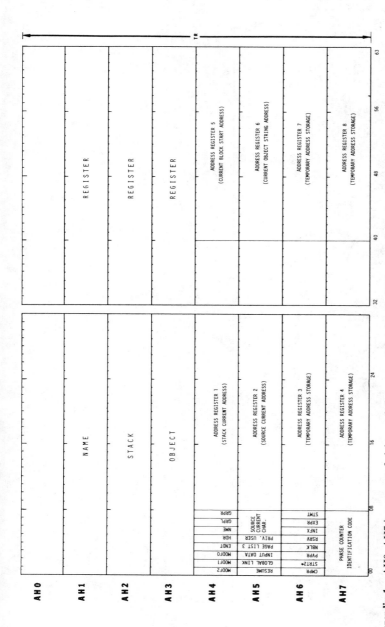

Appendix 1. AH0–AH7 is a group of eight words known as the A-header. Thirty-two A-headers (one for each terminal) occupy the second core page in main memory. The A-headers are usually used for storing initialization, completion, and status information for the CP, IP, and TR.

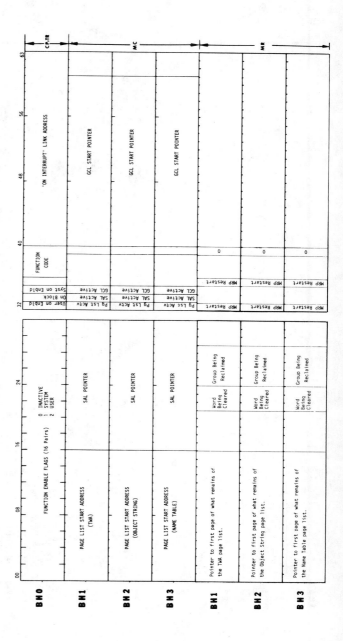

BH 4

Restricted
Non Restricted
Error if UDCLR

SS - SOFTWARE

RESTRICTED SYSTEM NAME TABLE ADDRESS

COMMUNICATION WORD (See Detail)

NON RESTRICTED SYSTEM NAME TABLE ADDRESS

BH 5

Pointer to page in which indicated group was being reclaimed.

Pointer to Forward Group Tree Link

BH 6

MRG Restart Flags
Word Being Examined
Group Being Reclaimed
Page List for MR

MRG Fwd. Act.
MRG Back. Act.
MR Flag

BH 7

I/O OPERATION CODE (See CHO)
Display Status
Transmit Unit Flags
TERMINAL STATUS
Status Sent
BUFFER CHAR. ADDRESS

Block Transfer
UNIT NUMBER

BC BUFFER WORD ADDRESS

JC
TR
MR
CC

Appendix 2. BH0–BH7 is a group of eight words known as the B-header. Thirty-two B-headers (one for each terminal) occupy the third page in main memory. They are used for storing memory allocation and reclamation control words as well as additional miscellaneous control information for the processors as shown.

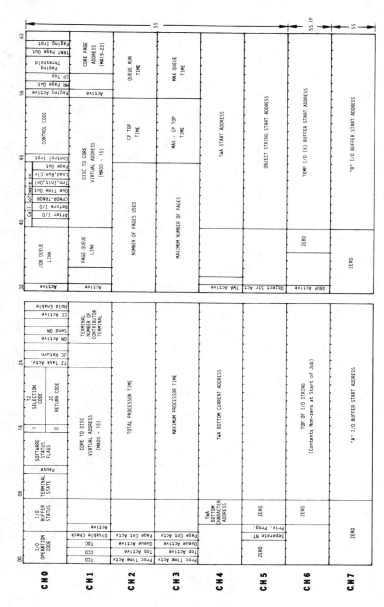

Appendix 3. CH0–CH7 is a group of eight words known as the C-header. Thirty-two C-headers (one for each terminal) occupy the fourth page in main memory. They contain control information used primarily by the system supervisor as indicated.

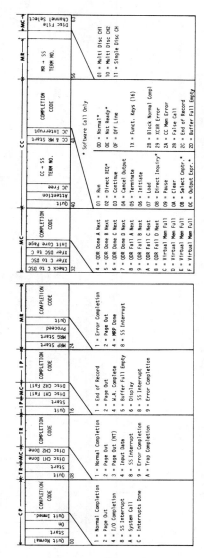

Appendix 4. Allocation of main data bus bits during control exchange cycles.

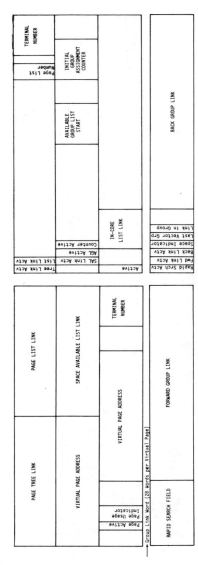

Appendix 5. Page-header-control format (first four words in each virtual page—one word not used) and group-link-word format.

	CPNDR	A8 TRNDR	TR TRAP	TZ I/O Errors	Queuing Error (JC)	Page Out Error	Page Out Interrupt	Memory Full
B0	Page Usage Overflow Space Word	Input/Output Command from CP	Load Complete	I/O Return to CP Interrupt	Accounting Interrupt	Disc Error	IPL (CHO TI)	I/O Buf Page Numbers
B8	System Available Space Word	AFU Queue Control Word	Paging Queue Control Word	Real-Time Clock	Standard BH0	Standard BH5	Standard CH0	Standard CH3
C0	TRERR (Name Table)	TRERR (Memory Error)	TRERR (Conditional st.)	TRERR (End)	TRERR (Comma)	TRERR (Semicolon)	TRERR (Comma or Semic)	TRERR (I/O Qualifier)
C8	TRERR (Left paren.)	TRERR (Right paren.)	TRERR (Bracket)	TRERR (Colon)	TRERR (Infix Operator)	TRERR (Interrupts, Name, Procedure, On)	TRERR (Data Structure)	TRERR (Switch)
D0	CPERR (OX)	CPERR (8X)	CPERR (2X)	CPERR (3X)	CPERR (4X)	CPERR (5X)	CPERR (6X)	CPERR (EX)
D8	CC Block Complete	CCERR (XCVR Err)	CCERR (Mem. Err)	CCERR (False Call)	NR Err (MR Detected)	IPERR	Power Off Interrupt	Real-Time Clock Underflow
E0	Run Error	Compile and Run (S46)	(Software Call) Direct Execute	(Hardware Only) Continue	(Hardware Only) Cancel Output	Terminate (S45)	Initiate (S45)	Load (S46)
E8	(Software Call) Direct Inquiry	(Hardware Only) Pause	Clear	(Software Call) Device Error (Type 2)	Restart (S46)	(Software Call) Normal	(Software Call) Edit Call (TTY)	Terminal Off-Line (S45)
F8	Sys. Funct. 0	Sys. Funct. 1	Sys. Funct. 2	Sys. Funct. 3	Sys. Funct. 4	Sys. Funct. 5	Sys. Funct. 6	Sys. Funct. 7
	Sys. Funct. 8	Sys. Funct. 9	Sys. Funct. 10	Sys. Funct. 11	Sys. Funct. 12	Sys. Funct. 13	Sys. Funct. 14	Sys. Funct. 15

Appendix 6. Groups 21–31 of the first page in main memory contain a set of messages selectable by the SS for transmission to users.

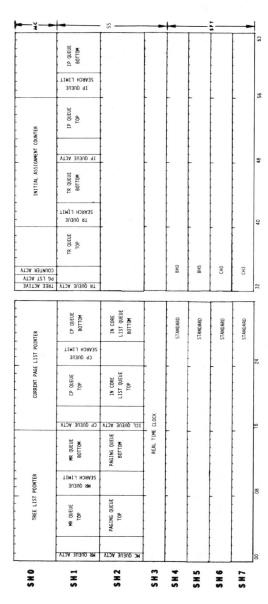

Appendix 7. SH0–SH7 is a group of eight words known as the *system header*. The system header resides in the first page of main memory and contains available page list information, the top and bottom pointers for the queues of the processor, and standard header information for initialization.

BUS PIN USAGE AND ALLOCATION

Pin	Usage	
1	-------- Spare	
2	-------- MC0	
3	-------- MC1	
4	-------- MC2	
5	-------- MC3	See Table Below
6	-------- MC4	
7	-------- MC5	
8 - 12 -- MT (0-4)	- Terminal Number Bus	
13 - 36 -- MA (00-23)	- Memory Address Bus	
37 - 100 -- MD (00-63)	- Memory Data Bus	
101	---------------------- System Clear Line	
102		
103	-------- MP1 -------- Syst. Super Memory Priority	
104	-------- MP2 -------- Interface Processor Memory Priority	
105	-------- MP3 -------- Central Processor Memory Priority	
106	-------- MP4 -------- Translator Memory Priority	
107	-------- MP5 -------- Main Bus Inhibit Line	
	(Data transfer on next clock)	
108	-------- MP6 -------- Control Cycle Request Line	
109	-------- MP7 -------- Memory Free Signal	
110	-------- MP8 -------- Memory Reclaimer Memory Priority	
111	-------- MP9 -------- Spare Memory Priority Line	

MC (0-5) During AFU→MC

MC (0-3)

MC0,1

MC2,3	00	01	11	10
00	NP	FF	DE	SA
01	AG	FR	DS	SO
11		FD	RG	SI
10	IG	FL	DL	SD

MC (4-5)

00	Non Page List Operation
01	Page List 1 (TWA)
10	Page List 2 (Object String)
11	Page List 3 (Name Table)

MC (0-5) During MC→AFU

000011	- Normal Completion
100011	- Normal Completion with New Page
000001	- Page Out
000010	- No Address Returned
000100	- Illegal Terminal Header Reference
001000	- Illegal Use of Group Link Word or Page Header
001100	- Absolute Address Error
010000	- Illegal Operation
100000	- Memory Hardware Failure

Appendix 8. (above) Main bus definition.

0000	NP	No operation	
0001	AG	Assign group	
0010	IG	Insert group	
0100	FF	Fetch and follow	
0101	FR	Fetch and reverse follow	
0110	FL	Follow and fetch	
0111	FD	Fetch direct	
1000	SA	Store and assign	
1001	SO	Store only	
1010	SI	Store and insert	
1011	SD	Store direct	
1100	DE	Delete to end	
1101	DS	Delete string	
1110	DL	Delete list	
1111	RG	Reclaim group	

Appendix 9. (above) Definition of the 15 memory operations available to all the processors through the memory controller.

IP OPERATION CODES

		OP REG	
OPERATION	SIGNALS	0123	4567
Word Align	WDA	0001	0000
Input String	INP, STR	0101	0000
Input List	INP, LIST	0100	0000
Input Data	INP, DATA	0110	0000
Input Load	INP, DATA	0111	0000
Output String	OUT, STR	1001	0000
Output List	OUT, LIST	1000	0000
Output Data	OUT, DATA	1010	0000
		1011	0000
Move Pointer FWD	MPF	01XX	0100
Move Pointer BKWD	MPB	01XX	0010
Remove	REM	01XX	0110
Insert	INS	01XX	0001
Display	DIS	01XX	1001
Move FWD Search	MPF, SRC	01XX	1100
Move BKWD Search	MPB, SRC	01XX	1010

NOTES: (1) EDIT is defined as OP4 + OP5 + OP6 + OP7
(2) X is don't care

Appendix 10. (above) Definition of interface processor operation codes.

Appendix 11. (right) I/O-buffer state diagram maintained by the system supervisor.

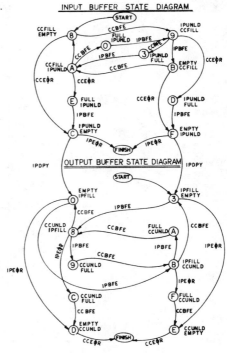

INPUT BUFFER STATE DIAGRAM

OUTPUT BUFFER STATE DIAGRAM

Appendix 12.   Type II terminal keyboard definition.

Edit Keyboard	Control Keyboard
PERFORM EDIT	F0–F15
EDIT LOAD	RESTART
SEARCH BACKWARD	CLEAR
MOVE BACKWARD	LOAD
REMOVE FORWARD	CANCEL OUTPUT
DISPLAY FORWARD	PAUSE
SEARCH FORWARD	RUN
MOVE FORWARD	CONTINUE
LINES	DIRECT EXECUTE
CHARACTERS	DIRECT INQUIRY
ALL	NORMAL
0, 1, 2, 3, 4, 5, 6, 7, 8, 9	EDIT ENABLE
	TERMINATE
	INITIATE
	TERMINAL CLEAR
	REMOTE
	LOCAL
	START
	STOP
	STEP
	BACKSPACE
	AUX1–AUX5
	LOAD CODE
	LOAD COMMAND
	CARRIAGE RETURN

Appendix 13.   SYMBOL syntax.

$digit ::= 1|2|3|4|5|6|7|8|9|0$
$letter ::= A|B|C|---|Z|a|b|c|---|z|$
$character ::= \_$ any character except $\dotplus$ $\_$
$break\text{-}char ::= \_$ a carriage return, tab, or space $\_$
$identifier ::= letter[[letter|digit|break\text{-}char] \ldots (letter|digit)]$
$label ::= identifier$
$decimal\text{-}number ::= digit \ldots [.]|[digit \ldots]. digit \ldots$
$exponent\text{-}part ::= {}_{10}[+|-] [digit] digit$
$number ::= decimal\text{-}number|exponent\text{-}part|decimal\text{-}number\ exponent\text{-}part$
$string\text{-}number ::= [+|-] [(digit|,) \ldots] number [EX|EM]$
$string ::= \_$ sequence of zero or more of any characters except $\langle \ \rangle$ $|$ and $\dotplus$ $\_$
$field ::= string\text{-}number|string$
$data\text{-}field ::= "|" field "|"$
$named\text{-}data ::= identifier (data\text{-}field|data\text{-}structure)$
$ds ::= [L "|" field]$
$data\text{-}structure ::= \langle ds [data\text{-}structure\ ds] \ldots \rangle$
$ls ::= [L "|" label]$
$label\text{-}structure ::= \langle ls [label\text{-}structure\ ls] \ldots \rangle$

Appendix 13. (*continued*)

as ::= [*L* "|" *exp*]
assignment-structure ::= ⟨*as*[*assignment-structure as*] . . .⟩
subscription ::= *identifier* "[" *L,exp* "]"
subfield ::= *identifier* "[" *L,exp:exp* "]"
designator ::= *identifier*|*subscription*|*procedure-call*|LIMIT
procedure-call ::= *identifier* ["(" *L*, [*reference*] ")"]
constant ::= *data-field*|*number*
value ::= *designator*|*subfield*|*constant*|IN(*subscription*|*subfield*)|LIMITED
reference ::= *designator* | *exp* | *label*
arithmetic-op ::= +|−|*|/
string-op ::= JOIN|FORMAT|MASK
binary-op ::= AND|OR
arithmetic-relation ::= GREATER[THAN]|GTE|EQUALS|NEQ|LTE|LESS[THAN]
string-relation ::= BEFORE|SAME|AFTER
relational-op ::= *arithmetic-relation*|*string-relation*
dyadic-op ::= *relational-op*|*arithmetic-op*|*string-op*|*binary-op*
monadic-op ::= +|−|ABS|NOT
exp ::= *value*|"("*exp*")"|*monadic-op exp*|*exp dyadic-op exp*
assignment-element ::= *assignment-structure*|*exp*|LINK *reference*
assignment-stm ::= *L,designator* = *assignment-element*
go-to-stm ::= GO[TO] (*label*|*subscription*|*procedure-call*|*identifier*)
call-stm ::= [CALL] *procedure-call*
break-stm ::= PAUSE|SYSTEM|TRAP
dummy-stm ::= [CONTINUE]
comment-stm ::= NOTE_any characters except ;_
output-stm ::= OUTPUT ([TO *exp*,]*L,exp*|STRING[TO *exp*,]*L,exp*|DATA[TO *exp*,]
    L,identifier)
input-stm ::= INPUT([EX|EM][FROM *exp*,]*L,designator*|STRING[FROM *exp*,]
    L,designator|DATA[FROM *exp*])
list-data ::= *L* ∔ (*field*|*data-structure*) ∔
string-data ::= *L* ∔ [*character* . . .] ∔
self-defined-data ::= *named-data* . . . ∔
initialization-stm ::= *named-data*
switch-stem ::= SWITCH *identifier label-structure*
for-clause ::= FOR *L*, (*exp*|*exp* WHILE *exp*)
step-clause ::= (FROM *exp*|BY *exp*|THRU *exp*|WHILE *exp*) . . .
loop-header ::= LOOP [*designator*] *L*, [*for-clause*|*step-clause*];
loop-stm ::= *loop-header body* END
on-element-list ::= *L*,(*identifier*|*label*|INTERRUPT)
on-header ::= ON *on-element-list;*
on-control-stm ::= (DISABLE|ENABLE) *on-element-list*
return-stm ::= RETURN [*reference*]
procedure-header ::= PROCEDURE *identifier* ["(" *L,identifier*")"];
conditional-stm ::= IF *exp* THEN *body* [ELSE *body*] END
scope-stm ::= GLOBAL *L,identifier*
block ::= (BLOCK|*on-header*|*procedure-header*) *body* END
stm ::= *label*: *stm*|*assignment-stm*|*go-to-stm*|*call-stm*|*break-stm*|*dummy-stm*
    |*comment-stm*|*output-stm*|*input-stm*|*initialization-stm*|*switch-stm*
    |*loop-stm*|*on-control-stm*|*return-stm*|*scope-stm*|*conditional-stm*|*block*

Appendix 13.   (*continued*)

$body ::= [L;stm]$
$program ::= body +$
$privileged\text{-}stm ::= (fetch|store|delete|assign)(identifier|subscription)$
$fetch ::= FF|FR|FL|FD|FT$
$store ::= SA|SO|SI|SD|ST$
$delete ::= DE|DS|DL$
$assign ::= AG|IG$

METALANGUAGE

$(X|Y)$ Select one alternative from group
$[X|Y]$ Select zero or one from group
$X \ldots$ Repeat zero or more times
L XY   List of Y's separated by X's
$\_X\_$ A comment
"X"   Not a metasymbol

REFERENCES

Agrawal, O. [1974]. "Applicability of Buffered Main Memory to SYMBOL 2R-Like Computing Structures." Ph.D. Thesis, Iowa State Univ., Ames, Iowa.

Alarilla, Jr., L. M. [1974]. "Storage Linking Techniques for the Automatic Management of Dynamically Variable Arrays." Ph.D. Thesis, Iowa State Univ., Ames, Iowa.

Anderberg, J. W. [1974]. Source program analysis and object string generation algorithms and their implementation in the SYMBOL 2R translator, Special Rep. NSF-OCA-GJ33097-CL7410. Cyclone Computer Lab. Iowa State Univ., Ames, Iowa.

Anderberg, J. W., and Smith, C. L. [1973]. High-level language translation in SYMBOL-2R, *Proc. Symp. High-Level Language Computer Architecture, Univ. Maryland, Nov. 1973* 11–19.

Bradley, A. C. [1973]. An algorithmic description of the SYMBOL arithmetic processor, Special Rep. NSF-OCA-GJ33097-CL7301. Cyclone Computer Lab., Iowa State Univ., Ames, Iowa.

Calhoun, M. A. [1972]. SYMBOL hardware debugging facilities, *Proc. SJCC 1972* 359–368.

Chesley, G. D., and Smith, W. R. [1971]. The hardware-implemented high-level language for SYMBOL, *Proc. SJCC 1971* 563–573.

Chu, Y. [1972a]. Significance of the SYMBOL computer system, *Dig. COMPCON 72* 33–35.

Chu, Y. [1972b]. Software into hardware, *Sci. Amer.* **226**, 42–43.

Cowart, B. E., Rice, R., and Lundstrom, S. F. [1971]. The physical attributes and testing aspects of the SYMBOL system, *Proc. SJCC 1971* 389–600.

Dakins, M. C. [1974]. "Nonnumeric Processing in the SYMBOL 2R Computer System." M.S. Thesis, Iowa State Univ., Ames, Iowa.

Falk, H. [1974]. Hard-soft tradeoffs, *SPECTRUM* **11** (3), 42–43.

Fowlie, J. L. [1972]. "The SYMBOL 2R Disk Controller," M.S. Thesis, Iowa State Univ., Ames, Iowa.

Hutchison, P. C., and Ethington, K. [1973]. Program execution in the SYMBOL 2R computer, *Proc. Symp. High-Level Language Computer Architecture, Univ. Maryland, Nov. 1973* 20–26.

Jefferis, J. L. [1973]. "Design of a Drum Controller for the SYMBOL 2R System." M.S. Thesis, Iowa State Univ., Ames, Iowa.

Jones, W. E. [1973]. The role of the interface processor in the SYMBOL 2R computer system, Special Rep. NSF-OCA-GJ33097-CL7304. Cyclone Computer Lab. Iowa State Univ., Ames, Iowa.

Laliotis, T. A. [1973a]. Implementation aspects of the SYMBOL hardware compiler, *Proc. First Annual Symp. on Computer Architecture* 111–115.

Laliotis, T. A. [1973b]. Main memory technology, *Computer* **6** (8), 21–27.

Rice, R. [1972a]. A project overview, *Dig. COMPCON 72* 17–23.

Rice, R. [1972b]. The hardware implementation of SYMBOL, *Dig. COMPCON 72* 27–29.

Rice, R., and Smith, W. R. [1971]. SYMBOL—a major departure from classic software-dominated von Neumann computing systems, *Proc. SJCC 1971* 575–587.

Richards, Jr., H. [1971a]. "SYMBOL 2R Programming Language Reference Manual." Cyclone Computer Lab., Iowa State Univ., Ames, Iowa.

Richards, Jr., H. [1971b]. Hardware invades software domain, *Electronics* **44** (4), 25.

Richards, Jr., H., and Wright, Jr., C. [1973]. Introduction to the SYMBOL 2R programming language, *Proc. Symp. High-Level Language Computer Architecture, Univ. Maryland, Nov. 1973* 27–33.

Richards, Jr., H., and Zingg, R. J. [1973]. The logical structure of the memory resource in the SYMBOL 2R computer, *Proc. Symp. High-Level Language Computer Architecture, Univ. Maryland, Nov. 1973* 1–10.

Smith, W. R. [1972]. System supervisor algorithms for the SYMBOL computer, *Dig. COMPCON 72* 21–26.

Smith, W. R., *et al.* [1971]. SYMBOL—A large experimental system exploring major hardware replacement of software, *Proc. SJCC 1971* 601–616.

Zingg, R. J., and Richards, Jr., H. [1972a]. Operational experience with SYMBOL, *Dig. COMPCON 72* 31–35.

Zingg, R. J., and Richards, Jr., H. [1972b]. SYMBOL: A system tailored to the structure of data, *Proc. Nat. Electron. Conf.* **27**, 306–311.

Conceptual Design of a Direct
High-Level Language Processor

Howard M. Bloom

Management Information Systems Group
Harry Diamond Laboratories
Adelphi, Maryland

1. INTRODUCTION

The development of high-level programming languages (e.g., FORTRAN) provided the impetus that made computer programming "easily available" to many types of disciplines. However, in the process of providing a convenient language to users, layers of system software had to be constructed to enable the high-level language to interact with the machine language of the computer. Chu, in the first chapter of this volume, described the development of high-level language systems from the initial compiler concept found on conventional machines to the *direct high-level language system* (DHLLS) to be described here.

In a *direct-execution, high-level language processor* (DHLLP), there are no intermediate languages and no translations on the input code. The processor takes as input a program written in a high-level language (ALGOL here) and executes it directly without any code generation. The fundamental reason for developing the DHLLP concept is to remove layers of conventional software. Thus, the programmer can understand the high-level language semantics by observing the direct response of the computer hardware. There is no need to know the entire spectrum of compilers, assemblers, loaders, and system supervisors. The entire operation of the computer can be controlled by one language.

The subsequent sections describe, through a series of examples, the method for executing the language semantics and data structures needed for the DHLLP.

2. CONCEPTUAL DEVELOPMENT

This section introduces the DHLLP concept and describes the elements that are needed to construct the DHLLP.

2.1   Basic DHLLP Concept

A high-level language program can be represented by the string

$$\$c_1 c_2 \cdots c_m \$$$

where $\$$ is used as a program delimiter and c_i $(i = 1, \ldots, m)$ is a character in the language.

The processor accepts this program string as input and performs operations as determined by the semantics of the string characters.

Example.   A program string in ALGOL may take the form

```
$begin
    integer A, B, C;
    A := B + C
end$
```

The important characteristic of the DHLLP is that it operates directly on the program string and not on any intermediate translation. Hence, there is never any other form of the program string except the original one.

2.2   Syntax-Checking Technique

The fundamental structure of the DHLLP is the syntax-checking design. Every language consists of a set of rules, called "productions," that determine how the basic characters in the language, called "terminals," can be combined into special forms, called "nonterminals." Syntax-checking involves examining the program string to see if any of these rules of the language have been violated.

Example.   In ALGOL, terminals might be digits, letters, and operators $(+, -,$ etc.), and nonterminals might be "terms" $(A \times B)$, "factors" $(A \uparrow B)$, etc.

The technique used in this DHLLP (Bloom [1971]) requires the language to have an operator precedent grammar. The two distinguishing features of the grammar are the rules: (a) no adjacent nonterminals may appear in any production, and (b) at most one precedence relationship can exist between any two terminals T_i and S_j that can appear in a program string of the form $\cdots T_i \langle \text{nonterminal} \rangle S_j \cdots$. Precedence relationships are used to determine the order in which operations are performed.

Example.   Given the string $\$A + B \times C\$$, if $\times$ has higher precedence than $+$, the expression $B \times C$ must be considered before the expression $A + B$.

The first rule is used in setting up the basic structure of the syntax-checker flowchart (Fig. 1), and the second rule is used in developing the terminal precedence relationships.

2.2.1 Precedence Relationships

The technique used to determine terminal precedence assumes that a unique relationship exists between any two terminals T_i and S_j that can appear

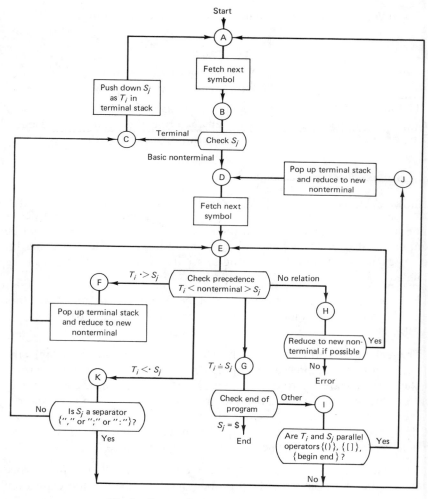

Fig. 1. Syntax-checking algorithm flowchart.

adjacent to a given nonterminal. A table of terminal precedence relationships must be established for each nonterminal in the language. This table can be constructed for a given nonterminal by simply applying the three precedence relationship definitions ($<$, $\doteq$, $>$) to all the productions in which the nonterminal can appear on the right side (see Gries [1971] for development of precedence relationships). Here, it will be assumed that the precedence tables for the DHLLP language have already been developed (see Section 4 of Bloom [1971] for an example of precedence-table construction).

2.2.2 Syntax-Checking Algorithm

The algorithm, a natural development of the precedence relationship tables, can best be expressed in the flowchart shown in Fig. 1. The algorithm operates on two types of data areas, stacks and tables, which can be defined as follows.

Stack. A linear array of elements in which only the top element can be accessed. Given a stack X consisting of elements $x_1, x_2, \ldots, x_m$, x_m must be accessed before x_{m-1}, x_{m-1} before x_{m-2}, etc. The index m is called the pointer to the top of the stack. There are three operations commonly performed upon a stack X whose pointer is m. (A notation for the operation is shown after the operation is defined.)

(1) PUSH X, Y. Push down a new element Y onto the stack:

$$m \leftarrow m + 1$$
$$x_m \leftarrow Y$$

(2) POP X. Pop up the top element of the stack:

$$m \leftarrow m - 1$$

(3) POPS X, Y. Pop up the top element of the stack and store in element Y:

$$Y \leftarrow X_m$$
$$m \leftarrow m - 1$$

Table. A linear array of elements in which all elements can be accessed. Given a table P consisting of elements $p_1, p_2, \ldots, p_n$, any of the p_i ($i = 1, \ldots, n$) can be accessed. There are two pointers associated with the table. There is the index n pointing to the top of the table, and the index i pointing to the element currently being accessed in the table. All the stack operations can also be applied to the table. There are three operations commonly performed upon a table P.

(a)   GETI P, Y. Get the element pointed to by i and store it in Y, then increment i:

$$Y \leftarrow p_i$$
$$i \leftarrow i + 1$$

(b)   PUT P, Y. Put the element Y into the ith element in the table:

$$p_i \leftarrow Y$$

(c)   GET P, Y. Get the element pointed to by i and store it in Y:

$$Y \leftarrow p_i$$

The syntax-checker interacts with two data areas: (a) the *character table* (CT), and (b) the *terminal stack* (TS) (see Fig. 2). The character table contains the program string and, upon request from the checker, outputs a symbol S_j representing the current symbol being scanned. This symbol can consist of one or more characters from one of two categories, operators and operands. Operators are all the terminals in the language that cause specific operations to be performed (e.g., $+$, $-$, begin). They may consist of one or more characters depending on the limitations of the character set implemented on the processor. Operands are either identifiers or unsigned numbers. The operators will be called "terminals" and the operands will be called "basic nonterminals." Hence the digits and letters that are used to form operands have been excluded from the definition of a terminal.

The terminal stack temporarily saves incoming terminals until they can be used in nonterminal reductions. The symbol T_i is used to indicate the terminal at the top of the stack. Reductions in general involve performing some operation as determined by the terminal and then creating a new nonterminal as determined by the syntax (e.g., performing $X \uparrow 2$ causes a reduction to the nonterminal "factor").

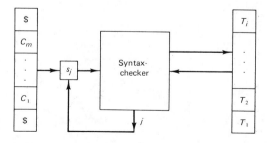

Fig. 2.   Basic structure of the syntax-checker.

The scanning of any production always begins at the flowchart start position point A. The first symbol scanned, S_j, will be the first symbol on the right side of the production. There are two possibilities:

(a) *S_j is a terminal.* Since no reduction can yet take place, the terminal must be temporarily saved by pushing it down into the terminal stack.

(b) *S_j is a basic nonterminal.* After recognition of a nonterminal, the precedence-checking can now take place. However, a new symbol, T_i, must be fetched first so that the terminal comparisons can be made (point D).

In checking precedence between T_i and S_j (point E), there are four cases to consider:

(a) *T_i has higher precedence (point F).* A reduction can take place involving T_i and one or more previous nonterminals that have already been scanned. This operation involves popping up the terminal stack and the formation of a new nonterminal.

(b) *T_i has less precedence (point K).* In this case, no reduction can take place and the symbol S_j must be saved. However, there is a special case for when the symbol S_j is a separator (comma, semicolon, or colon). Separators are artificial symbols that are used to help make the syntactical productions appear in a more precise form; they have no intrinsic meaning of their own. Hence, they can be ignored in the syntax-checking algorithm.

(c) *T_i has equal precedence (point G).* The first check is for $\langle$program$\rangle\$$ so that the algorithm can be ended. If T_i and S_j are parallel operators (i.e., parenthesis, brackets, or "begin"–"end"), a reduction can take place since S_j is the rightmost symbol of the production [e.g., $\langle p \rangle ::= \langle ae \rangle$]. However, T_i must be popped up from the stack. Since a new nonterminal has just been formed, the next symbol must be fetched. If T_i and S_j are not parallel operators (e.g., "if" and "then" in a conditional statement), it is not necessary to save S_j. The reduction to the nonterminal that contains more than one terminal on the right-hand side of the production need only keep the first terminal as a key to which reduction should take place.

(d) *No precedence relation (point H).* If neither T_i nor S_j appears adjacent to the nonterminal in any production, no precedence relations can be checked, and the nonterminal is reduced to another nonterminal as determined by the grammar (e.g., $\langle$factor$\rangle ::= \langle$primary$\rangle$). If no "default" production exists, there is a syntax error.

The part of the flowchart showing the precedence check (points E–A and E–D) expresses the general form of execution. For each nonterminal there is actually a specific flowchart that expresses the possible relationships that can exist between those terminals that can appear adjacent to the given nonterminal (see Bloom [1971, Section 4] for an example of the syntax-checking flowcharts).

2.3 Data Structure

Now that the syntax-checking phase has been developed, the execution phase can begin. At this point, it is necessary to consider what data structure elements are needed for the processor to function. The terminal stack and the character table have already been mentioned. Since the nonterminals are now being considered, a stack must be used to save values of the nonterminals. This stack is called the *work stack* (WS). In addition to saving nonterminal values, the WS is also used in special operations that will be described throughout this chapter. Two other tables, the *block table* (BT) and the *node table* (NT) are also needed, but a description of these tables will be postponed to a later section. The functions of these data structures appear in Table I.

The format of data elements TS, WS, and CT appears in Fig. 3. The terminal stack has a pointer TSP to the top of the stack. The terminal code is the symbol code for the terminal. The character table has two pointers, CCTP and TCTP. Each word in the table contains ten fields, one per character. The table outputs two symbols, S_j and S_{j+1}. The work stack has a pointer WSP to the top of the stack. Each entry contains three fields:

(a) *form:* the type of information that is stored in the stack,
(b) *value:* data of interest,
(c) *type:* specification of value type.

The different forms will be introduced as they appear.

TABLE I

Functions of Data Structures

Structure name	Function
terminal stack (TS)	Temporary storage for incoming terminals that cannot be used immediately in a reduction.
block table (BT) consisting of subareas:	Dynamic storage for block declarations.
(a) dynamic storage allocation table (DSAT)	(a) Storage of identifier declaration.
(b) value table (VT)	(b) Assigned identifier values.
(c) block-level stack (BLS)	(c) Storage of block-level pointers.
work stack (WS)	Temporary storage for nonterminals and special conditions (see NT).
character table (CT)	Storage for program string.
node table (NT)	Storage for special conditions in "for" statements, labels, and conditionals.

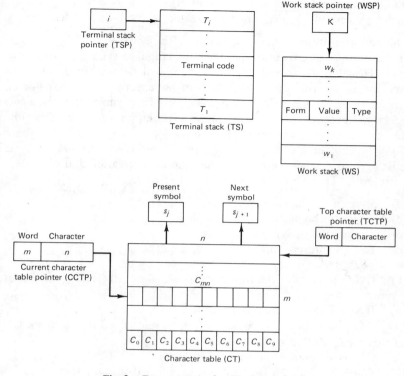

Fig. 3. Data structure for TS, WS, and CT.

2.4 Language Semantics

The syntax-checker flowchart Fig. 2 can now be updated to allow for semantics. The following changes must be made:

(a) After checking S_j (point B) and before fetching the next symbol (point D), add an operation that pushes the nonterminal onto the work stack.

(b) In addition to popping up the terminal stack (point F), perform semantic operation as determined by T_i. This may include operations on the work stack.

(c) After checking for the end of the program (point G), perform semantic operations as determined by T_i and S_j. These may include operations on the work stack.

(d) Since the separators are to be ignored (point K), any semantic operation as determined by T_i should be performed before returning to point A.

(e)   In checking for terminals (point B), a special case occurs if $S_j =$ "begin." A new block level must be created in the block table.

The new algorithm is shown in Fig. 4.

In Sections 3–10, execution processes of language semantics will be presented. The algorithms and data structures will be described, and an example will be used to show the details of the execution process. For each example, the program will be stepped through to show how the syntax-checker and execution algorithm applies, with emphasis on the description of the execution of the language semantics.

To help explain the design of the processor, the *execution table* (ET) will be used to illustrate how the data structures are altered at each step of the program. There are ten columns in the table.

(a)   *Step:* program step number,

(b)   *Symbol:* the present symbol S_j being scanned,

(c)   *J:* the present symbol number,

(d)   *TS:* the present top of the terminal stack, T_i,

(e)   *TSP:* index of the top of the *TS*,

(f)   *WS:* contents of the top of the work stack; the fields are separated by commas,

(g)   *WSP:* index of the top of the *WS*,

(h)   *BT:* contents of the present location referenced in the block table; the fields are separated by commas,

(i)   *CBTP:* present location used in the BT,

(j)   *Remarks:* indicates operations performed in data structures other than those listed in the table.

2.5   High-Level Language

The language chosen for the DHLLP is ALGOL 60 (Baumann [1964]) with the following changes in syntax and semantics to permit a simpler processor design:

(a)   Forward labels must be declared in a label declaration. A label is defined as forward if it appears as "goto label; ... ; label: ...."

(b)   The "own" statement has been omitted.

(c)   Expressions used as actual parameters cannot be used as call-by-name in the procedure declaration.

(d)   Arrays and procedures used as actual parameters must be used as call-by-name in the procedure declaration.

(e)   Designational expressions cannot be used as procedure parameters.

(f)   Comments have been omitted.

(g)   The "empty" statement has been omitted.

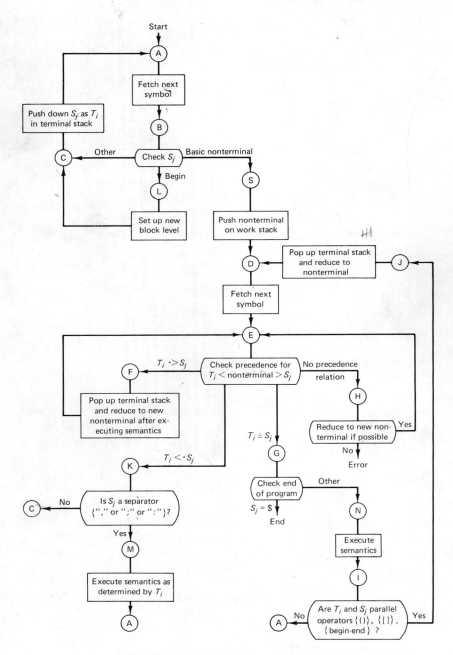

Fig. 4. Syntax-checking and execution algorithm.

In the conventional ALGOL syntax description (Baumann [1964]) there are productions that do not obey the rules needed for an operator precedent grammar. Hence, it was necessary to develop a new syntax description of ALGOL. Based on this new syntax, a set of flowcharts (not included here) was developed to describe the specific path from D to A in Fig. 4 in terms of the nonterminals defined for the ALGOL language.

2.6   An Example of Precedence

A language that consists of the following four rules of grammar is chosen here to illustrate the concept of precedence. This concept is important because the design of the DHLLP depends on it.

$$\langle primary \rangle ::= A|B| \ldots |Z$$
$$\langle factor \rangle ::= \langle primary \rangle|\langle factor \rangle \uparrow \langle primary \rangle$$
$$\langle term \rangle ::= \langle factor \rangle|\langle term \rangle \times \langle factor \rangle$$
$$\langle program \rangle ::= \$\langle term \rangle\$$$

For this example, $\langle primary \rangle$ would be the basic nonterminal and \$, $\uparrow$, and $\times$ the terminals.

The precedence relationships for each nonterminal are the following (where one assumes the form $T_i \langle nonterminal \rangle S_j$):

(a) $\langle primary \rangle: \uparrow > S_j$
(b) $\langle factor \rangle: \times < \uparrow, \times > S_j$ (other than $\uparrow$)
(c) $\langle term \rangle: T_i < \times, \$ \doteq \$$

Whenever T_i and S_j are such that neither terminal appears in the precedence relationships for a given nonterminal, a default reduction is made (e.g., $\langle primary \rangle$ defaults to $\langle factor \rangle$). If a default production does not exist, then there is an error in the program syntax.

Consider the string $\$E \times F \uparrow G \times H\$$. The execution of the string can be followed by using the syntax-checking and execution algorithm in Fig. 4. The state flow is shown in Table II. The table contains three columns: (1) the symbol being scanned, (2) the state flow through the algorithm—each point on the flowchart is represented by a letter and when the actual nonterminal state is reached the point is enclosed in parentheses [e.g., $\langle primary \rangle$(D)], and (3) the stack operation. One can follow the advancement of a $\langle primary \rangle$ to $\langle factor \rangle$ and $\langle term \rangle$ under the appropriate conditions. The advancement is, of course, determined by terminals T_i and S_j that surround the nonterminals and by the precedence between these terminals. Notice that the basic nonterminal E advances all the way to $\langle term \rangle$ but that F advances only to $\langle factor \rangle$ and G only to $\langle primary \rangle$. This allows the operation $F \uparrow G$ to be performed since this is a rule for

TABLE II

State Flow Table

Symbol	State flow	Stack operation	
$	A → B → C → A	PUSH	TS, $
E	B → ⟨primary⟩(D)	PUSH	WS, E
×	E → H → ⟨factor⟩(E) → H → ⟨term⟩(E) → K → C → A	PUSH	TS, ×
F	B → ⟨primary⟩(D)	PUSH	WS, F
↑	E → H → ⟨factor⟩(E) → K → C → A	PUSH	TS, ↑
G	B → ⟨primary⟩(D)	PUSH	WS, G
×	E → F → ⟨factor⟩(E)	POP	WS
		POP	WS
		PUSH	WS, F↑G
		POP	TS
		POP	WS
		POP	WS
		PUSH	WS, E × F↑G
		POP	TS
H	B → ⟨primary⟩(D)	PUSH	WS, H
$	E → H → ⟨factor⟩(E) → F → ⟨term⟩(E) → G	POP	WS
		POP	WS
		PUSH	WS, E × F↑G × H
		POP	TS

⟨factor⟩, and the operation E × (F ↑ G) to be performed since this is the rule for ⟨term⟩.

In all the following sections, the state flow will be implied and not specifically indicated. The important aspect will be the semantics attached to all the terminals. It is only important to understand that there is a precedence relationship between the terminals that will determine the order in which reductions (i.e., operations) are performed. The general precedence for arithmetic and Boolean operators has been defined in the ALGOL report (Baumann [1964]) and the precedence for the other types of terminals is obvious. Hence it is assumed throughout that whenever an operation is performed the proper precedence conditions have been reached. Therefore, the reader will no longer have to concern himself with the state-flow structure of the program. One need simply understand that the logic structure of the DHLLP is built upon the set of precedence relationships for each nonterminal.

It is important to understand that the stack operations in state-flow Table II are not program instructions generated when the original program is translated into a parse string code such as might appear in a stack-oriented machine like the Burroughs B5500. These operations would be built into the hardware logic (or microcode), and executed when a program symbol such as operator + is scanned by the processor.

3. BLOCK STRUCTURE DESIGN

This section describes the design of the basic ALGOL concept, the block.

3.1 Block Structure

A block table (BT) has been designed for the block structure design (Fig. 5). The table has a *top-block table pointer* (TBTP), which keeps track of the top location in the table, a *current-block table pointer* (CBTP), which indicates the present location being referenced in the table, and a *block-level word* (BLW), which keeps track of the present block level. At each block level, the three subtables of the BT (VT, DSAT, and BLS) are stored in the order shown in the figure.

When the BT functions as a stack, the TBTP will keep the location of the top entry made in the innermost block. All future entries into the VT (or DSAT overflow, to be explained later) cause this pointer to advance. When the BT functions as a storage and retrieval table, the CBTP is used as the current location pointer. More will be said about the data structure as the example is described.

The use of the block table will be illustrated by an example (Fig. 6). Appearing under each symbol in the program (Fig. 6a) is the symbol index *j* to aid the reader in following the execution table. The character table appears under the program. An abbreviated precedence table (Table III) is included to enable the reader to follow the syntax-checker and execution

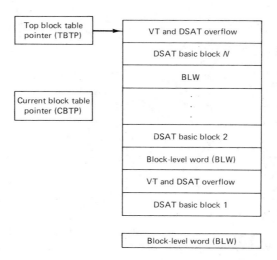

Fig. 5.   Block table data structure with *N*-order block nesting.

```
$     begin  real   A    ,    B    ;    integer  C    ;
(1)   (2)    (3)    (4)  (5)  (6)  (7)  (8)      (9)  (10)


      A    :=   1.   ;    B    :=   2.   ;    C    :=   3    ;
      (11) (12) (13) (14) (15) (16) (17) (18) (19) (20) (21) (22)


      begin real   E    ,    B    ;    E    :=   B    :=   A    end  ;        (a)
      (23)  (24)   (25) (26) (27) (28) (29) (30) (31) (32) (33) (34) (35)


      A    :=   B    end  $
      (36) (37) (38) (39) (40)
```

Word index	Character index									
	0	1	2	3	4	5	6	7	8	9
7	n	d	$							
6		e	n	d	;	A	:=	B		e
5		E	,	B	;	E	:=	B	:=	A
4	b	e	g	i	n		r	e	a	l
3	;	B	:=	2	.	;	C	:=	3	;
2	g	e	r		C	;	A	:=	1	.
1	I	A	,	B	;	i	n	t	e	
0	$	b	e	g	i	n		r	e	a

(b)

Fig. 6. Example of block structure: (a) ALGOL program with symbol count; (b) character table.

TABLE III

Precedence Table Needed for Block Example

Nonterminal	T_i	S_j	Relation
type declaration	real	,	real $<\!\cdot$,
compound tail	begin	;	begin $<\!\cdot$;
		end	begin $\doteq$ end
block head	begin	;	begin $<\!\cdot$;
right part	:=	S_j	:= $\cdot\!>$ S_j
left part	T_i	:=	$T_i <\!\cdot$:=

flowchart. The execution table appears in Table IV. Whenever possible, abbreviations will be used in place of the longer field names for any of the table or stack entries. A summary of these abbreviations is given in the appendix.

3.2 Block Entry Execution

After $ is scanned and stored in the terminal stack, the "begin" (step 2) is scanned. This causes a special operation to be performed on the block

TABLE IV

Execution Table for Block Structure

Step	Symbol	J	TS	TSP	WS	WSP	BT	CBTP	Remarks
1	$	1	$	1					Set BLW 0, 0, 0–0
2	begin	2	begin	2					
3	real	3	real	3					
4	A	4			D, A, R	1	A, 64, R, 0	1	
5	,	5			—	0			
6	B	6			D, B, R	1	B, 65, R, 0	2	
7	;	7	begin	2	—	0			
8	integer	8	integer	3					
9	C	9			D, C, I	1	C, 66, I, 0	3	
10	;	10	begin	2	—	0			
11	A	11			V, 64, R	1			
12	:=	12	:=	3	C, 1,, R	2			
13	1.	13			C, 1,, R	1			
14	;	14	begin	2			1.	64	
15					—	0			
16	B	15			V, 65, R	1			
17	:=	16	:=	3	C, 2,, R	2			
18	2.	17			C, 2,, R	1			
19	;	18	begin	2			2.	65	
20					—	0			
21	C	19			V, 66, I	1			
22	:=	20	:=	3	C, 3, I	2			
23	3	21			C, 3, I	1			
24	;	22	begin	2			3	66	
25					—	0			

#		#							
26	begin	23	begin	3					
27	real	24	real	4					
28	E	25	E		D, E, R	1	0, 0, 0, 01110–0	127	Set BLW 2, 4, 0, 0–0
29	,	26	,		—	0			
30	B	27	B		D, B, R	1		133	
31	;	28	begin	3	—	0		130	
32	E	29	E	4	V, 192, R	1	E, 192, R, 0		
33	:=	30	:=						
34	B	31	B	5	V, 193, R	2	B, 193, R, 0		
35	:=	32	:=						
36	A	33	A	3	V, 64, R	3			
37	end	34	end	3	C, 1, R	3			
	:=		:=	2	C, 1, R	2	1.	193	
	begin		begin	1	C, 1, R	1	1.	192	Restore BLW 0, 0, 0, 0111–0
38		35		2	—	0			
39	begin	36	begin		V, 64, R	1			
40	;	37	;						
41	A	38	A	3	V, 65, R	2			
42	:=	39	:=	2	C, 2, R	2	2.	64	
43	B		B	1	C, 2, R	1			
44	end	40	end	0	—	0			Empty BLW
45	$		$	1					End of program

(handwritten annotation with brace: multiple assignment)

table. An initial set of 64 words (beginning at an integer multiple of 64) is assigned to the new block with the TBTP pointing to the top word. Identifiers will be stored as they are declared in this 64-word set with a hash code entry (the hash code function sums the ASCII code of all the characters of the identifier and keeps the rightmost 6 bits for an address value 0–63) rather than sequential storage. Since the addresses for identifiers are not saved (because the execution always uses the original source code), it would be very inefficient to use a sequential search through the table every time an identifier is scanned. It is not inefficient to have most of the 64-word set empty for two reasons.

(a)   The table is dynamic and hence the block is erased when exited.

(b)   Most of the BT space will be allocated to storing the values assigned to arrays, and hence the number 64 becomes insignificant.

After setting up the new block, a special block-level word is created. It contains four fields.

(a)   *first location (FL)*. This is the first location in the set of 64 in terms of multiples of 64. This value is needed so that the hash code can be added to it to obtain the correct entry into the block table.

(b)   *block identification (ID)*. Each block needs a unique number associated with it. Later on, it will be shown how labels need to be associated with block identifications. The word index in the character table (e.g., zero or four in Fig. 6b) of the "b" in "begin" is used for the identification.

(c)   *procedure or block indicator (I)*. Procedures and blocks are treated in almost the same manner with regard to the declarations. The indicator value for block is zero and for procedure, one.

(d)   *hash table activity (HTA)*. This is actually a set of 64 indicators determining the status of each word in the hash entry set. When an identifier is hashed into an address, a check must be made to see if there is a previous entry in that address. If yes, then if the key (i.e., name of identifier) just hashed is not the same as the key in the table, a collision has occurred and some further action must be taken. Hence, it is necessary initially to zero out the status indicators so that there are no entries as yet. As an entry is made, the activity indicator involved is set to one. The collisions are stored in the block table in the first free locations after the hash set of 64 (i.e., the TBTP is incremented). Collisions involving the same hash code are linked together through a field within the words stored in the table.

3.3   Simple Variable Declaration Execution

When an identifier is scanned, if it is in a declaration (step 4), it is first stored in the work stack. The fields have the following values:

(a) *form:* declaration (D),
(b) *value:* identifier name (e.g., A),
(c) *type:* declaration type (e.g., R).

When the "," or ";" is scanned, the identifier is moved into the DSAT in a location determined by its hash code value. The DSAT section of the block table contains four fields.

(a) *key (K):* Quantity (i.e., identifier name) used to obtain hash code. In this case the key is A (i.e., the 6 rightmost bits of ASCII code for A).

(b) *value link (VL):* Pointer to first available location (i.e., the TBTP is incremented) after the hash code entry set where potential numerical value for the key could be stored. In this case, the first available location is 64.

(c) *type (T):* Declaration type. In this case, R.

(d) *collision link (CL):* Pointer to next location in the block table where a different key with same hash code entry is stored. In this case, there is no collision and the link is zero. The collision entries and value table portion of the BT are, in general, intermixed.

3.4 Assignment Statement Execution

When an identifier is scanned (step 11) and it has previously been declared (the DSAT is checked to see if the identifier is stored there), it is stored in the work stack with the following fields:

(a) *form:* variable pointer to value location in block table (V),
(b) *value:* location in block table where identifier value is stored (e.g., 64),
(c) *type:* identifier type (e.g., R).

When the := is executed the contents of the top element in the work stack is stored in the *value table* (VT) in the location indicated by the second field of the next-to-top element in the work stack (steps 11–13). The top element is then placed into the next-to-top element and the stack is popped. The assignment value is retained until one is sure that there are no more multiple assignments. In step 14, the value "1." is stored in location 64, which is the storage word for the value of A. Notice the multiple assignment operation in steps 32–37. When the assignment value is a variable link, the value must be changed to a "constant" value (step 37). The work stack fields for a constant, using step 18 as an example, are as follows:

(a) *form:* constant (C),
(b) *value:* actual value (e.g., "2."),
(c) *type:* constant type (e.g., R).

3.5   Nested Block Execution

When a nested block is encountered (step 26), the block-level word from the outer block must be saved before the new block-level word is created. This word is put into the last position of the words allocated to the outer block in the block table. Since all allocation is made in blocks of 64 and since location 67 is the first free location, the block level is stored in location 127 with the new block starting in 128. Notice that in storing the word, the value of the 2nd–4th positions of the hash table activity field is one to indicate that A, B, and C are occupying the locations.

The new identifiers are declared and stored in the new hash table set of 64 (locations 128–191). Whenever an identifier is scanned and the block table is searched to see if it is already declared, the search begins from the locations referenced by the present block-level word. If the identifier cannot be found in this section, other sections of the block table are scanned by using the previous block-level words, with the last word stored referenced first.

3.6   Block Exit Execution

When a block is exited (e.g., "end" is scanned), the only operation required is to restore the previous block-level word (step 41). This effectively erases all the space allocated to the old block.

4.   ARITHMETIC AND BOOLEAN EXPRESSION EXECUTION

In this section, arithmetic and Boolean-expression-type execution will be described. The two most significant features of this type of execution are the strong dependence on terminal precedence and the use of an arithmetic unit to perform the basic operations.

4.1   Arithmetic Unit

Whenever a reduction takes place involving any arithmetic or Boolean terminal (e.g., + or =), the operation must involve the actual execution of the semantics of the terminal. As an example, in the case of + the two arguments must actually be added and the resulting sum retained. The function of the *arithmetic unit* (AU) is to perform this execution. If the terminal is a binary operator, the top element and the next-to-top element of the work stack are sent as operands to the AU. If the terminal is a unary operator, only the top element of the WS is needed. The AU performs the following tasks:

(a)   Checks the operands to see if they are actual values (i.e., the form field in WS is C) or links (i.e., the form field in WS is V). All links must be changed to actual values.

(b)   Checks the operands to see if the type field in WS agrees with the basic operator type (e.g., arithmetic or Boolean).

(c)   For arithmetic operations, checks to see if the operand types agree (e.g., both real or both integer). If not, the integer operand value is converted to a real value.

(d)   Executes based on operator semantics. For a unary operator, the result is returned in the top element of the WS. For a binary operator, the result is returned in the next-to-top element of the WS (the top element will then be popped).

4.2   Use of Precedence

The arithmetic operator precedence relationships offer a good example to illustrate how the syntax-checking is formed and how one can follow the specific flowcharts for each nonterminal. The precedence relationships needed for this example are shown in Table V.

Remember that whenever a precedence check is made, and T_i appears adjacent to the nonterminal while S_j does not, the reduction is made. Also, if S_j appears adjacent to the nonterminal but T_i does not, S_j is automatically pushed down onto the terminal stack. The table reflects the order in which reductions could be made. After recognition of a variable, the next reduction would be to a ⟨primary⟩ followed by a ⟨factor⟩ through to an ⟨arithmetic expression⟩. A parenthesized expression results in a reduction to ⟨primary⟩ and the loop begins again.

4.3   Arithmetic Expression Example

Assume the assignment statement shown in Fig. 7 was inserted into the block example at symbol index 23 (Fig. 6a). Although this example illus-

TABLE V

Abbreviated Precedence Table for Arithmetic Expression Example

Nonterminal	T_i	S_j	Relation
⟨primary⟩	↑		$↑ ⋗ S_j$
⟨factor⟩	$\{× \|/\| ÷\}$	↑	$\{× \|/\| ÷\} ⋖ ↑$
⟨term⟩	$\{+\|-\}$	$\{× \|/\| ÷\}$	$\{+\|-\} ⋖ \{× \|/\| ÷\}$
⟨simple arithmetic expression⟩		$\{+\|-\}$	$T_i ⋖ \{+\|-\}$
⟨arithmetic expression⟩	(	)	($≐$)
⟨right part⟩	:=		$:= ⋗ S_j$
⟨left part⟩		:=	$T_i ⋖ :=$

A	:=	B	×	(	A	+	C	/	B	)	+	2 .	↑	B	;
(23)	(24)	(25)	(26)	(27)	(28)	(29)	(30)	(31)	(32)	(33)	(34)	(35)	(36)	(37)	(38)

Fig. 7.   Arithmetic expression example.

trates the execution of arithmetic operators, all comments also apply to Boolean operators, since they are executed in a similar fashion. The execution table (Table VI) has been included to help the reader follow the execution.

The assignment statement begins with the left part, "A," getting put onto the work stack and the := being pushed down onto the terminal stack. The assignment operation will be the last one to be executed in the statement. The scan of the right part of the assignment statement begins with "B" being pushed down onto the work stack. In being pushed down, "B" has reached the state of a ⟨term⟩ nonterminal. The new symbol $S_j = \times$ is scanned and pushed down onto the terminal stack. One can follow the steps by assuming each new basic nonterminal scanned reaches the ⟨primary⟩ state. One then scans the T_i and S_j columns until one finds a match with the actual T_i stored on the stack or the actual S_j being scanned. The decision on what is to be done when a match is found is shown in the execution algorithm flowchart (Fig. 4). Assume a reduction always leads to the next nonterminal listed in the table.

In the current example, all the terminals must be stored until finally the) is scanned. At this point, the table shows that if $T_i = /$, a reduction can take place from ⟨factor⟩ to ⟨term⟩ (step 36). Before any arithmetic can be done, the contents of the work stack must be checked to see that actual values are stored in the two top entries. In this case, pointers to the value table for B (entry 5) and C (entry 4) are stored in the stack. The pointers are used now to obtain the values from the value table and the values for B and C are stored back into the work stack.

Once the values are obtained, the actual execution of the / operation can take place in the arithmetic unit. In this case the value 1.5 will be stored in location 4 at the top of the stack when the / operation is completed and the reduction is made to ⟨term⟩.

Now the + will also be performed and the reduction to ⟨simple arithmetic expression⟩ made. The pair (and) results in the reduction to ⟨primary⟩. Now the × can be performed, resulting in a reduction to ⟨term⟩. The terminal stack gets new entries + and ↑ (steps 44 and 46). Finally, when the semicolon is scanned, successive reductions involving ↑ and + are made, the assignment is made, and the value 9.0 is stored in the value table for A.

TABLE VI

Execution Table for Arithmetic Expression Example

Step	Symbol	J	TS	TSP	WS	WSP	BT	CBTP	Remarks
26	A	23			V, 64, R	1			
27	:=	24	:=	3					
28	B	25	×	4	V, 65, R	2			
29	×	26	(	5					
30	(	27							
31	A	28			V, 64, R	3			
32	+	29	+	6					
33	C	30			V, 66, I	4			
34	/	31	/	7					
35	B	32			V, 65, R	5			
36	)	33	+	6	C, 2,, R	5			
37					C, 3,, R	4			
38					C, 1.5, R	3			
39					C, 1,, R	3			
40			(	5	C, 2.5, R	6			
41			×	4		2			
42			:=	3	C, 2,, R	2			
43		34			C, 5.0, R	2			
44	+	35	+	4		3			
45	2.			5	C, 2,, R	3			
46	↑	36	↑			4			
47	B	37	+	4	V, 65, R	4			
48	;	38	+	4	C, 2,, R	4			
49					C, 4,, R	3			
50			:=	3	C, 9.0, R	2			
51			begin	2	C, 9.0, R	1	9.	64	
52					—	0			

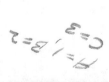

5. CONDITIONAL EXPRESSIONS AND STATEMENT EXECUTION

There are many types of conditional expressions and statements that appear in ALGOL. They will all be placed under the general classification "conditional." The semantics are straightforward: if the Boolean expression is true, execute the "then" clause and skip to the end of the conditional; if the expression is false, skip the "then" clause and execute the "else" clause, if it exists. Because of the characteristics of the DHLLP (i.e., the source language is executed with no transformation), it would be inefficient to scan the skipped clause on every pass through the conditional. Hence, a special table has been developed to store the necessary information about the conditional so that the scan need only be made once during the entire execution.

5.1   Node Table Data Structure

This table, called the *node table* (NT), is used not only for conditionals but also for "for" statements and for label declarations (to be described later). This table, unlike the block table, does not expand and contract with the block level. Upon the scanning of any new conditional (or "for" statement or label), an entry is made into the table and never erased. The general structure of the NT (Fig. 8) is similar to the BT in that the entries are hash-coded into their locations. The first 64 locations are used for the hash code function and the collisions are stored in the first free location (i.e., TNTP is incremented) after the basic set. There is a *node activity word* (NAW)

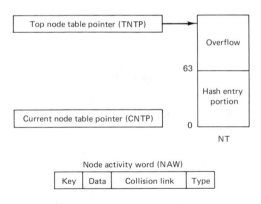

Fig. 8.   Data structure for the node table.

A	:=	if	B	=	C	then	8.	else	4.	;	
(23)	(24)	(25)	(26)	(27)	(28)	(29)	(30)	(31)	(32)	(33)	(a)

Word index	Character index										
	0	1	2	3	4	5	6	7	8	9	
6	.	;									(b)
5	h	e	n	8	.	e	l	s	e	4	
4	A	:=	i	f		B	=	C	.	t	

Fig. 9. Conditional expression example: (a) ALGOL program; (b) character table.

that serves the same purpose as the hash table activity field in the block-level word. The basic format of node table entries is as follows:

(a)   *key (K):* quantity used to obtain hash code value,

(b)   *data (D):* information needed for node type,

(c)   *collision link (C):* pointer to next word in NT that has the same hash code value for a different key,

(d)   *type (T):* type of node (e.g., C—conditional, F—"for" statement, L—label).

5.2   Conditional Entries in Node Table

In this example (Fig. 9), the node type is C for conditional. The key used is the word index for the "t" in "then" (e.g., "t" is in word index 4). The data field contains three subfields.

(a)   *"end" pointer:* the word and character index of the first character after the end of the conditional (e.g., 61 for the position of the semicolon).

(b)   *"else" clause indicator:* indicates presence (value 1) or absence (value 0) of an "else" clause.

(c)   *"else" pointer:* the word and character index of the "e" in "else" (e.g., 55).

In Section 2.4, the general format of the work stack was outlined. The form for the conditional is N and the type is C. However, the value field has six subfields.

(a)   *Boolean expression value:* the value of a Boolean expression from the "if" clause. If the value is one, the "then" clause is executed.

(b)   *key:* described for conditional node.

(c)   *"end" pointer:* described for the conditional node.

(d)   *"else" clause indicator:* described for the conditional node.

TABLE VII

Execution Table for Conditional Example

Step	Symbol	J	TS	TSP	WS	WSP	BT	CBTP	Remarks
26	A	23			V, 64, R	1			
27	:=	24	:=	3					
28	if	25	if	4					
29	B	26		5	V, 65, R	2			
30	=	27	=						
31	C	28			V, 66, R	3			
32	then	29	if	4	C, 3, R	3			Set up cond. node in WS / Scan to "else"
33					C, 2, R	2			
					C, 0, B	2			
34		29			N, 0, 4, 0, 0, 0, 1, C	2			
35	8,	30							
36	else	31			N, 0, 4, 0, 1, 55, 1, C	2			Add else clause info to node
37	4.	32			C, 4, R	3			
38	;		:= 3		C, 4, R	2			Store node in NT, 4: 4, 61, 1, 55, 0, C; turn position 5 in NAW on
39	begin		begin	2	C, 4, R	1	4.	64	
40					—	0			

(e)   *"else" pointer:* described for the conditional node.

(f)   *first-time indicator:* if the conditional has never been stored in the node table, this indicator has value 1 (otherwise, it is set to zero).

5.3   Conditional Example

Consider the example of the conditional expression used to compute an arithmetic expression (see Fig. 9). Assume that this statement is inserted into the program described for the block example (see Fig. 6). The new terminals to be considered are "if," "then," and "else." They are all of equal precedence and, when compared (point E of Fig. 4), the path will lead through point G to N to I and then to A. The first few symbols (steps 26–31, Table VII) are handled in the usual fashion. When "then" is scanned, the = is executed, leaving a Boolean value in location 2 of the work stack after the stack is popped. At this point, location 2 is converted into the node form for conditional. The node table is checked to see if the conditional is already there. It is not, and so the various fields must be initialized. The form field is changed to N, the type field to C, and in the value field the Boolean expression value is kept. All other subfields are zeroed except the key field, which is set to four (the word position of "then"), and the first time indicator, which is set to one.

Since it is the first time, the conditional must be scanned without execution until an "else" is encountered. Otherwise, the new character word index could automatically be set to the "else" position, since this information would be available in the work stack. At this point, since the first-time indicator is on, the "else" information is added to the node in the work stack. This includes turning the "else" clause indicator to one and storing the "else" position, 55. The execution algorithm is now activated, since the Boolean expression was false. When the semicolon is scanned, the conditional node is stored in the node table, and "if" is popped up. The "end" pointer (i.e., 61 for the position of the semicolon) is stored in the NT in place of the Boolean expression.

In the case of a conditional expression, the top two elements in the work stack must be switched before the node operation can be performed, since an expression value is presently on top (i.e., the constant 4). After the transfer is completed, the assignment operation can be performed.

If the Boolean expression had been true, the only difference would have been that when "8." was scanned, it would have been put on top of the work stack and the "4." in the "else" clause would have been ignored. All other operations would have been performed in precisely the same way.

6.   LABELS AND TRANSFER EXECUTION

This section is divided into two main areas, discussing (1) how labels are declared and (2) how the transfer is implemented. Since the two areas are so closely related, they have been combined into one section.

6.1   Algorithm for Nonterminal Pushdown on Work Stack

In Section 2.5, the syntax-checking algorithm was altered to allow for the execution phase (see Fig. 4). One block that was added, "Push Nonterminal on Work Stack" (points S–D), has already been described in general terms in the execution diagrams of the earlier section. However, with the introduction of labels it is now time to formalize the block operation into a flowchart algorithm (see Fig. 10). At this time, the nonlabel portion of the

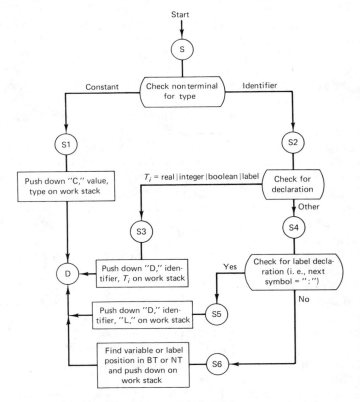

Fig. 10.   Algorithm for nonterminal pushdown on work stack.

flowchart will be explained. The label portion will be explained as the label example (Fig. 12) is described.

If the nonterminal is a constant, its value is pushed onto the stack (point S1). An example is step 37 in Table VII, where "4." is pushed down. If the nonterminal is an identifier, a check is made to see if it is in a declaration (point S2). If it is, the identifier name is pushed down (point S3). An example is step 4 in Table IV, where "A" is pushed down. The explanation of the label-declaration check (point S5) will be postponed. If the identifier has already been declared, its position in the block table is stored on the stack (point S6). An example is step 26 in Table VII, when the position of "A" in the BT, 64, is stored.

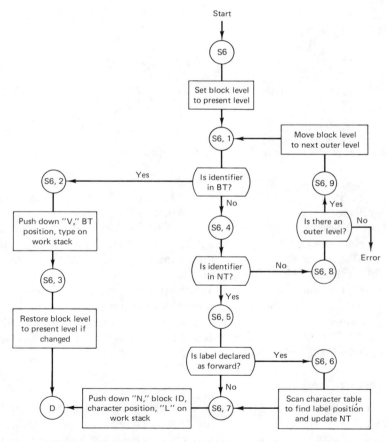

Fig. 11.   Algorithm for finding variables and labels in the BT or VT.

Word index	Character index									
	0	1	2	3	4	5	6	7	8	9
7	;	M	:	I	:=	3	e	n	d	$
6	g	o	t	o		M		e	n	d
5	n		l	a	b	e	l		M	;
4	o	t	o		L	;	b	e	g	i	(a)
3		l	=	1	t	h	e	n		g
2	;	L	:	l	:=	l	+	1	;	if
1	e	g	e	r		l	;	l	:=	0
0	$	b	e	g	i	n		i	n	t

$ (1)	begin (2)	integer (3)	I (4)	; (5)	I (6)	:= (7)	0 (8)	; (9)
L (10)	: (11)	I (12)	:= (13)	I (14)	+ (15)	1 (16)	; (17)	
if (18)	I (19)	= (20)	1 (21)	then (22)	goto (23)	L (24)	; (25)	(b)
begin (26)	label (27)	M (28)	; (29)	goto (30)	M (31)	end (32)	; (33)	
M (34)	: (35)	I (36)	:= (37)	3 (38)	end (39)	$ (40)		

Fig. 12.   Example illustrating labels and transfers: (a) character table; (b) ALGOL program.

The block S6–D can be further expanded to show the significance of the block level (see Fig. 11). The block structure of ALGOL allows the same variables to be declared at different levels of the program. When referencing a variable, the declarations should be checked from the present level outwards. Hence, the algorithm for finding the identifier must loop through all the block levels. The label segment S6, 4–D will be explained later.

Label and transfer execution will be illustrated using a simple example (see Fig. 12). The execution diagrams for the program are shown in Table VIII. Execution is approximately the same as the early example until step 11 is reached. Since the next symbol is a colon, "L" is stored as a label (see Fig. 10, points S–S2–S4–S5–D).

6.2   Label Declaration

When the colon is scanned as the next symbol, the node table must be checked to see if the label has already been declared on a previous scan. Once the label is stored in the NT, it is never removed. This condition keeps scanning by the interpreter, after transfers occur, to a minimum. On backward transfers (i.e., label appears before the "goto" statement) there is no scanning required. On forward labels (i.e., label appears after the "goto" statement), there is only one scan necessary and that occurs only if the "goto" statement is ever executed.

The node table format was described in Section 5.1. The data field for the label entry is as follows:

(a) *block identification:* This is the identification in the block-level word (see Section 3.2). Since labels with the same name can occur at many levels, a particular block must be associated with every label.

(b) *character table position:* This is the word and character index of the first character after the colon. When the "goto" statement is executed, the character table pointer is reset to this value.

The key field is the label name and the hash code function is the same as for the DSAT. However, when the keys match, a further match of the block identification is also required.

In this example, the following information is stored in the NT:

$$\text{position } 12: \quad L, 0, 23, 0, L$$

where L is the identifier name, 0 the block ID, 23 the character table pointer, 0 the collision link, and L the type.

Execution continues with the updating of I and the execution of the conditional statement. Since the Boolean expression is true, the transfer statement is executed (steps 27–28).

6.3   Transfer Execution

When the label following "goto" is scanned (step 28), its information must be retrieved from the node table (i.e., Fig. 10, point S6). Each block level is checked in sequence until the label is found in the NT. When the semi-colon is scanned, the transfer is performed. The following operations must be considered after "goto" is popped up from the terminal stack (Fig. 4, point F):

(a)   If transfer is from within a "for" or conditional statement, the terminal (i.e., "if" or "for") is popped up and, after switching with the label node, the node in the work stack corresponding to the terminal is also popped up.

(b)   If transfer is out of present block, all terminals pushed down during that block must be popped up including the "begin." Any node corresponding to "if" or "for" must also be popped up. Also, the BLW from the next outer block is removed from the BT and used as the present BLW.

TABLE VIII

Execution Table for Transfer Example

Step	Symbol	J	TS	TSP	WS	WSP	BT	CBTP	Remarks
1	$	1	$	1					
2	begin	2	begin	2					
3	integer	3	integer	3					
4	I	4			D, I, I	1	I, 64, I, 0	9	
5	;	5	begin	2	—	0			
6	I	6			V, 64, I	1			
7	:=	7	:=	3					
8	0	8			C, 0, I	2			
9	;	9	begin	2	C, 0, I	1	0	64	
10					—	0			
11	L	10			D, L, L	1			1—Store label in NT 12: L, 0, 23, 0, L
12	:	11			—	0			
13	I	12			V, 64, I	1			
14	:=	13	:=	3					
15	I	14			V, 64, I	2			
16	+	15	+	4					
17	I	16			C, 1, I	3			
18	;	17	:=	3	C, 1, I	2			
19			begin	2	C, 1, I	1	1	64	
20					—	0			
21	if	18	if	3					
22	I	19			V, 64, I	1			
23	=	20	=	4					
24	I	21			C, 1, I	2			
25	then	22	if	3	C, 1, B	1			2—Set up conditional node in WS

Step	Token	Node	Stack sym	Lvl	Generated code	n	Value	Action
26	goto				N, 1, 3, 0, 0, 0, 1, C	1		
27	L	23	goto	4	N, 0, 23, L	2		3—Switch 1 and 2 in WS and pop. Reset CCTP to 23.
28	;	24	if	3	N, 0, 23, L	1		
29		25	begin	2	N, 0, 23, L	0		
30					—	1		
31	I	12	:=	3	V, 64, I	0		
32	:=	13	+	4	V, 64, I	1		
33	I	14	I	3	C, 1, I	3		
34	+	15	+	4	C, 2, I	2		
35	I	16	I	3	C, 2, I	1	2	
36	;	17	;	2	—	0	64	
37		18	if	3	V, 64, I	1		
38		19	I	4	C, 1, I	2		
39		20	=		C, 0, B	2		
40	if	21	I	3	N, 0, 3, 0, 0, 0, 1, C	1		4—Set up conditional node in WS and scan to ";"
41	I	22	then					
42	=							
43	I							
44	then							
45								
46	goto	23		2	begin		0	5—Store WS in NT 3: 3, 45, 0, 0, 0, C
47	L	24						
48	;	25					127	6—Save BLW in BT
49	begin	26		3	begin		0, 0, 0, 0...010...0 (10th position)	
50	label	27		4	label			

TABLE VIII (continued)

Step	Symbol	J	TS	TSP	WS	WSP	BT	CBTP	Remarks
51	M	28			D, M, L	1			7—Store label in NT 13: M, 4, 0, L
52	;	29	begin	3	—	0			
53	goto	30	goto	4					
54	M	31			N, 0, 73, L	1			8—Find M in CT. Store new info in NT
55	end	32	begin	3					9—Reset CCTP to 73 and restore old BLW
56		36	begin	2	—	0			
57	I	37			V, 64, I	1			
58	:=	38	:=	3	C, 3, I	2			
59	3	39			C, 3, I	1		64	
60	end		begin	2	—	0	3		
61									
62	$		$	1					
63	$	40							10—Program completed

(c)   Step (b) is repeated until the block ID in the BLW matches the block ID in the label node in the work stack.

(d)   Pop up label node in work stack and reset character table pointer to value in label node.

The algorithm is shown in Fig. 13.

Because execution of the transfer statement occurs inside the conditional statement, the conditional node being constructed in the work stack does not get stored in the NT. However, on the next pass through the conditional, it is stored (step 48).

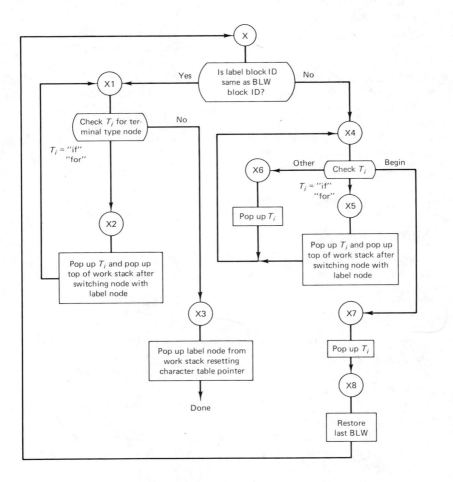

Fig. 13.   Algorithm for executing transfers.

6.4   Forward-Label Declaration

A special case occurs when the label appears before a colon in a statement after it first appears in a transfer statement. This case is called the forward-label declaration. One way of handling label declarations is simply to begin scanning the program characters to find the label followed by a colon and at the same time to search the NT for a label declaration. This operation must be performed once for every label encountered after a "goto." It is obviously very inefficient, especially for a long block where the label appears early in the block. An efficient solution is to require forward-label declaration to be explicit, i.e., the label must appear in a label declaration statement.

When the declaration is executed (step 52) the label is stored in the NT with the block ID and the character table position both set to zero. Later, just before the transfer is executed (step 54), the label is scanned again and this time a forward search is initiated (i.e., Fig. 11, points S6, 6–S6, 7) to find its declared position following the colon. This scan need only be made the first time, for the next time the label declaration is scanned the node table is first checked to see if the label had been entered previously.

In this example, the transfer is outside the block and the outer block-level word must be restored (step 55).

7.   ARRAY DESIGN

7.1   Array Storage

Arrays are reduced when stored in the VT from an n-dimensional configuration into a one-dimensional structure. The form of the storage is shown in Fig. 14. There are six types of information stored.

(a)   *Pointer to first element:* This is the first location allocated to the array and its location is stored in the *link field* (VL) of the DSAT for that array. It points to the first location where the actual array element values are stored.

(b)   *Lower bound (lb):* The lower bound for each bounds-pair in the declaration is stored in the table.

(c)   *Upper bound (ubd):* The upper bound for each bounds-pair in the declaration is stored in the table.

(d)   *Base (b):* This is a special computed quantity used to determine the number of elements in the $(n - 1)$ previous dimensions (i.e., for the nth dimension, the base is $(n - 1)!$).

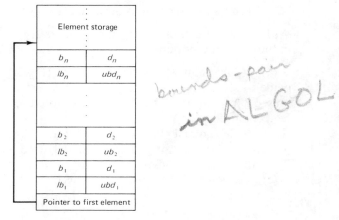

Fig. 14.   Storage allocation of arrays in value table.

(e)   *Difference (d):* This is the computed difference between the upper and lower limits.

(f)   *Element storage:* This is the storage area for the actual array elements.

The elements are stored with the left-most dimension changing the fastest. For an n-dimensional array, $2n + 1$ locations are needed for the parameter information (i.e., lb, ubd, b, d) in addition to the space for the array elements themselves. For an array declared as $A[0:1,0:1]$, the elements in consecutively increasing locations are $A[0,0]$, $A[1,0]$, $A[0,1]$, and $A[1,1]$.

The formula used for computing the base is

$$b_1 = 1$$

$$b_i = b_{i-1} \cdot d_{i-1}$$

The ith difference d_i is defined as

$$d_i = ubd_i - lb_i + 1$$

When an array is referenced, the location of the specific element within the array is computed and used as the VT pointer in the value field of the work stack reference (where the form is V). The following equation is used where se_i is the value of the ith subscript expression and n the number of dimensions:

$$\text{location} = \text{location (first element)} + \sum_{i=1}^{n} (se_i - lb_i) \cdot b_i$$

7.2   Changes in Execution Algorithm

With the introduction of arrays, there are a few changes that must be made in the execution flowchart.

(a)   After point M has been executed (Fig. 4), a special check must be made to see if $T_i = [$ for the case when $S_j = $ ":". If $S_j = $ ":", the transfer must be to point C, since ":" must be stored so that the upper bound can be recognized.

(b)   After point I (Fig. 4), if $S_j = $ "array" and $T_i = $ "real," "Boolean," or "integer," instead of going immediately to point A, S_j is pushed in with T_i on the terminal stack.

(c)   At point S2 (Fig. 10), the T_i check should now include "real array," "Boolean array," "integer array," and "array."

(d)   After point S4 (Fig. 10), if $S_j = $ ":", an additional check must be made before stating that the identifier is a label. Since ":" is used to separate bounds-pairs, T_i must be checked for [. The terminal stack is scanned from top to bottom until one of two events occurs.

(1)   *Terminal is [:* identifier is not a label and the flowchart proceeds to point S6.

(2)   *Terminal is "begin" or semicolon:* identifier is a label and flowchart proceeds to point S5.

7.3   Program Execution

The example used to illustrate array implementation is shown in Fig. 15. The execution table follows (Table IX). Execution proceeds normally until the terminal "array" is scanned. At this point the two terminals, "real" and "array," are packed together on the terminal stack. Now the array declaration can begin.

7.3.1   *Array Segment Execution*

There are two types of array segments: (1) the array name followed by "," and (2) the array name followed by [. In the former, nothing can be done until the latter has been scanned. This is the situation at step 6. The identifier A remains on the work stack and the next array identifier will be scanned (step 7).

The scan of the [initializes the construction of the bounds-pair list within the array segment. At this time the array identifier is stored in the DSAT as a normal identifier and the VT pointer is stored back on WS (step 8). The base b_1 and difference d_1 parameters are initialized for the first dimension (i.e., $b_1 = 1$, $d_1 = 0$) in step 9. Further discussion of array segments must be postponed until the bounds-pair list has been described.

Word index	Character index									
	0	1	2	3	4	5	6	7	8	9
4	,	1	]	:=	0	e	n	d	$	
3	1	:	2	]	;	A	[	1	,	1
2	B	[	0	:	2	,	0	:	1	,
1	I		a	r	r	a	y		A	,
0	$	b	e	g	i	n		r	e	a

(a)

$	begin	real	array	A	,	B	[	0	:	2
(1)	(2)	(3)	(4)	(5)	(6)	(7)	(8)	(9)	(10)	(11)

,	0	:	1	,	1	:	2	]	;
(12)	(13)	(14)	(15)	(16)	(17)	(18)	(19)	(20)	(21)

(b)

A	[	1	,	1	,	1	]	:=	0
(22)	(23)	(24)	(25)	(26)	(27)	(28)	(29)	(30)	(31)

end	$
(32)	(33)

Fig. 15. Illustration of array execution: (a) character table; (b) ALGOL program.

7.3.2 Lower-Bound Execution

When the lower limit is scanned its value will be stored on top of the work stack (step 10). When the colon is scanned, the bounds-pair is set up on the WS replacing the lower bound. This introduces a new form to the WS:

(a) *form:* array parameter pair (A),
(b) *value:* (1) the lower bound and upper bound, (2) base and difference,
(c) *type:* (1) *bounds-pair* (BD), if value (1) is used, (2) *base pair* (BS), if value (2) is used.

7.3.3 Upper-Bound Execution

After the upper bound is scanned (step 12), the bounds-pair in the WS can be finalized by storing the top of the WS in the right side of the next-to-top of the WS (i.e., the A–BD) and popping the stack.

7.3.4 Bounds-Pair Execution

When the comma is scanned, the bounds-pair can be finalized (step 14). This means computing d_i for the base pair from the upper- and lower-bounds-pair values. At this point both the bounds and base pairs can be stored in the VT in consecutive locations beyond the first location assigned to the array identifier. The pointer to the BT (TBTP) is incremented by two.

The execution of the bounds-pair is repeated in steps 16–21 and 22–27. The only difference from the initial bounds-pair is that the new base must be computed at the , or] (see steps 20 and 26).

TABLE IX

Execution Table for Array Example

Step	Symbol	J	TS	TSP	WS	WSP	BT	CBTP	Remarks
1	$	1	$	1					
2	begin	2	begin	2					
3	real	3	real	3					
4	array	4	real array	3					Pack real array
5	A	5			D, A, A	1			
6	,	6				2			
7	B	7			D, B, A	2			Declare B
8	[	8	[	4	V, 64, A	2	B, 64, A, 0	2	Set up base pair
9	0	9			A, 1, 0, BS	3			
10					C, 0, I	4			
11	:	10	:	5	A, 0, 0, BD	4			Set up lb_1 in A–BD
12	2	11			C, 2, I	5			
13			[	4	A, 0, 2, BD	4			
14	,	12			A, 1, 3, BS	3	0, 2	65	Store BD and BS
15							1, 3	66	
16	0	13			C, 0, I	4			
17	:	14	:	5	A, 0, 0, BD	4			
18	1	15			C, 1, I	5			
19			[	4	A, 0, 1, BD	4			
20	,	16			A, 3, 2, BS	3	0, 1	67	
21							3, 2	68	
22	1	17			C, 1, I	4			
23	:	18	:	5	A, 1, 0, BD	4			
24	2	19			C, 2, I	5			
25			[	4	A, 1, 2, BD	4			

Line	Token	No.	Keyword	N1	Instruction	N2	Value	N3	Comment
26	1	20	real array	3	A, 6, 2, BS	3	1, 2	69	Store array pointer
27							6, 2	70	
28	;	21			V, 64, A	2	71	64	Increment TBTP by 12
29					V, 83, A	1	A, 83, A, 0	1	Transfer array parameters
30							0, 2	84	from B to A
31							1, 3	85	
32							0, 1	86	
33							3, 2	87	
34							1, 2	88	
35							6, 2	89	
36					V, 64, A	1	90	83	
37			begin	2	—	0			
38	A	22			V, 83, A	1			Initialize subscripts
39	[	23	[	3	V, 84, R	1			
40					C, 90, I	2			
41					A, 1, 3, BS	3			
42					A, 0, 2, BD	4			
43	1	24			C, 1, I	5			
44	,	25			C, 1, I	4			
45					C, 1, I	3			
46					C, 91, I	2			
47					V, 86, R	1			Perform *se* operation
48					A, 3, 2, BS	3			
49					A, 0, 1, BD	4			
50	1	26			C, 1, I	5			
51					C, 1, I	4			
52					C, 3, I	3			
53					C, 94, I	2			
54					V, 88, R	1			
55		27			A, 6, 2, BS	3			

TABLE IX (continued)

Step	Symbol	J	TS	TSP	WS	WSP	BT	CBTP	Remarks
56					A, 1, 2, BD	4			
57	1	28			C, 1, I	5			
58	]	29			C, 0, I	4			
59					C, 0, I	3			
60					C, 94, I	2			
61			begin	2	V, 94, R	1			Set array pointer
62	:=	30	:=	3					
63	0	31			C, 0, I	2			
64	end	32	begin	2	C, 0, I	1	0	94	
65					—	0			
66			$	1					
67	$	33							

7.3.5   Bounds-Pair List Execution

After all the pairs have been computed and stored in the VT, the value of the BT pointer (TBTP) plus one is stored in the original location assigned to the array (see step 28).

The TBTP is now incremented by the amount $b_3 \cdot d_3$ (i.e., 6 × 2 or 12).

7.3.6   Type 1 Array Segment Execution

At this point, WS is checked to see if there are other array identifiers. Since A is on the work stack, it is now declared (step 29) in the same manner as B, and the work stack entry now points to the VT where A values will be stored. Now all the parameters for B are stored in locations similar to the locations for A (steps 29–36). Since there are no more arrays, the work stack can be popped.

7.3.7   Subscripted-Variable Execution

The following steps 38–60 are concerned with setting up a subscripted variable. At the end of the execution, a pointer to the value location in the VT of the particular element of the array being referenced will be stored in the work stack. Once this reference is stored, there is no apparent difference between a simple variable and a subscripted variable.

When the array identifier is scanned, its VT pointer is stored on the WS (step 38). When the [is scanned, the VT pointer in the WS (location 1) is moved to point to the first set of bounds-pairs (location 84 in the VT) and the top entry in the work stack is set up with a pointer to the location in the VT where the first element is stored (location 90). The pointer is updated after each subscript expression is computed to get the new element location. The pointer to the set of bounds-pairs is incremented by two to get the next set.

7.3.8   Subscript Expression Execution

After the subscript has been computed (step 43) and stored on top of the WS, many operations are performed as the comma is scanned.

(a)   *Test range of subscript.* Check that $ubd - se > 0$ (step 44). If not, there is a range error.

(b)   *Compute se − lb.* If the quantity is negative, there is a range error. Pop up the top of the WS and store $se - lb$ in place of the bounds-pair ("1" is stored in the WS in step 44).

(c) *Compute (se − lb) · b.* This gives the displacement from the first location. The result is stored in the base-pair position in the WS and the stack is popped ("1" is stored in the WS in step 45).

(d) *Add displacement to array element location pointer.* The updated element pointer is set ("91" is stored in the WS in step 46).

(e) *Move array pointer to the next set of bounds-pairs.* ("86" is stored in the WS in step 47).

After each expression is computed, the array element location pointer is modified, and when the] is scanned (step 58), the final operation is to switch the location pointer with the pointer to the bounds-pair and pop up the WS. The final value is 94. This location corresponds to the storage of A(1, 1, 1).

8.   "FOR" STATEMENT DESIGN

The "for" statement semantics, as defined for ALGOL (Baumann *et al.* [1964]), can be illustrated in the following:

initialize; test; statement S; advance; successor

for list exhausted

"Initialize" means to perform the first assignment of the "for" clause variable. "Advance" means to perform the next assignment of the variable. "Test" determines if the last assignment has been done. If so, the execution continues with the successor of the "for" statement. If not, "statement S" following the "do" is executed. In performing the assignment, control can proceed from one "for" list element to the next when the element is exhausted.

8.1   Data Structure

To implement the "for" statement, the following data structure is needed when the "for" statement is recognized, and information must be stored in the WS. The "for" statement uses the node table structure:

(a) *form:* N
(b) *value:* (1) *key:* the word position of the := following the "for" control variable,

(2) *"end" pointer:* the position of the first character following the "do statement S,"

(3) *"for" list element pointer:* the position of the first character in the present "for" list element,

(4) *"do" pointer:* the position of the first character following the "do,"

(5) *first-time indicator:* indicates the presence or absence of
the "for" statement information in the NT. If it is the
first scan, the indicator is set to one,

(6) *first time "do" indicator:* indicates whether it is the first
scan of the "do" statement. If yes, the indicator is set
to one,

(7) *initial condition indicator:* indicates first execution of a
given "for" list element,

(8) *sign indicator:* saves the sign in the (V–C) operation.

(c)   *type:* "for"

The "for" statement entry into the NT takes the following form:

(a)   *key:* defined above
(b)   *data:* "end" pointer⎫
              "do" pointer ⎬ defined above
(c)   *collision link:* see node table format (Section 5.1)
(d)   *type:* F

8.2   Program Execution

The implementation of the various nonterminals used to describe "for"
statements (i.e., "for" list element, "for" list, and "for" clause) has been
described elsewhere (Bloom [1973]), and will not be described here.

9.   PROCEDURE DESIGN

Procedures are implemented in much the same fashion as blocks. Each time
a procedure is executed, a new block level is set up with storage available
for the procedure's formal parameters. The procedure implementation is
illustrated through an example (Fig. 16). The execution will be illustrated
with execution table X.

A few restrictions have been placed on procedure parameters to keep
the processor design simple. These restrictions do not inhibit the full use
of ALGOL, but only force the programmer to alter his code.

TABLE X

Execution Table for Procedure Example

Step	Symbol	J	TS	TSP	WS	WSP	BT	CBTP	Remarks
1	$	1	$	1					
2	begin	2	begin	2					
3	procedure	3	procedure	3					
4	F	4			D, F, P	1			
5	(	5		4	V, 64, P	1	F, 64, P, 0	6	
6	A	6			D, A, (	2			
7	)	7	procedure	3	V, 64, P	1	A, 0, 0, 1	64	Store parameter A in FPS
8	;	8							
9	real	9	real	4					
10	A	10			D, A, R	2			
11	;	11	procedure	3	V, 64, P	1	A, 0, R, 1	64	Set type field for A
12	value	12	value	4					
13	A	13			D, A, V	2			
14	;	14	procedure	3	V, 64, P	1	A, 1, R, 1	64	Set value field for A
15			begin	2		0	37	65	Save procedure body position in FPS
16							0	66	Save block ID in FPS and skip to end of procedure declaration
17	real	33	real	3	D, B, R	1			
18	B	34				0			
19	;	35	begin	2		1	B, 67, R, 0	2	
20	B	36			V, 67, R				

Src#	Tok	Gen#	GenOp	L1	Operand	L2	Code	Addr	Comment
21	:=	37	:=	3	V, 64, P	2	0, 0, 0, 00100010-0	127	Store **BLW**; new **BLW**: 2, 0, 1, 0—0 for procedure
22	F	38	F						
23	(	39	(	4					
24	2	40		3	C, 2, I				Set up formal parameter in DSAT with actual parameter value
25	)	41	:=	3	A, 1, R, 1	4			
26					D, A, R	4			
27					C, 2, I	3	A, 192, R, 0	129	
28					C, 2, I	4			
29					V, 192, R	3			
30					V, 64, P	2	2.	192	
31	:=			3	V, 65, P	2			CCTP points now to 37 — Return CTP is saved
32	F				R, 81, I	2			
33	(	15			V, 64, P	3			
34	:=	16	:=	4					
35	if	17	if	5					
36	A	18			V, 192, R	4			
37	>	19	>						
38	1	20		6	C, 1, I	5			
39	then	21	if		C, 1, B	4			
40				5	N, 1, 4, 0, 0, 0, 1, C	4			
41	A	22			V, 192, R	5			
42	×	23	×						
43	F	24	F	6	V, 64, P	6	2, 0, 1, 010—0	255	Save **BLW**; New **BLW**: 4, 0, 1, 0——0
44	(	25	(						
45	A	26		7	V, 192, R	7			

TABLE X (continued)

Step	Symbol	J	TS	TSP	WS	WSP	BT	CBTP	Remarks
46	−	27	−	8					
47	1	28		7	C, 1, I	8			Same as steps 24–32
48	)	29	(		C, 1, I	7			Return CTP is 58
49				×	6	A, 1, R, 1	8			
50						D, A, R	8			
51						C, 1, I	7	A, 320, R, 0	257	
52						C, 1, I	8			
53						V, 320, R	7			
54						V, 64, P	6	1	320	
55						V, 65, P	6			
56						R, 58, I	6			
57	F	15			V, 64, P	7			
58	:=	16	:=	7					
59	if	17	if	8					
60	A	18			V, 320, R	8			
61	>	19	>	9					
62	1	20			C, 1, I	9			
63	then	21	if	8	C, 0, B	8			Create C node; Since false, skip to else
64						N, 0, 4, 0, 0, 0, 1, C	8			
65	else	30			N, 0, 4, 0, 1, 58, 1, C	8			Update C node

Step	Node	Token		Code		Comment
66		1		C, 1, I	9	Store C node in NT
67	31	;	7	C, 1, I	8	Procedure leaves value in WS; value switches with return word
68	32	:= ×	6	C, 1, I	7	
69				C, 1, I	6	CCTP updated to 58 and BLW is restored
70				R, 58, I	7	
71	30	else			6	Multiplication is done; A value used is in 192
72		if	5	C, 1, I	5	
73				C, 2, I		Set WS; 4—node; 1, 4, 0, 1, 58, 1, C and skip to end
74	32	;	4	C, 2, I	4	Store node in NT
75		:=	3	C, 2, I	3	Do procedure assignment as step 68
76				C, 2, I	2	
77				R, 81, I	3	
78	42	end	2	C, 2, I	2	Same as step 70
79		begin	1	C, 2, I	1	
80		$				
81	43	$				

2.   67

$	begin	procedure	F	(	A	)	;	real	A	;	
(1)	(2)	(3)	(4)	(5)	(6)	(7)	(8)	(9)	(10)	(11)	
	value	A '	;								
	(12)	(13)	(14)								
	F	:=	if	A	>	1	then	A	×		
	(15)	(16)	(17)	(18)	(19)	(20)	(21)	(22)	(23)		
	F	(	A	−	1	)	else	1	;		
	(24)	(25)	(26)	(27)	(28)	(29)	(30)	(31)	(32)		
	real	B	;	C	:=	F	(	2	)	end	$
	(33)	(34)	(35)	(36)	(37)	(38)	(39)	(40)	(41)	(42)	(43)

(a)

Word index	Character index									
	0	1	2	3	4	5	6	7	8	9
8	)	e	n	d	$					
7				B	;	C	:=	F	(	2
6	s	e	1	;	r	e	a	l		
5	A	x	F	(	A	−	1	)	e	l
4	f		A	>	1	t	h	e	n	
3	a	l	u	e	A	;	F	:=	i	
2	)	;	r	e	a	l		A	;	v
1	c	e	d	u	r	e		F	(	A
0	$	b	e	g	i	n		p	r	o

(b)

Fig. 16. Procedure example: (a) ALGOL program; (b) character table.

Actual Parameter Restrictions

(a) Expressions must be call-by-value (i.e., no thunks). To overcome this restriction, simply define the expression as a procedure.

(b) Arrays must be call-by-name. To overcome this restriction, copy the array before entering it as an actual parameter.

(c) Procedures must be call-by-name.

9.1 Changes in Execution Algorithm

With the introduction of procedures, there are a few changes that must be made in the execution flowchart.

(a) After point I (Fig. 4), if S_j = "procedure" and T_i = "real," "Boolean," or "integer," instead of going immediately to point A, S_j is pushed in with T_i on the terminal stack.

(b) At point S2 (Fig. 10), the T_i check should now include "real procedure," "Boolean procedure," "integer procedure," "procedure," and the special case where T_i = (and T_{i-1} is a procedure-type terminal.

(c) At point S6,9 (Fig. 11), the move-to-next-block is altered if the present level is "procedure." The move is to the block whose ID is stored in the procedure BLW.

9.2 Procedure Declaration Execution

When the procedure identifier is scanned (step 4) in the declaration, it is initially treated as a normal identifier and stored on the WS in the D form. When the next symbol (is scanned, the procedure identifier is stored in the DSAT and given the type P. The procedure is allocated a starting position in the VT (location 64), but will actually use $n + 2$ locations for n formal parameters (Fig. 17). If the next symbol had been a semicolon, the procedure would be parameterless and the CT pointer would be moved to the end of the procedure declaration.

There are three types of information stored in the VT in the area called *formal parameter storage* (FPS).

(a) *Block ID:* The ID for the block in which the procedure is defined (this ID is now in the present BLW) must be saved. The explanation of the significance of the ID will be postponed until procedure execution is described.

(b) *CT pointer to procedure body:* Each time the procedure is referenced in a statement, the CT pointer must be moved to the procedure for execution. Since all the information in the procedure head is already saved in the VT, control can go immediately to the procedure body for execution.

(c) *Formal parameter table:* As each formal parameter is scanned (step 6) it is stored in the WS. However, the type field is (to remind the processor that this variable is a formal parameter. When the) is scanned (or a comma if there is more than one parameter), the parameter is stored in the table set aside for it in the VT (Fig. 17). There are four fields.

(1) *N:* name field (e.g., A),
(2) *V:* call-by-value (one is stored) or call-by-name (zero is stored) field,

Block ID			
CT Pointer to procedure body			
N_m	V_m	T_m	1
	·		
	·		
N_2	V_2	T_2	0
N_1	V_1	T_1	0

Fig. 17. Formal parameter storage (FPS) in value table.

(3)   *T:* type field (e.g., R),
(4)   *L:* last parameter field (all parameters have value 0 except last, which has value 1).

Since the symbol is) and not , the last parameter field is set to one (step 7).

The specification part and type list are scanned next. As each identifier is scanned, the parameter table must be scanned to find a match between the N field and the identifier name stored in the WS. After the match, the corresponding field, V or T, can be set. The type field of the WS entry form D will be either V or one of the type terminals such as R.

After this section is completed (step 14) by checking to see that there are no new value or specification parts, the CT is scanned without execution to the first symbol beyond the end of the procedure body. This completes the declaration of a procedure. The procedure body position and the block ID are now stored in the FPS (steps 15–16).

9.3   Procedure Assignment Execution

When a procedure identifier is followed by a := (steps 33–34), it is treated as a normal variable until the assignment is executed (step 67). The value on the right side is left on top of the WS and the procedure identifier is popped from the WS without any storage in the VT. This value can now be used in the expression in which the procedure-call appeared.

9.4   Procedure as Parameter Execution

Procedures are treated as any other identifiers if used as a formal parameter or actual parameter.

9.5   Procedure Execution

When the procedure identifier is scanned, the present BLW is stored in the BT with a new block setup. The new BLW is for a procedure rather than a begin–end block (see Section 3.2). The block ID is initially set to the previous block ID whose BLW was just put into the BT. After the formal parameters have all been stored, the block ID will be set to the value indicated in the VT storage of the procedure. The indicator field is set to one for "procedure." A special flag is set to inhibit scanning this new block for identifiers while the actual parameters are being scanned. (Otherwise, the formal parameter *X* just stored might be used in matching with the actual parameter *X*, which could have an entirely different meaning.) Now the actual parameter list is scanned (step 24). As each parameter is stored in WS, the corresponding formal parameter is retrieved from the

VT formal-parameter table. If it is call-by-value, the formal parameter is stored in the VT in a normal, identifier-declaration operation (A is stored in location 192). If it is call-by-name, the formal parameter is stored in the VT with a pointer to the actual-parameter VT storage rather than incrementing the BT pointer. After each actual parameter is scanned, the procedure pointer (V, value, P) stored in location 2 in the WS is incremented. After all the actual parameters have been scanned, the DSAT for the new block will consist of all the formal-parameter names.

The procedure pointer is now incremented to get the CT pointer value from the VT (i.e., 37). Control will transfer to the procedure body. The block ID field in the BLW is now set to the value in the VT.

When the identifiers are scanned in the procedure body, the DSAT search begins in the present procedure block. If the identifier is not stored there, the next block searched is not necessarily the block in which the procedure is called, but rather the block in which the procedure is declared. Hence, the block ID in the procedure BLW points the way to the next search in the proper block.

The procedure entry in the WS is now changed to set up the information needed to get a proper return from the called procedure. The CT position (81) of the symbol following the end of the procedure-call is stored. This introduces the new WS form:

(a) *form:* R—indicates that this is a return CT pointer value,
(b) *value:* CT pointer value of the character after the procedure call,
(c) *type:* I

9.6 Procedure Recursion

Now the procedure body is scanned (step 33). When the identifier F is scanned (step 43), the entire operation set defined in Section 9.5 is repeated. This includes setting up a new block. The value used for the actual parameter is 2, obtained from the outer procedure block. The new value for the formal parameter A is now A − 1, or 1. The return pointer is stored with the value 58. This will cause a return to within the procedure. Hence, procedure recursion involves stacking up a set of return pointers in the WS and saving the formal parameter values in a set of nested blocks in the BT.

9.7 Procedure Return

On this pass through the procedure body (steps 59–67), there is no recursion-call since the Boolean expression is false. When the semicolon is scanned (step 67), the procedure assignment can be made. The top two elements on the work stack are then switched so that the R element is on top.

A special check must be made whenever a statement has been scanned to see if it is a procedure body. This is performed by checking the top of the WS for the R element. Control then goes to the position in the CT indicated by the value field.

Now the expression $A \times F(A - 1)$ can be evaluated since the value of $F(A - 1)$ has been returned as 1. The operation $\times$ is performed when "else" is scanned (step 71), yielding the value 2 in WS position 5. F can now be assigned the value 2 for the final return. Control finally goes back to the original call (step 78) and the final assignment to B can be made.

On each return, the BT is reduced to the status just before the procedure was entered.

10. SWITCH DESIGN

In another paper (Bloom [1973]), the implementation of the switch design was described. This included an example illustrating switch declaration, switch designator, and switch list execution.

APPENDIX—TABLES OF ABBREVIATIONS

TABLE A.1

Work Stack Forms

Form (F)	Value (V)	Type (T)
declaration (D)	identifier name (IN)	declaration type (DT)
variable (V)	VT pointer (VTP)	identifier type (IT)
constant (V)	constant variable (CV)	constant type (CT)
node (N)	Boolean expression value (BEV), key (K), end pointer (P), "else" clause indicator (ECI), "else" pointer (EP), first-time indicator (FTI).	conditional (C)
node (N)	block identification (BI), character table position (CTP).	label (L)
array (A)	lower bound (*lb*), upper bound (*ub*).	bounds-pair (BD)
array (A)	base (*b*), difference (*d*).	base pair (BS)
node (N)	key (K), "end" pointer (EP), "for" list element pointer (FLEP), "do" pointer (DP), first-time indicator (FTI), first-time "do" (FTD), initial condition indicator (ICI), sign indicator (SI).	"for" statement (F)
return (R)	return CT pointer (RP)	integer (I)

TABLE A.2

Node Table Forms

Key (K)	Data (D)	Collision link (CL)	Type (T)
word index for "then" (WIT)	"end" pointer (P), "else" clause indicator (ECI), "else" pointer (EP)	CL	conditional (C)
label name (NM)	block identification (BI), character table position (CTP).	CL	label (L)
word index for := (WIA)	"end" pointer (EP), "do" pointer (DP)	CL	"for" statement (F)

TABLE A.3

Type List

Declaration types	Identifier types	Constant types
real (R)	real (R)	real (R)
integer (I)	integer (I)	integer (I)
Boolean (B)	Boolean (B)	Boolean (B)
real procedure (P)	real procedure (P)	switch (S)
procedure (P)	procedure (P)	
Integer procedure (IP)	integer procedure (IP)	
Boolean procedure (BP)	Boolean procedure (BP)	
real array (A)	real array (A)	
array (A)	array (A)	
integer array (IA)	integer array (IA)	
Boolean array (BA)	Boolean array (BA)	
switch (S)	switch (S)	
value (V)		
label (L)		

REFERENCES

Baumann, R., *et al.* [1964]. "Introduction to ALGOL." Prentice-Hall, Englewood Cliffs, New Jersey.

Bloom, H. M. [1971]. A syntax-directed FORTRAN interpreter for ALGOL 60, HDL-TM-71-12. Harry Diamond Labs. Washington, D.C.

Bloom, H. M. [1973]. Conceptual design of a direct high-level language processor. Tech. Rep. TR-239. Computer Sci. Center, Univ. Maryland, College Park, Maryland.

Gries, D. [1971]. "Compiler Construction for Digital Computers." Wiley, New York.

Architectural Design of an APL Processor

Bernard J. Robinet

Institut de Programmation
Université Pierre et Marie Curie
Paris, France

1. INTRODUCTION

A methodology proposed by Chu [1973] recognizes the existence of two separate and distinct phases of software engineering: architectural design and implementation. These two phases are interfaced by a formalized specification described by a language called ADL. An ADL description of a direct interpreter for mini-ALGOL has demonstrated that a software description can be machine independent, precise, concise, and complete.

Computing machines that directly execute the statements of a high-level language have been proposed in the past. In particular, for the APL language (Iverson [1964]), many microprogrammed implementations have been proposed (Hassitt *et al.* [1973]; Zaks *et al.* [1971]), but all these solutions are expressed in terms of specific languages. The aim of this chapter is to describe the main lines of the architectural design of a processor for a subset of APL. This processor has two separate and distinct parts: the *scanner* and the *interpreter*. The scanner scans each statement from left to right to create symbol table entries for new identifiers, to generate constant vectors, to analyze headers of functions, and to convert each statement into a code string of pointers. The interpreter scans the former strings from right to left, recognizes the syntactic elements, and executes the statements.

243

2. DESCRIPTION OF THE APL SUBSET

In this section we describe a subset of APL that serves as the language of the designed APL processor. In subsequent subsections, the metalanguage is introduced, with subsections describing the lexicon, the syntax, and the semantics. For more details about the full APL, the reader is invited to consult the references.

TABLE I

Symbols of the Metalanguage

Symbol	Representation
⟨ . . . ⟩	a syntactic unit
:=	is defined as
|	choice of either the left or right side
{ . . . }*	choice of zero or more times

TABLE II

Symbolic Names for Nonterminals

Symbolic name	Representation of nonterminals	Symbolic name	Representation of nonterminals
AS	assignment	LET	letter
B	branch	LST	labeled statement
CR	carriage return (⊛)	MOOP	mixed dyadic operator
D	dummy	MHT	monadic header type
DHT	dyadic header type	MMOP	mixed monadic operator
DIG	digit	MOP	monadic operator
DOP	dyadic operator	NHT	niladic header type
E	expression	NUM	number
F	function	OUTP	outer product
FB	function body	P	primary
FC	function-call	PROG	program
FH	function header	REDOP	reduction operator
FN	function name	S	space, blank
HT	header type	SDOP	scalar dyadic operator
ID	identifier	SMOP	scalar monadic operator
IND	index	ST	statement
INDV	indexed variable	SV	simple variable
INP	inner product	UST	unlabeled statement
INT	integer	V	variable
IO	input/output symbols	VEC	vectorial constant
LAB	label		

2.1 Metalanguage

The symbols that are used to describe the syntax of the metalanguage are shown in Table I.

Symbolic names for the nonterminals to be used in subsequent subsections are listed in Table II. They are essentially the first characters of the names they represent.

2.2 Syntax Description

This subsection will be devoted to a brief description of the current state of the APL subset. In Fig. 1 we give a set of rules describing the language.

A program consists of a set of functions, possibly empty, followed by a statement. It has as its effect the calculation of that statement; generally, this effect is used to call a function (Fig. 1, rule 41).

A function is invoked by mentioning its name in an expression, together with the appropriate number of parameters (rule 31).

Labels of statements are variables; they may be used in arithmetic expressions.

Constants can be either scalar or vector; a vector constant is denoted by a sequence of numbers separated by blanks (rule 9).

The only rules of grammar used in the scanner are the following:

  1–3: miscellaneous symbols
  4–6: numbers
  7–8: identifiers
    9: vector
   18: labeled statement
22–30: operators
33–34: function header and closing function quote

Data are either scalar or arrays of scalars. A scalar is a numerical quantity represented either as an integer or as a decimal fraction. A negative sign can be associated with a number and is written above the line, to distinguish it from the operator of opposite.

2.3 Semantics of the Terminals

The semantics of the APL subset is defined in Table III. The symbol ≡ is a metasymbol used to describe the semantics and must be read as "by definition, is equal to."

Miscellaneous

1. $\langle CR \rangle := ®$ (carriage return)
2. $\langle S \rangle :=$
3. $\langle 10 \rangle := \square$

Number

4. $\langle NUM \rangle := \langle INT \rangle \mid \langle INT \rangle . \langle INT \rangle \mid {}^{-}\langle NUM \rangle$
5. $\langle INT \rangle := \langle DIG \rangle \mid \langle INT \rangle \langle DIG \rangle$
6. $\langle DIG \rangle := 0 \mid 1 \mid \ldots \mid 8 \mid 9$

Identifier

7. $\langle ID \rangle := \langle LET \rangle \mid \langle ID \rangle \langle LET \rangle \mid \langle ID \rangle \langle DIG \rangle$
8. $\langle LET \rangle := A \mid B \mid \ldots \mid Y \mid Z$

Constant

9. $\langle VEC \rangle := \langle NUM \rangle \mid \langle VEC \rangle \langle S \rangle \langle NUM \rangle$

Variable

10. $\langle SV \rangle := \langle ID \rangle$
11. $\langle IND \rangle := \langle E \rangle \mid \langle IND \rangle ; \langle E \rangle$
12. $\langle INDV \rangle := \langle SV \rangle [\langle IND \rangle]$
13. $\langle V \rangle := \langle SV \rangle \mid \langle INDV \rangle \mid \langle I/O \rangle$

Expression

14. $\langle E \rangle := \langle P \rangle \mid \langle MOP \rangle \langle E \rangle \mid \langle P \rangle \langle DOP \rangle \langle E \rangle \mid \langle FC \rangle \mid \langle AS \rangle$
15. $\langle P \rangle := \langle VEC \rangle \mid \langle V \rangle \mid \langle FN \rangle \mid (\langle E \rangle)$
16. $\langle AS \rangle := \langle V \rangle \leftarrow \langle E \rangle$

Statement

17. $\langle ST \rangle := \langle UST \rangle \langle CR \rangle \mid \langle LST \rangle \langle CR \rangle$
18. $\langle LST \rangle := \langle LAB \rangle : \langle UST \rangle$
19. $\langle UST \rangle := \langle E \rangle \mid \langle B \rangle$
20. $\langle B \rangle := \rightarrow \langle E \rangle$
21. $\langle LAB \rangle := \langle ID \rangle$

Operators

22. $\langle MOP \rangle := \langle SMOP \rangle \mid \langle MMOP \rangle \mid \langle REDOP \rangle$
23. $\langle REDOP \rangle := \langle SDOP \rangle /$
24. $\langle SMOP \rangle := + \mid - \mid \times \mid * \mid \div$
25. $\langle MMOP \rangle := \iota \mid , \mid \rho$
26. $\langle DOP \rangle := \langle SDOP \rangle \mid \langle MOOP \rangle \mid \langle INP \rangle \mid \langle OUTP \rangle$
27. $\langle SDOP \rangle := + \mid - \mid \times \mid * \mid \div \mid = \mid \neq \mid \leq \mid < \mid > \mid \geq \mid \Lambda \mid V$
28. $\langle MOOP \rangle := \iota \mid , \mid \rho$
29. $\langle OUTP \rangle := {}^{\circ} . \langle SDOP \rangle$
30. $\langle INP \rangle := \langle SDOP \rangle . \langle SDOP \rangle$

Fig. 1. Syntax description.

3.   THE APL PROCESSOR

An APL program is a set of functions and a function is a group of related statements. The APL processor executes statements one after another, and executes functions when they are called.

3.1   Overview

The directly executed APL processor is composed of two separate and distinct parts, which are used sequentially: the scanner and the interpreter.

The scanner takes each statement as it is held in its buffer (see Fig. 4), scans it from left to right, and performs the following tasks:

1.   Creates symbol table entries for new identifiers (table STAB).

2.   Converts scalar constants or vector constants into data entries (array D).

3.   Converts each statement into a code string of pointers to appropriate entries in STAB (identifiers), D (constants), MOPTAB, REDTAB, DOP-TAB (operators), and CHARTAB (characters). These pointers are stored in code syllables (two-field table SP), the first field containing a code specifying the syntactic class of the element, the second containing the pointer defined above.

4.   Inserts as the leftmost symbol in every code string a special symbol to be used by the interpreter as a statement terminator.

5.   When a function quote (∇) is encountered, the processor sets an internal flag to change from the *immediate* to the *function* mode. In the latter

---

Fig. 1.   (*continued*)

Function

31. $\langle FC \rangle := \langle FN \rangle \langle S \rangle \langle E \rangle \,|\, \langle P \rangle \langle S \rangle \langle FN \rangle \langle S \rangle \langle E \rangle$
32. $\langle FN \rangle := \langle ID \rangle$
33. $\langle F \rangle := \langle FH \rangle \langle FB \rangle \nabla \langle CR \rangle$
34. $\langle FH \rangle := \nabla \langle HT \rangle \langle CR \rangle$
35. $\langle FB \rangle := \langle ST \rangle \,|\, \langle FB \rangle \langle ST \rangle$
36. $\langle HT \rangle := \langle NHT \rangle \,|\, \langle MHT \rangle \,|\, \langle DHT \rangle$
37. $\langle NHT \rangle := \langle D \rangle \leftarrow \langle FN \rangle \,|\, \langle FN \rangle$
38. $\langle MHT \rangle := \langle D \rangle \leftarrow \langle FN \rangle \langle S \rangle \langle D \rangle \,|\, \langle FN \rangle \langle S \rangle \langle D \rangle$
39. $\langle DHT \rangle := \langle D \rangle \leftarrow \langle D \rangle \langle S \rangle \langle FN \rangle \langle S \rangle \langle D \rangle \,|\, \langle D \rangle \langle S \rangle \langle FN \rangle \langle S \rangle \langle D \rangle$
40. $\langle D \rangle := \langle ID \rangle$

Program

41. $\langle PROG \rangle := \{ \langle F \rangle \}^* \langle ST \rangle$

TABLE III

Semantics of Terminals

Terminals	Semantics
$0 \ldots 9$	digits
$A \ldots Z$	letters
"end of line" or $\circledR$	carriage return; each statement must begin on a new line
" "	blank, space; used to write constant vectors and headers of functions
$\square$	input or output symbol assignment to $\square$ causes the value assigned to be printed; if $\square$ is a primary there is a request of input
.	separator for real numbers; between integer part and decimal part (see also, inner product and outer product)
;	separator of indices in an indexed variable
$[\ldots]$	square brackets are used to enclose a list of indices in an indexed variable; let H be an array such that $\rho H \equiv n_1, \ldots, n_p$; let $\{T_j\}$ be a family of integer arrays such that any element of $T_j \, \varepsilon \, \{1 : n_j\}$ and $\rho T_j \equiv m_i{}^j, \ldots, m_{r_j}{}^j$, for any $j \, \varepsilon \, \{1 : p\}$; then $H[T_1, \ldots, T_p]$ is an array such that $$(H[T_1, \ldots, T_p])[i_1{}^1, \ldots, i_{r_p}{}^p] \equiv$$ $$H[T_1[i_1{}^1, \ldots, i_{r_1}{}^1], \ldots, T_p[i_1{}^p, \ldots, i_{r_p}{}^p]]$$ and $$\rho H[T_1, \ldots, T_p] \equiv (\rho T_1), \ldots, \rho T_p$$ $$\rho\rho H[T_1, \ldots, T_p] \equiv (\rho\rho T_1) + \ldots + \rho\rho T_p$$
$(\ldots)$	parentheses used in the normal way to alter the order of evaluation of an expression, which is from *right to left*
$\leftarrow$	operator of assignment; assigns the value of the right expression to the left variable
:	separator between a label and a statement
$\times$	operator of BRANCH; used to alter the flow of control in the execution of a function; let v be the value of the expression to the right of the arrow; if ε is the first element (in rows order) of the array whose value is v and if ε is within the subset $[1 :$ number of lines of the currently executed function$]$ then control passes to the statement on the εth line; if ε is out of this range, the function is exited and control is passed to the point from which the function was entered; if ε is an empty quantity, control is passed to the next statement if such exists; otherwise the function is exited as above; if none of these cases applies, the statement is undefined and an error is indicated

TABLE III (continued)

Terminals	Semantics
/	this symbol is used in the so-called operation of *reduction*;

(a) if A is a vector then, for any dyadic scalar operator d, d/A (read d reducing A) is defined as follows:
if

$$X \equiv d/A$$

then

$$X \equiv A[1]d\ A[2]d \ldots A[\rho A]d$$

where the order of execution is from right to left, as usual; if A is a vector with a single element ($\rho A \equiv 1$), then $d/A \equiv A$; if A is empty, then X is the right identity element of d; the reduction is only defined for:

Operators	Right identity element
+	0
−	0
×	1
÷	1
*	1
∧	0
∨	1

(b) if $(\rho\rho A) > 1$, reduction can be carried out over the last coordinate of an array; this construction can be defined as follows:
if

$$X \equiv d/A$$

then

$$\rho\rho X \equiv 1 + \rho\rho A$$

$$\rho X \equiv (\rho A)[\iota^-1 + \rho\rho A]$$

$$X[i_1;\ldots;i_{-1+\rho\rho A}] \equiv d/A[i_1;i_2;\ldots;i_{-1+\rho\rho A};\iota(\rho A)[\rho\rho A]]$$

for all combinations of the indices over the ranges:
$$1 \leq i_j \leq (\rho A)[J], \text{ for all } J \equiv 1,\ldots,^-1 + \rho\rho A$$

 monadic scalar operators; they are *identity, opposite signum, exponential, inverse,* and *not,* respectively; so: $+3 \equiv 3$, $-3 \equiv 0 - 3$, $\times^-2 \equiv \ ^-1$, $\times 0 \equiv 0$, $\times 3.5 \equiv 1$, $\div 2 \equiv 0.5$, $\sim 1 \equiv 0$, $\sim 0 \equiv 1$; if A is not scalar, then the operations defined above are applied to A element-by-element to produce a result with the same rank; for example, $\times 3\ ^-5\ 0 \equiv 1\ ^-1\ 0$

TABLE III (continued)

Terminals	Semantics
ι	monadic mixed operator, called *index generator*; $\iota N \equiv$ undefined for nonintegral N and $N < 0$; empty vector if $N \equiv 0$; $(\iota N - 1)$, N if $N > 0$
,	monadic mixed operator, called *ravel*; , B is a vector whose components are the components of the right argument taken in index sequence (row order)
ρ	monadic mixed operator called *size*; $\rho A \equiv$ a vector whose components represent the number of values each index of A has; the expression $\rho\rho A$ gives the *rank* of A
$+, -, \times, *, \div\,^a$	dyadic scalar operators; they are *addition, subtraction, multiplication, exponentiation,* and *division,* respectively
$=, \neq, <, \leq, \geq, >^a$	dyadic scalar operators; usual meaning; the result is always 0 or 1
$\wedge, \vee^a$	dyadic scalar operators; the usual "and" and "or"; the operands must be 0 or 1
ι	dyadic mixed operator, called *index of*; if $R \equiv A \iota B$, then $\rho R \equiv \rho B$ and $\rho\rho R \equiv \rho\rho B$; $R[J]$ is the smallest index I such that $A[I] \equiv B[J]$; if no component of A has the value $B[J]$ then $R[J] \equiv 1 + \rho A$; only defined if A and B are vectors; for example,
	$$4\ 7\ 3\ \iota\ 7 \equiv 2, \quad 4\ 7\ 4\ 3\ \iota\ 4\ 2 \equiv 1\ 5$$
,	dyadic mixed operator, called *catenation*; $A, B \equiv$ a vector formed by appending the components of B to the components of A; so
	$$3\ 2, 1\ 2\ 4 \equiv 3\ 2\ 1\ 2\ 4$$
ρ	dyadic mixed operator, called *restructuring*; $A\rho\ B \equiv$ an array where dimensions are A and where elements, if any, are taken from B in the order defined by $,B$
$\circ.$	dyadic mixed operator, called *outer product*; if $X \equiv A \circ. dB$ (d is any dyadic scalar operator) then
	$$X[i_1; \ldots; i_{\rho\rho A}; j_1; \ldots; j_{\rho\rho B}] \equiv$$ $$A[i_1; \ldots; i_{\rho\rho A}]dB[j_1; \ldots; j_{\rho\rho B}]$$ for all values of the indices in the ranges $$1 \leq i_k \leq (\rho A)[k], \qquad k \equiv 1, \ldots, \rho\rho A$$ $$1 \leq j_m \leq (\rho B)[1], \qquad m \equiv 1, \ldots, \rho\rho B$$ so $\rho X \equiv (\rho A), \rho B$ and $\rho\rho X \equiv (\rho\rho A) + \rho\rho B$

TABLE III (continued)

Terminals	Semantics
	used in the dyadic mixed operator called *inner product*; if d_1 and d_2 are any two dyadic scalar operators, then

$$(Ad_1 \cdot d_2 B)[i_1; i_2; \ldots; i_{(\rho\rho A)-1}; j_2; j_3; \ldots; j_{\rho\rho B}] \equiv$$

$$d_1/A[i_1; i_2; \ldots; i_{(\rho\rho A)-1}; \iota(\rho A)[\rho\rho A]]d_2$$

$$B[\iota(\rho B)[1], j_2, \ldots, j_{\rho\rho B}]$$

for all values of the indices over the ranges

$$1 \le i_k \le (\rho A)[k], \quad k \equiv 1, \ldots, (\rho\rho A) - 1$$

$$1 \le j_m \le (\rho B)[m], \quad m \equiv 2, \ldots, \rho\rho B$$

A and B must be compatible, that is to say,

$$(\rho A)[\rho\rho A] \equiv (\rho B)[1]$$

the familiar matrix product of linear algebra is given by $A + \cdot \times B$ if A and B are matrices; in any case,

$$\rho Ad_1 \cdot d_2 B \equiv (\rho A)[\iota^-1 + \rho\rho A], (\rho B)[1 + \iota^-1 + \rho\rho B]$$

$$\rho\rho Ad_1 \cdot d_2 B \equiv {}^-2 + (\rho\rho A) + \rho\rho B$$

| ∇ | a function is defined by a head followed by a body of statements; the entire function is enclosed in function quotes ∇ called "del" |

[a] If A and B are arrays with identical rank vectors, then the 13 dyadic scalar operations defined above are applied to A and B element-by-element to produce a result with the same rank vector. For example,

$$1\ 2\ 3 \times 1\ 2\ 3 \equiv 1\ 4\ 9$$

If one argument is a scalar and the other an array, the scalar is extended to match the other operand rank:

$$1\ 2\ 3\ 4 * 2 \equiv 1\ 4\ 9\ 16$$

mode, the header of the function is analyzed, and the names of the formal parameters and the function are determined. As each statement is scanned, it is processed as described in steps 1–4. The function name is stored with the information obtained from the header in a special table (FTAB) and has as its value an integer vector whose $(k + 1)$st element is a pointer to the rightmost code syllable of statement k. When labels are encountered, they are given the value of the number of the rightmost code syllable of the current statement. At last, when a closing function quote is found, the scanner returns to the immediate mode and the next statement is scanned as above.

6.   When the end of an immediate statement is reached, control is passed to the interpreter for statement execution.

The interpreter performs syntactical analysis of statements and controls execution using a series of interpretation rules.

The only syntax built into the grammar of productions is for a statement; the flow of control between statements is done by the end-of-statement interpretation rule. Note that for the interpreter, the syntactic analysis is performed from *right to left*.

Interpretation rules, most of which are trivial, make up the main part of the processor. There is a *value stack* (SVAL, pointed to by SV), which holds all temporary values (pointers to D). An examination of a typical rule will be instructive. The following rule is a simplified version of MO-NADIC that is encountered in traversing an expression after having seen a primary (P) with a monadic operator (MOP) on its left side.

procedure MONADIC;
   AUX := SVAL(SV);
   Z := DA;
   while $Z \leq D(AUX) + 1 + D(AUX + 1)$
   do $D(Z) := D(Z - D(AUX))$; $Z := Z + 1$ *end*;
   /*copy of the descriptor: the result has the same rank and size as the
      operand*/
   while $Z \leq DA + D(AUX) - 1$
   do /*loop to compute and copy the values*/
      $V := D(Z - D(AUX))$;
      case CODE *of* /*perform the operation*/
         1: NOT(V);
         3: V := $-V$;
         4: SIGN(V);
         5: INV(V);
         6: V := $2.71828 \uparrow V$;
      end /*of case*/;
      $D(2) := V$; $Z := Z - 1$;
   end /*of do*/;
   SVAL(SV) := DA;
   DA := Z;
end /*of MONADIC*/

When this rule is encountered, the stack looks like its representation in Fig. 2a. The procedure MONADIC performs the operation coded in CODE on AUX and assigns the result to SVAL (Fig. 2b).

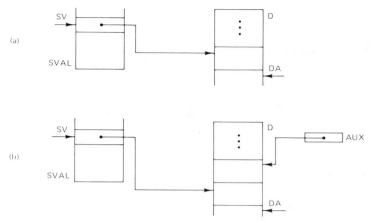

Fig. 2. The stack: (a) when MONADIC is encountered; (b) after performing the procedure.

Within the interpreter, there is a table, SF, that records the name of the called function and the address of the return point. The formal parameters of the called function (if any) are linked with the top elements of two stacks, SD1 and SD2, that point to the values of the actual parameters. When the called function is exited, the previous stacks are popped, if necessary, and execution continues from the return point.

Figure 5 shows the result of scanning the program FACTORIAL M (see Figs. 3 and 4). For clarity, the code syllables of the operators have been replaced by their symbols. Figure 6 gives the result of the interpretation of the call of FACTORIAL by F 5.

3.2   The Scanner

3.2.1   *Data Structures*

The functional elements required for the scanner include tables SP, FTAB, and VTAB, arrays D and VFUNC, procedures IDEN, NUMBER, LOOK-

$$\nabla N \leftarrow F\ M$$
$$N \leftarrow I \leftarrow 1$$
$$BIS: \rightarrow E \times \iota I = M$$
$$N \leftarrow N \times I \leftarrow I + 1$$
$$\rightarrow BIS$$
$$E: \rightarrow 0$$
$$\nabla$$
$$F\ 5$$

Fig. 3.   FACTORIAL M.

Fig. 4. Value of the input string buffer S for the program FACTORIAL M.

UP, and ERROR, and several buffers, pointers, and tables (see Fig. 7). These elements are summarized by the following statements:

/*description of the functional elements of the scanner*/

string buffer	S(J)	$store input program
table	SP(I)	$store the code syllables
	FTAB(F)	$store the function headers
	VTAB(VAR)	$store identifiers
	MOPTAB(M)	$store the monadic operators
	TILDE(T)	$store the operator ∼
	REDTAB(R)	$store the reduction operators
	DOPTAB(D)	$store the dyadic operators
	CHARTAB(C)	$store the miscellaneous characters
	TVAL	$store the elements of a scanned vector
array	D	$store the values
	VFUNC	$store the address of the statements
pointer	J,I,F,VAR,M,T,R,D,C	
character buffer	Q,Q1,Q2,Q3,Q4	$symbol accumulators
integer buffer	Z,LENG,L,K	$temporarily store pointers
	U	$store the sign of a code syllable
	DA	$store index to D
	VAL	$store index to VFUNC
	SIGN	$store the value of the sign of a number
real buffer	VALUE	$store the absolute value of a number
logic buffer	FLAG,B,W	$store logic values
counter	COUNT	
procedure	IDEN	$recognize identifiers
	NUMBER	$recognize and compute numbers
	LOOKUP	$look up a table
	ERROR	$print error message

The functions of these elements and their formats are now described.

3.2.1.1 *Input String Buffer*. Buffer S stores the input string, which is an APL program. The location of the characters of the string is pointed to by

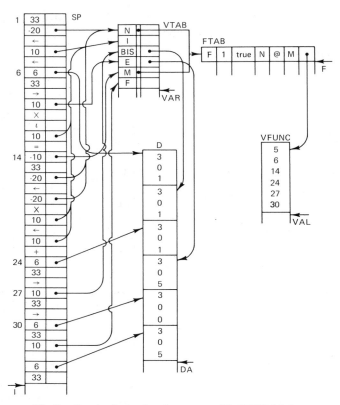

Fig. 5. Result of scanning the program FACTORIAL M.

pointer J (see the example shown in Fig. 4). It is assumed that the input program is already in buffer S when scanning begins.

3.2.1.2   *Table of Code Syllables.*   The table SP stores the code syllables that are emitted by the scanner. Each entry stores an integer, the code of the syntactical unit, and a pointer to the associated table or array (Fig. 8).

3.2.1.3   *Table of Functions.*   The table FTAB stores the information obtained from the analysis of the function header. As shown in Fig. 8, it is a table with seven fields: the first contains the name of the function; the second contains a 0, 1, or 2 depending on whether the function is niladic, monadic, or dyadic, respectively; the third contains a logical value ("true" if the function is explicit, "false" otherwise); the next three fields contain the names of the formal parameters (if any); and the seventh contains a pointer to the array VFUNC.

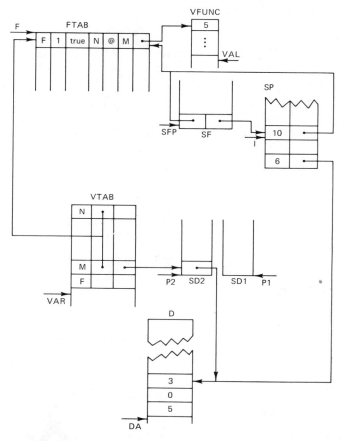

Fig. 6. Linkage of the different functional elements by executing the call of FACTORIAL by F 5.

3.2.1.4   *Array VFUNC.*   This array contains the "value" of a function, that is, an integer vector whose $(k + 1)$st element is a pointer to the right-most code syllable of the kth statement. This vector is updated whenever an end-of-statement symbol is encountered (Fig. 9).

3.2.1.5   *Array D.*   Each data entry in D contains the rank and size vectors of the data being stored. During the scanning process, only scalars and vectors are stored. But during the interpretation, for multidimensional arrays M, the $\times/\rho M$ entries are stored in row-major order following the size vector; that is, the mapping function used is exactly the base-value

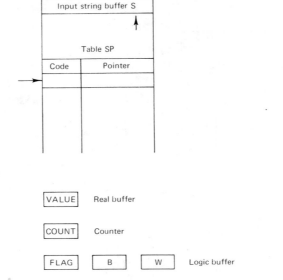

Fig. 7. Some functional elements of the scanner.

function with the size vector as the radix. For example, if A is an array, the element

$$A[i_1, i_2, \ldots, i_{\rho\rho A}]$$

has the index

$$DA + 3 + \rho\rho A + (\rho A) \perp (i_1, \ldots, i_{\rho\rho A}) - 1$$

that is to say,

$$DA + 3 + D(DA + 1) + (D(DA + 2), \ldots,$$
$$D(DA + D(DA + 1)) \perp (i_1, \ldots, i_{\rho\rho A}) - 1$$

where $\perp$ is the APL operator called "base value," which is not implemented

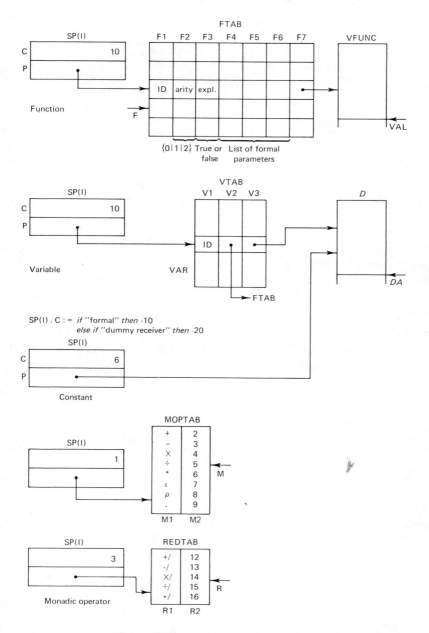

Fig. 8. Some code syllables and their relation to the functional elements.

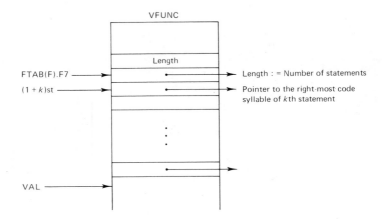

Fig. 9. Array VFUNC.

here (Robinet [1971b]). In Fig. 10, the structure of array **D** is shown. According to P. S. Abrams [1966], we call the set of length, rank, and size the "descriptor."

3.2.1.6 *Table VTAB.* The table **VTAB** is used to store the names of the identifiers. As shown in Fig. 8, there are three fields in each entry: (a) the identifier name, (b) a pointer to **FTAB** (if any), and (c) a pointer to array **D** or special stacks.

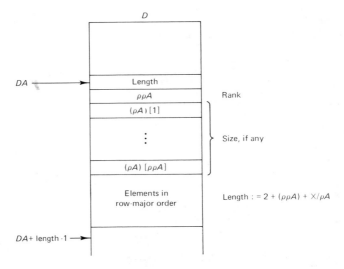

Fig. 10. Array *D*.

During scanning, if an identifier corresponds to a formal parameter, the second field points to the name of the associated function; this is to avoid any confusion between formal parameters of different functions that have the same identifier. The third field is set at interpretation time: if the identifier corresponds to a variable, its value points to the associated value; if the identifier is a formal parameter, its value points to the top of the stack, which contains the address of the corresponding actual parameter.

3.2.1.7 *Tables of Operators.* The tables MOPTAB, TILDE, REDTAB, and DOPTAB have two fields in each entry: (a) symbol characters and (b) integer code. The tables are used by both the scanner and the interpreter. The value of the code will be used to switch between the different sections of program that perform the operations.

3.2.1.8 *Miscellaneous Elements.* In addition to these functional elements, there are 21 other elements:

the table CHARTAB, which contains the other available characters of the APL language (the code part of the table is not used);

the array TVAL, which contains the different elements of a scanned vector;

the character buffers Q, Q1, Q2, Q3, and Q4, which are used during the packing of an identifier name;

the integer buffers DA and VAL, which are used to pack identifiers, to pack numbers, to consult tables of symbols, and to print out error messages (in which case, the processor stops);

and other auxiliary buffers.

3.2.2 The Scanning Process

The scanner scans the input string from left to right, recognizes some syntactical units, and generates the code syllables.

3.2.2.1 *Initial point.* The *initial point* or IP is where the scanning of the first character of the right-hand side of any production (these are only used in the scanning process; see Section 2) begins. If the first character is a function quote, the scanner sets the flag to change its mode. If the flag is off, the scanner must analyze the header of a function. If the flag is on, the scanner must analyze an immediate statement.

3.2.2.2 *Identifiers.* When an identifier is recognized, the succeeding characters are concatenated into a name in character buffer Q. There are now four possibilities: the identifier is the name of (a) a function defined previously, (b) a formal parameter, (c) a global variable (or a function defined later), or (d) a label.

The table VTAB is searched in case the identifier has previously been stored. If the search fails, the name is created. If the search succeeds and if the identifier corresponds to a formal parameter, the identifier is linked to the name of its function. When the identifier does not correspond to a label, a code syllable is created with value 10 for a global variable, -10 for a formal argument, and -20 for a formal result. If the identifier corresponds to a label, the value of the number of the statement is assigned to the variable. Then the process returns to the IP.

3.2.2.3 *Headers of Functions,* When a function is encountered, the header is analyzed to define the arity of the function (0, 1, or 2), the names of the formal parameters, the name of the function, and the existence of an explicit result.

According to the grammar there are six types of syntax for functions: explicit or implicit niladic, explicit or implicit monadic, and explicit or implicit dyadic. All of this information is stored in the table FTAB.

When the end of the header is encountered, the length of the function (number of statements) is set to zero in the vector VFUNC.

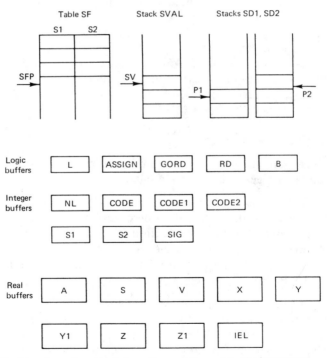

Fig. 11. Some functional elements specially used by the interpreter.

3.2.2.4 *Numbers.* When a number is recognized, the succeeding digits are packed and converted to a number in the real buffer VALUE. If a sequence of numbers is encountered, this corresponds to a vector, and a copy is made in array D with the definition of the associated descriptor. The process returns to the IP after making this copy.

3.2.2.5 *Operators.* By searching the different tables of operator symbols, the scanner outputs the associated code syllable with the code field equal to one if the operator is monadic and four if it is dyadic. For reduction processing the code is equal to three, and for the special operator "not" the code is one (this monadic operator receives special treatment: it is the only monadic operator having no dyadic form). For all these cases, the pointer field points to the row number of the table in which it appears.

3.2.2.6 *Other Units.* For the other characters, a check is made and when the character is the end-of-line marker (ⓒ), the "value" of the function (the pointer to the rightmost syllable of the scanned statement) is updated. If the scanned line is an immediate statement, the process of interpretation is activated.

3.3 The Interpreter

3.3.1 *Data Structures*

Some of the functional elements required for the interpreter are shown in Fig. 11. These include the table SF, stacks SV, SD1, and SD2, and several buffers and pointers. These elements are summarized by the following statements:

/*description of the functional elements of the interpreter*/

table	SF(SFP)	$store a pointer to the called function and the address of return
stack	SVAL(SV)	$store a pointer to the value of a primary
	SD1(P1)	$store a pointer to the value of a primary; this stack is associated with the left parameter of a function, if any
	SD2(P2)	$same purpose as previous for the right parameter

pointer	AUX, AUXV, AUX2	
	AUX3, PT, K	
	OPG, OPD	
integer buffer	NL	$store the number of a statement
	CODE, CODE1, CODE2	$store the codes of operators
	S1, S2, SIG	$store the number of elements of an array
	NPV	$store the number of semi-colons in an indexed expression
real buffer	A, S, V, X, Y, Y1, Z, Z1	$store the value of elements
	IEL	$store the identity element

The functions of these elements and their formats are now described.

3.3.1.1 *Table of Called Functions.* The table SF stores references to called functions. Each entry stores (a) a pointer to the table FTAB, which contains all the information defining the syntactical type of the function, and (b) a pointer to the next syntactical unit. When a function is exited, there is a return to the calling statement and the top element of SF is erased.

3.3.1.2 *Stack for Evaluation.* The stack SVAL stores pointers to the values (stored in D) of the operands of operators. When a dyadic operand is encountered, the corresponding operation is performed, the two top elements are popped, and a pointer to the result is pushed. For a monadic operand, the operation is performed, the top element is popped, and a pointer is pushed, as above.

3.3.1.3 *Stacks of Actual Parameters.* The stacks SD1 and SD2 store pointers to the values of the actual parameters of a function; the formal parameters point, for each call, to the corresponding top elements.

3.3.1.4 *Miscellaneous Elements.* In addition to the previous elements, there are 25 other elements that are essentially auxiliary buffers.

3.3.2 *The Interpretation Process*

The interpreter analyzes, from *right to left,* the string of code syllables generated by the scanner, performs the operations, and executes the expressions ready for execution. The algorithm is shown in Robinet [1974b].

3.3.2.1 *Initial Point.* The initial point of the interpreter is where the analysis of an expression begins. The only syntax built into the BNF grammar is for a statement; flow of control between statements is handled by the end-of-statement interpretation rules SUCCESSOR and BRANCH.

3.3.2.2 *Flow of Control.* The right-arrow symbol (→) designates a branch and is used to alter the flow of control in the execution of a function. Let NL be the value of the expression to the right of the symbol → ; this value is pointed to by SVAL(SV) and is equal to D(SVAL(SV) + 1). If this value is an empty quantity, control is passed to the interpretation rule SUCCESSOR. If the value is a nonintegral quantity, an error is indicated. If the symbol occurs in an immediate statement (the stack SF is empty), the interpretation process stops. Otherwise, if the value is within the range of the address numbers in the currently executed function, control passes to the statement at the associated address. If the value is out of this range, control is passed to the interpretation rule RETURN.

If the statement is not a branch or if there is a branch to an empty quantity, the procedure SUCCESSOR is called and control is passed to the next statement, if one exists. Otherwise, the function is exited or, for an immediate statement, the process stops.

When a function that was declared explicit is exited, the result is stacked, the pointers to the formal parameters are reset, and control is passed to the point at which the function was entered.

3.3.2.3 *Expression.* An expression may appear in any one of five productions: primary, function-call, assignment, or expressions invoking monadic or dyadic operators.

The value of an expression being on the top of SVAL, the interpreter performs monadic operators by calling the procedure MONADIC. If the operator is dyadic, the interpreter calls the procedure DYADIC, which is applied to the top two elements of SVAL.

3.3.2.4 *Primary.* A primary is a vector, the call of a niladic explicit function, a variable, or an expression between parentheses as shown in Fig. 1. If it is a function-call, the procedure CALL is activated and the result, if any, is pushed on the top of SVAL. For the other cases, the associated values are pushed by executing the procedures VEC, V, or E, respectively.

3.3.2.5 *Function-Call.* In the general case, a function-call is the call of a monadic or dyadic function. For the two cases, the procedure CALL is invoked and the result, if any, is pushed on the top of stack SVAL.

3.3.2.6 *Assignment.* After recognizing an expression, the interpreter tests to see if there is a left arrow (←) with a variable on its left-hand side. The function of the logic buffer ASSIGN is to distinguish between variables that are primary and variables that are assigned.

3.3.2.7 *Monadic Operators.* After recognizing a monadic operator, the interpreter invokes the procedure MONADIC, which performs the recognized operation with the data pointed to by SV.

If the operator is scalar, the descriptor of the result is the same as the operand's and a copy is made in array D. Then a loop enables us to compute and copy the values. As with other operations, the top of SVAL points to the beginning of the data entry.

If the operator is a *reduction* by a dyadic scalar operator, the construction of the result is defined as follows: the rank of the result is the rank of the operand minus one $[D(DA + 1) := D(AUX + 1) - 1]$ and the size of the result is the size of the operand with the last element omitted. Each element of the result is obtained by performing the reduction on the last coordinate using the mapping function defined in subsection 3.2.1.5. Note that if the operand is an empty array, the result is the right identity element of the associated dyadic operation.

If the operator is mixed, three cases are possible in this APL subset: it could be a *ravel* operator, an *index* generator, or a *size* operator, according to the semantics of these operators.

3.3.2.8   *Dyadic Operators.*   Recognition of dyadic operators gives the information to compute the value of the results. Four main cases are possible: the interpreter can recognize an inner product, an outer product, a scalar operator, or a dyadic mixed operator.

If the operator is scalar, the operation is meaningful if and only if the operands have the same size or if one of them is scalar. For scalars and arrays not having the same descriptor (the size is empty for scalar), a special case called SCAL is arranged. For the other cases, the process is trivial.

If the operator is mixed, there are three cases: it could be an *index* operator, a *catenation* operator, or a *restructuring* operator. For the first, the descriptor of the result is obtained by copying the operands and loops are executed to search the index of the first occurrence, if any, of the values of the right operand in the left operand. For the second, the operation is meaningful if the two operands have ranks less than two. The result is always a vector $[D(AUX) := 1]$ and a copy of the elements of the operands is made. Finally, for the third, the rank of the result is the size of the left operand $[D(AUX) := Z - 1$ where Z is equal to $D(OPG + 2)$ and AUX equals $DA + 1]$. The result is composed with elements, if any, taken from the right operand in the row-major order.

For an outer product, the rank of the result is the sum of the ranks of the operands, and the size is obtained by concatenating their sizes. It is sufficient to execute two loops to obtain the elements of the result.

Finally, an inner product is obtained by performing reductions, with the aid of the first operator, on the vectors that result from the execution of the second operator with the "rows" of the first operand and the "columns" of the second operand, according to the semantics of the inner-product generalization of the matrix product.

3.3.2.9   *Name of Function.*   An identifier in a statement can be the identifier of a function to be declared later. If this is the case, the procedure FN, invoked by FC, searches this correspondence and stacks a pointer to the name and a pointer to the calling point in the specific stack SFP, which is used to stack the calls. This process enables the use of recursive functions.

3.3.2.10   *The Procedure CALL.*   The purpose of this procedure is to define the links between the formal parameters, if any, and the actual parameters. The procedure uses two specific stacks, SD1 and SD2, which contain pointers to the values of the actual parameters. The third field of table VTAB contains, for the invoked formal parameters, a pointer to the top of the associated stack—SD1 for the left argument, SD2 for the right argument.

Figure 6 is an illustration of the activation of this procedure for the call F 5 of FACTORIAL M (Fig. 3).

3.3.2.11   *Variable.*   A variable can be a "transmitter" or a "receiver." The syntactic analysis is the same for the two cases, but the semantic processes are different. If the variable is a primary, we have to stack a pointer to the array defined by the variable; if the variable is on the left-hand side of a left arrow, we have to link it with the data entry defined by the top of SVAL.

The activation of the procedure SV results in the linkage of the different kinds of variables: global, dummy receiver, and argument.

3.3.2.12   *The Procedure STACK.*   The body of this procedure, used when a variable is a primary, is, in fact, the process of computing the value of the mapping function.

In an APL-type language, the process of computing the sequence of indices in D to access the elements of, say, $A[H_1, \ldots, H_k]$, is a generalization of Horner's schema. The sequence of indices is the value of S after executing

$$S \leftarrow 0$$

$$for\ k \leftarrow 1\ until\ \rho\rho A\ do\ S \leftarrow S \times (\rho A)[k]\circ. + , H_k - 1$$

3.3.2.13   *The Procedure LINK.*   The purpose of this procedure is to link various kinds of variables (global, dummy receiver, or actual parameters) with the data entries pointed to by SVAL(SV).

The only case of an assignment to an indexed variable allowed in this APL subset is the assignment of a scalar to an indexed variable with scalar indices. If the variable is not indexed, we can assign all kinds of arrays.

3.3.2.14 *The Procedures INPUT and OUTPUT.* These procedures are activated by analyzing the symbol □. If □ is a primary, a request of inputs is performed by INPUT until a ⊕ appears. The set of values is stored as a vector in D and SVAL(SV) points to these values. If □ is a receiver, the data entry pointed to by SVAL(SV) is displayed.

3.3.2.15 *Other Procedures.* The procedures RARROW, CR, RIGHT-PAR, LEFTPAR, LARROW, S, IO, PV, LBRACKET, and RBRACKET are used by the interpreter to check if the syntactical units are →, ⊕,), (, ←, " " (space), □, ; (semicolon), [, and], respectively.

The procedures NOT, INV, SIGNUM, AND, OR, and DIV compute the monadic operators "not," "reciprocal," "sign," and the dyadic operators "and," "or," and "division," respectively.

The procedure INTEGER tests to see if a value is an integer and the procedure COPY copies a set of values in some other place. When there is a branch to STOP, the directly executed APL processor stops.

REFERENCES

Abrams, P. S. [1966]. An interpreter for Iverson notation, Tech. Rep. CS47. Stanford Univ., Stanford, California.

Chu, Y. [1973]. A methodology for software engineering, Tech. Rep. TR-256. Computer Sci. Center, Univ. Maryland, College Park, Maryland.

Chu, Y. [1974]. Architectural design of a mini-ALGOL interpreter, Tech. Note 74-56. Computer Sci. Center, Univ. Maryland, College Park, Maryland.

Chu, Y., and Yeh, J. [1974]. Description of architectural design language, Tech. Note 74-55. Computer Sci. Center, Univ. Maryland, College Park, Maryland.

Hassitt, A., Lageschulte, J. W., and Lyon, L. E. [1973]. Implementation of a high-level language machine. *Commun. ACM* **16,** 199–212.

Iverson, K. E. [1964]. "A Programming Language." Wiley, New York.

Robinet, B. [1971a]. "Semantique d'APL. Actes du Colloque APL." I.R.I.A., Paris.

Robinet, B. [1971b]. "Le langage APL." Technip. Editors, Paris.

Robinet, B. [1974a]. Description of an APL subset, Tech. Note 74-68. Computer Sci. Center, Univ. Maryland, College Park, Maryland.

Robinet, B. [1974b]. Architectural design of a directly executed APL processor, Tech. Rep. TR-320. Computer Sci. Center, Univ. Maryland, College Park, Maryland.

Zaks, R., Steingart, D., and Moore, J. [1971]. A firmware APL time-sharing system. *Proc. SJCC* **38,** 178–190.

Index

Ballen